A GRIM ALMANAC OF

THE BLACK COUNTRY

Winson Green Prison. (Author's collection)

A GRIM ALMANAC OF

THE BLACK COUNTRY

NICOLA SLY

The
History
Press

The Market Place, Dudley. (Author's collection)

First published 2013

The History Press
The Mill, Brimscombe Port
Stroud, Gloucestershire, GL5 2QG
www.thehistorypress.co.uk

British Library Cataloguing in Publication Data.
A catalogue record for this book is available from the British Library.

ISBN 978 0 7524 7979 8

Typesetting and origination by The History Press
Printed in Great Britain
Manufacturing managed by Jellyfish Solutions Ltd

CONTENTS

ALSO BY
THE AUTHOR

INTRODUCTION & ACKNOWLEDGEMENTS

The first obstacle in writing about the Black Country is determining exactly where it is, since its location is not precisely defined. For example, some would argue that it doesn't include Wolverhampton, Smethwick or Stourbridge, while others say that it is anywhere within the Metropolitan District Council areas of Dudley, Sandwell, Walsall and Wolverhampton. I sincerely hope that I haven't taken too many liberties with the geography of the area.

All of the stories within this book are true and were sourced entirely from the contemporary newspapers listed in the bibliography at the rear. However, much as today, not everything was reported accurately and there were frequent discrepancies between publications, with differing dates and variations in names and spelling.

As always, there are a number of people to whom I owe a debt of gratitude for their assistance. Dennis Neale, who runs a fascinating website called 'Black Country Muse', was extremely helpful and knowledgeable and very kindly gave me permission to use one of his illustrations, as did the *Wolverhampton Express and Star*, who permitted me to use their illustrations pertaining to the 'Hagley Bella' case. On a personal level, my husband Richard provided constructive criticism – and countless cups of tea! I would also like to thank Matilda Richards, my editor at The History Press, for her help and encouragement in bringing this book to print.

Every effort has been made to clear copyright; however, my apologies to anyone I may have inadvertently missed. I can assure you it was not deliberate but an oversight on my part.

Nicola Sly, 2013

JANUARY

Dudley police station. (Author's collection)

1 JANUARY

1869 Schoolmistress Elizabeth Fereday faced magistrates at Wolverhampton Police Court charged with assaulting a pupil. Eight-year-old Nancy Ann Jones's parents complained that, just before Christmas, Mrs Fereday had struck their daughter in the face with a cane. Nancy was brought into court still sporting a black eye, and the Magistrates' Clerk testified that the bruising had been much worse when the summons against the teacher was taken out soon after the incident.

Mrs Fereday denied hitting Nancy, saying that the child was injured by falling onto a bench. She claimed that Nancy was impudent and refused to do her school work, prompting her to tell the girl that she would not be spoken to in that way. Mrs Fereday said that she was about to 'box the child's ears' when Nancy accidentally fell and hit her face.

The magistrates found in Nancy's favour, fining Mrs Fereday £2 plus costs.

2 JANUARY

1889 Richard Walters and Fanny Cornock left home to go for a walk and never returned. The following morning, a walking stick and a woman's muff were found lying on the towpath of the canal at Nine Locks, Brierley Hill.

When the canal was dragged, the bodies of twenty-six-year-old Walters and his nineteen-year-old fiancée were found a few yards apart. An inquest held by coroner Mr E.B. Thorneycroft on 5 January surmised that the couple had accidentally walked into the canal during a thick fog, and the jury returned two verdicts of 'accidental death'.

3 JANUARY

1884 Twenty-one-year-old Eliza Cartwright from Bradley felt safe walking to work, until she noticed a man crawling towards her across a field on his hands and knees. She was forced to ask for protection from a couple of men in front of her, and from that day onwards, she changed her route to one that was less isolated.

On 3 January, a postman heard a woman shouting and, moments later, he came across Eliza lying senseless on the ground. She died that evening from a compound fracture of the skull. A search of the area where she was found suggested that a great struggle had taken place and the police found two large pieces of furnace cinder, one covered in clotted blood and hair, the other tied with half of Eliza's work apron.

An inquest was opened and adjourned to allow the police time to investigate. However, when the inquest finally concluded, the police were no nearer to finding Eliza's killer(s) and the jury's verdict was 'murder by person or person's unknown'.

Several arrests were made but everyone was released due to lack of evidence. Eliza had not been robbed, nor sexually assaulted and whoever killed her struck entirely at random, using the first thing that came to hand rather than a specific weapon. A reward of £100 was offered for information leading to the apprehension of her killer(s) but it went unclaimed and Eliza's murder remains unsolved.

4 JANUARY

1917 Tramcar driver Richard Davies was a few minutes early arriving at the terminus at the top of Tipton Road, Dudley. He left his tram briefly and, while he was away, conductress Maggie Jefferson reversed the pole used to conduct live electricity to the controls and boarded the tram. Unaware that Davies was not in his seat, Miss Jefferson then released the brake. The runaway tram careered down Tipton Road, gathering speed as it went, and when it reached a bend, it jumped the rails and overturned.

Twenty-five passengers were injured, most of them crushed or cut by flying glass. Annie Payne was trapped beneath the rear of the tram and it took some time to free her. She was eventually lifted through a window by a nurse and doctor, but was so badly injured that she died shortly after admission to hospital.

The accident was unusual in that it replicated almost exactly another fatal accident that occurred at the same spot a year earlier – in each case, even the tramcar was the same.

5 JANUARY

1894   Robert and Mary Goodwin appeared at the Guildhall in Walsall charged with neglecting their five children. Magistrates were told that the children came to the attention of the Society for the Prevention of Cruelty to Children in August 1893, when the society's inspector had visited their home seven times, each time finding the children dirty, hungry and inadequately clothed.

The chief magistrate called it 'an abominable case' but his colleague, former mayor, Mr J. Wheway, seemed fixated on whether the inspector had the right to enter the Goodwins' house.

'Even a poor man's house is his castle, or ought to be,' insisted Wheway, who seemed unable to grasp the inspector's repeated assertions that he had permission to go in. 'It is not right to examine a man's rooms' persisted Wheway, adding, 'I would not allow it in my own house and will not suffer it in anybody else's.'

Although his colleagues on the Bench voiced their disagreement, Wheway continued to object, even though the society's solicitor tried to

The Guildhall,
Walsall, 1867.
(Author's collection)

reason with him, reiterating that permission was always obtained and pointing out that it would be very difficult to prove a case of neglect or cruelty if a house was not entered. Eventually, in the face of Wheway's nit-picking, the case collapsed and all the society could do was to watch the Goodwins carefully, to see how things progressed. The society's solicitor sarcastically promised that they would endeavour to do so in a manner to which Wheway could not possibly object.

6 JANUARY

1890 Eighteen-year-old Emma Greaves appeared before magistrates at Dudley charged with assaulting and wounding Elizabeth Darbey with a red hot iron. Elizabeth and her sister Mary rented space in a nail-maker's workshop in Dudley, from Emma's mother, but were told to leave after an argument. When they went back to collect their tools, the argument started afresh.

Castle Street, Dudley, 1950s. (Author's collection)

Elizabeth and Mary threatened Emma with violence and she picked up a piece of red hot iron with which to defend herself. Both sisters were burned, one on the nose, the other on the eye.

Magistrates decided that there was blame on both sides and dismissed the case.

7 JANUARY

1865 Emmanuel Davis and Francis Longmore went to Swan Village Station and while Davis went to purchase their tickets to Wednesbury, Longmore crossed the wooden bridge to the opposite platform.

While walking across the bridge, Longmore slipped and fell head first through the side, landing on the platform 10ft below. Davis asked if he was hurt, to which Longmore replied, 'I shall die.' He was taken to a nearby pub, where a surgeon rendered first aid, after which he was sent home in a cab.

Longmore did die the following morning from a broken neck. At the inquest on his death, held by coroner Edwin Hooper, the main question for the jury was whether or not Longmore was sober at the time of the accident.

He and Davis had been conducting some business in the pub and Davis was quite prepared to admit that they had been drinking but insisted that they were both sober. Other witnesses gave varying accounts, and Longmore was said to have been 'drunk but able to walk straight and take care of himself', 'slightly tipsy', 'perfectly sober' and 'drunk and incapable'.

The inquest jury ruled that death was caused by a fall from the bridge, and expressed an opinion that Longmore was capable of taking care of himself, and that the bridge needed better fencing. Longmore left thirteen children, six of whom were too young to work, and his widow later sued the Great Western Railway Company for damages at the Staffordshire Assizes. She was awarded £500.

8 JANUARY

1864   An inquest was opened at Tipton into the death of thirteen-year-old Minnie Smart. When Minnie was taken ill while visiting Tabitha Cambridge, her married sister at Netherton, Mrs Cambridge gave her some 'surfeit water' and took her back to their parents' home, where Minnie subsequently died.

Rumours began to circulate that Minnie had been poisoned, so coroner Edwin Hooper adjourned the proceedings for a post-mortem examination.

When the inquest reopened, surgeon Thomas Underhill reported that although Minnie was emaciated, there were no marks of violence on her body and no trace of poison. In Underhill's opinion, Minnie died from scarlet fever and Mrs Cambridge confirmed that there was fever in the house when Minnie visited – two of her brother's children had recently died and a third child was currently at death's door.

The 'surfeit water' she gave her sister was a traditional Black Country recipe used for 'bringing out eruptions' and curing indigestion. It was made from water, sugar, spirits and cinnamon, and Underhill confirmed that he had tested a sample taken from the same batch given to Minnie and found it perfectly harmless.

The inquest jury returned a verdict of 'death from natural causes' and Underhill begged the coroner to direct the attention of the public to two very important points. Firstly, he pointed out the folly of taking an infected child among those who hadn't yet succumbed to the illness, and secondly, had Minnie been kept warm and not taken home in the cold, her life would probably have been spared. Sensitive to Mrs Cambridge's feelings, the coroner agreed with Underhill's opinions but added that he did not believe that Mrs Cambridge was aware that Minnie had caught the fever when she took her home.

9 JANUARY

1878   After courting for two years, twenty-one-year-old William Henry Griffiths and Elizabeth Beeston were engaged to be married.

On 9 January, Griffiths called for his fiancée at her home in Wolverhampton, and the couple went out for a walk together. When they reached Goldthorn Hill, Griffiths suddenly cried 'Stop!'

Elizabeth asked him what he wanted but Griffiths didn't reply. Instead, he threw his left arm around her neck, covering her mouth with his left

Goldthorn Hill,
Wolverhampton.
(Author's collection)

hand and cut her throat with his right hand. Elizabeth bit the fingers covering her mouth and Griffiths let her go, but before she could run away he stooped down, grabbed her ankles and tipped her over. As she lay on her back, he tried to cut her throat a second time.

Elizabeth screamed 'Murder!' and several people ran to her. 'Here's somebody coming,' she said loudly, hoping that Griffiths would stop what he was doing.

'Is there, Betsy?' he asked calmly, before getting up and walking away.

Fortunately, Elizabeth survived the attempt on her life but Griffiths was found dead in a gateway, having cut his throat.

An inquest was opened and adjourned for a month in the hope that Elizabeth Beeston would be able to attend. When it reopened, she was unable to explain her fiancé's actions. It was assumed that the motive for the attack was jealousy but Elizabeth swore that she had never given Griffiths any cause, nor had there been any quarrel between them on that or any other occasion. The only unusual thing that Elizabeth noted was that, when her fiancée called for her on 9 January, he was wearing his work clothes and no collar.

With no ready explanation for Griffiths's behaviour, the inquest jury returned a verdict of suicide while temporarily insane.

10 JANUARY

1870   Samuel Tonks appeared before magistrates at Dudley charged with manslaughter. On a visit to his aunt at Brockmoor on New Years' Day, Samuel picked up a gun and, as a joke, pointed it at his six-year-old cousin, Louisa Heath. Unbeknown to Samuel the gun was loaded and he accidentally shot the little girl, blowing away most of her face and killing her almost instantly.

Tonks was arrested but magistrates recognised that the shooting was a terrible accident and discharged him with a caution to be more careful when handling firearms in the future.

11 JANUARY

1864   At the Bridge End Colliery in Bromley, six men began their descent to the coal face in a skip. Meanwhile, on the surface, Thomas Jones was about to bridle one of the pit horses.

As Jones entered the stable, something spooked the horse, which spun round, knocking Jones over, before bolting through the stable door. As it neared the mouth of the pit, it slipped on a metal plate and plummeted down the shaft. Halfway down, the horse landed on the skip and the supporting chain snapped, sending the men crashing 400ft to the bottom of the shaft.

Joseph Baker (29), Job Round (26), Zachariah Barker (53), George Terry (33), Thomas Bate (40) and John Page (27) were killed instantly, their bodies terribly mutilated, while the horse was said to be 'smashed to atoms.' Bate lived in Worcestershire, so there was a separate inquest on his death, but Staffordshire coroner Mr T.M. Phillips opened an inquest on 14 January and adjourned it to permit the Mine Inspector to visit the scene of the accident. When the inquests concluded, the juries returned six verdicts of accidental death.

At the time of the accident, the banksman was not at his post at the top of the shaft, and the juries wondered if he might have been able to stop or turn the horse had he been there. Although regulations stated that pit shafts should be fenced, one side of the iron rail surrounding the shaft had been removed to allow the men to board the skip.

The luckiest man of all was collier Richard Aston, who got off the skip because he thought there were too many men on board.

12 JANUARY

1888 Seventeen-year-old Kate James of Wednesfield returned home from her job in London and was collected by her father, Henry, at High Level Station, Wolverhampton. It was a foggy night and, by the side of the canal bridge at Wood End, there was an open gate leading to the towpath. Instead of crossing the bridge, the horse turned through the gate and pulled the trap straight into the canal.

Kate's father managed to get out of the water and shouted until help arrived. He was found on the bank in a state of exhaustion, but sadly Kate drowned and an inquest later returned a verdict of 'accidental death'.

Canal at New Bridge, Wolverhampton, 1913. (Author's collection)

13 JANUARY

1864 Jane Glover saw a group of small boys at Bagnall's Pool, Tipton. The pond was frozen and one boy was testing the strength of the ice at the edge with his clog. The ice broke and Mrs Glover advised the boy to stay well away from the pool, but eleven-year-old Reuben Clifton told her that he thought that it would be fine for sliding.

As soon as Reuben ventured onto the ice it gave way, sending him into the water. Unable to reach him, Mrs Glover ran to raise the alarm and Harry Jukes hurried to the pond with drags. Reuben's body had drifted almost 10 yards from the bank and sunk in 12ft of water and, by the time it was recovered, he was beyond any medical help. An inquest held by coroner Edwin Hooper returned a verdict of 'accidental death'.

14 JANUARY

1854 Coroner Mr T.M. Phillips held an inquest at the Shinglers' Arms Tavern at Brierley Hill into the death of fourteen-year-old James Rowley.

The boy was killed by a fall of coal while working underground at a pit owned by Lord Ward, Earl of Dudley, and the verdict of 'accidental death' was a relatively straightforward decision for the jury.

It was revealed at the inquest that both of Rowley's brothers were tragically killed in almost identical mining accidents, when they were roughly the same age as James.

High Street, Brierley Hill, 1911. (Author's collection)

15 JANUARY

1864 Coroner Edwin Hooper held an inquest into the death of sixteen-year-old miner John Whitehouse, who drowned in the canal at West Bromwich on 13 January – an exceptionally foggy day. Lock keeper Richard Parks recalled the arrival of two boys at his cottage, informing him that someone had fallen into the water. Parks went to fetch the drags but was unable to find them and so grabbed a rake, with which he retrieved Whitehouse's body.

There was no public road or path at the point where the body was found but people often went that way as a short cut. There was little doubt that John had wandered into the canal in the dense fog, and the jury returned a verdict of accidental death.

After the inquest, Hooper and Parks immediately moved to another pub for the inquest on the death of foundry labourer Richard Bradley, whose body was found just a few yards from that of Whitehouse. As soon as he began giving evidence, Parks apologised to the coroner, saying that he was confused and that the evidence he had just given at the first inquest actually applied to Bradley, whose was the first body found. The mix-up made no difference to the jury's verdict of 'accidental death', since it was obvious that Bradley had also drowned on his way to work after losing his bearings in the fog and walking into the canal.

16 JANUARY

1864 The case of *Green v Smith* was heard at the Wolverhampton County Court, in which the Misses Green, who kept a boarding school, tried to recoup outstanding fees of £26 7s 6d.

In 1857, Mr Smith sent three of his children to the school, at a cost of £8 17s 6d a quarter for their board and education. The children were withdrawn from the school in late 1863, and the sum claimed by the Greens was for three quarters, during the first of which the children attended the school and during the second of which they left. The third quarter was charged in lieu of notice of intent to remove the children.

Mr Smith, whose allegations were corroborated by the school maid, claimed that for breakfast his children each received one slice of dry bread with broth or porridge, seasoned with nettles or onions. Meat was only provided for dinner three or four times a week, and then only around an ounce of mutton, pig face or bacon per child, with vegetables. Pudding was served only twice a week and soup made from rice, sheep's lungs or nettles – which the children had to pick themselves – was served at least three days every week.

The judge pointed out that the cost per child, including education, broke down to 5s 10d a week and he considered the diet good enough for the price. There was nothing wrong with nettle soup, insisted the judge, who seemed to be under the impression that Smith was exaggerating and that the testimony of his daughter, fourteen-year-old former pupil Eliza Smith, was largely a figment of her imagination.

The judge ordered Smith to pay for the two quarters during which his children had attended the school, waiving the third quarter's payment in lieu of notice.

17 JANUARY

A coatimundi.

1934 The Wolverhampton Monster's reign of terror was ended by seventeen-year-old George Goodhead, who threw a brick at it and then kicked it to death, after it sprang for his throat when he disturbed it while it was attacking a child.

The dead animal on wasteland at Brickkiln Croft was final proof of the existence of the strange, mythical creature that roamed the streets of Wolverhampton, terrorising the population and savaging children. Described as 'like a monstrous rat', it was said to be the size of a full-grown cat, with a shaggy coat, an upturned snout, a rat-like tail and fearsome protruding teeth.

The 'monster' was finally identified as a coatimundi by Dr S.C. Dyke, the pathologist at the Royal Hospital in Wolverhampton. Dyke explained that the animals came from Mexico and were imported to England as pets or kept in zoos.

When a second coatimundi was found dead at Brickkiln Croft it sparked fears that there was a colony of the animals in the area, particularly since this one was a female, while the one killed was male. However, the mystery of the dead female was quickly solved when an attendant at a travelling fair came forward to say that they had passed through the locality at Christmas and thrown away the body of a dead coatimundi. Even so, the council decided to err on the safe side and arranged for the official rat catcher to scour the area. In spite of being hampered in his work by crowds of sightseers, he found no more 'monsters'.

18 JANUARY

1893 As an underground fire burned at Heath End Colliery near Walsall, sixty-four-year-old John Holt was contracted to supervise the diversion of a brook into the pit, in the hope of extinguishing the blaze.

As Holt dug, a large hole suddenly opened up in his excavations. Holt began filling the hole but, as he did, the earth suddenly shifted again and he was buried alive. His workmates immediately dug down to try and rescue him but it took four hours before they reached him, by which time he was long dead. An inquest held by coroner Mr T.H. Stanley returned a verdict of 'accidental death'.

19 JANUARY

1877 Fifty-two-year-old Pardoe Hyde died in Lower Gornal, and was to be the subject of a controversial inquest held by coroner Mr W.H. Phillips.

Dudley surgeon Mr A. Jones had ordered a post-mortem examination, without first gaining the coroner's permission. Phillips accused Jones of 'improper interference' since, on death, the body became the property of the Crown and must not be meddled with, to avoid perverting the course of public justice.

Hyde broke his thigh on 28 November 1876 and the bone was set by Jones. The patient was progressing well until he died and, not knowing the cause of death, Jones felt unable to issue a death certificate without further investigation.

Mrs Hyde gave her permission for the post-mortem, which was carried out by Jones and another surgeon. The cause of death was found to be a twisted bowel and, although the inquest returned a verdict of 'death from natural causes', Phillips was still not happy, saying that the doctors had overstepped the bounds of their authority. After some grovelling apologies, the coroner eventually accepted that the doctors concerned had acted with the best intentions and stated that he did not intend to take the matter any further.

20 JANUARY

1858 Twelve-year-old Maria Powell died at Tipton. Among her chores was the collection of pieces of unburned coal from the ash mounds created by the Park Lane Furnaces and on 12 January, as Maria concentrated on her task, she failed to notice her petticoats trailing across some live embers.

Although the garments were quickly extinguished, Maria was badly burned. An inquest held by deputy coroner Edwin Hooper returned a verdict of 'accidental death' before warning parents in the strongest terms about the dangers of sending children onto the ash heaps.

21 JANUARY

1882   Susannah Jones took her father's supper to the Swan Village Gasworks near West Bromwich, then was seen at about 9.30 p.m. walking along the canal towards Dudley Port with her sweetheart William Fryer, who had his arm around her waist. The couple seemed to be on good terms but two hours later, Fryer met a policeman and told him that he wished to give himself up for murdering his girlfriend.

Fryer, who was dripping wet, explained to PC Davis that he had pushed a woman into the canal and thought she was drowned. The police went to the spot indicated by Fryer and found a woman's hat floating on the water and at first light Susannah's body was recovered.

Fryer had been courting Susannah for about eighteen months and, according to her father, they had not quarrelled prior to her death. Doctors who examined Fryer suggested that he was suffering from 'impulsive mania', the first manifestations of 'homicidal mania'. He had delusions, coupled with a tendency to destroy those he loved or commit suicide and, at the time of Susannah's death, would have been incapable of distinguishing right from wrong.

Fryer, who tried to commit suicide three times while incarcerated, told the doctors that the devil had ordered him to drown Susannah, saying that he loved her and would far rather have drowned himself. At his trial at the Staffordshire Assizes in May 1882, his defence counsel called several witnesses to describe Fryer's strange behaviour before the murder and he was acquitted due to insanity and ordered to be detained during Her Majesty's pleasure. He was sent to Broadmoor Criminal Lunatic Asylum.

22 JANUARY

1925   More than 4,000 people attended the funeral of twenty-five-year-old PC Albert Willitts at St Peter's Church, Wolverhampton. On 17 January, Willitts was patrolling his beat near Bilston Road police station when he saw three youths behaving suspiciously. Having spoken to them, he decided to follow them and the young men got as far as Vicarage Road before they realised that the policeman was behind them.

St Peter's Church, Wolverhampton. (Author's collection)

They began to run and Willitts chased them, managing to grab one boy. As he did, three gun shots rang out and Willitts fell to the ground mortally wounded.

Several other policemen had spoken to the three youths that night, having observed them loitering in the area, and the police quickly arrested George James Dixon (14), Edward Patrick Heggerty (17) and William Crossley (19). All three had absconded from a probation home for young offenders in Hertfordshire and, when the two older boys were jointly charged with the murder of PC Willitts, both blamed the other. 'It was Crossley who shot him,' insisted Heggerty, adding, 'I saw the flash from the other side of the road.'

'I never had the revolver. I don't know how to fire one,' countered Crossley.

Both youths were tried at the Stafford Assizes on 27 February, where each was still blaming the other. Dixon appeared as a witness for the prosecution, after all charges against him were dropped, and stated that it was Crossley who fired the fatal shots. However, whether the trigger was pulled by Crossley or Heggerty, each was equally responsible in the eyes of the law and, when both were found guilty, they were sentenced to death.

Notice of an appeal was immediately given on the grounds that the proper verdict should have been guilty of manslaughter. Crossley was said to have the mental age of a nine-year-old and a petition was raised in his hometown to try and save him from the gallows. The appeal took place on 23 March but was unsuccessful and the date of the double execution was set for 7 April. In the event, the Home Secretary commuted the death sentences to life imprisonment.

23 JANUARY

1861 Coroner Edwin Hooper held an inquest at Crookhay, West Bromwich, into the death of twenty-one-year-old Thomas Morgan.

Morgan worked at a forge and happened to notice that a large crank wheel attached to a steam engine was loose. Without stopping the engine, he tried to fix the wheel by driving wedges behind it, and the crank handle hit his head, knocking him onto the revolving wheel.

Although the engine was quickly stopped, Morgan was literally cut to pieces by the machinery and died instantly. He was known as a sober, steady man, who was due to be married a few days after his fatal accident.

24 JANUARY

1900 At Bent's Brewery in Bilston, one of the heavy horses took fright and bolted. Still pulling its dray, it galloped out of the yard, through an orchard and into the main street, where it crashed through the enormous plate glass window of Messrs Leeke, Provision Merchants.

At the time, Mr Lawson was idling away a few minutes while waiting for a train to Wolverhampton by doing some windowshopping. The horse collided with Lawson, driving him through the window, through the wood partition at the back of the window and onto the shop floor.

By a miracle, Lawson escaped with cuts and bruises and, after being treated by a local surgeon, was able to continue his homeward journey. The fate of the horse is not recorded.

25 JANUARY   **1848**   An inquest held at The Royal Oak, Portobello, Willenhall, into the death of Elizabeth Wootton returned a verdict of 'accidental death'. Elizabeth's father was a butty collier (mining subcontractor) at the Bull Pleck Coal Pit and, like most butties, he regularly employed members of his own family.

On 24 January, Elizabeth was working with him and overbalanced as she was pushing a skip. Feeling herself falling down the shaft, she grabbed another girl's skirt to save herself but the girl quickly shook Elizabeth off, for fear of being dragged down herself. Elizabeth plunged right to the pit bottom and was literally dashed to pieces.

26 JANUARY   **1929**   The funeral of Harry Park Temple took place at St Matthew's Church, Wolverhampton, and the crowds who turned out were so large that 40 yards of railings surrounding the churchyard collapsed, injuring two women. More than 5,000 people later watched Temple's interment in Bilston Cemetery.

Temple died on 20 January, after a heroic attempt to rescue two youths from drowning. Joseph Elmore, Harold Heath and Reginald Bond were playing football on a frozen pool in Wolverhampton when the ice beneath them gave way and all three fell through. Reginald managed to haul himself back onto the ice and pulled Joseph out after him. Together, the boys were pulling Harold out when the ice broke again and Harold and Joseph went back into the water.

By now, several people had come to help and Thomas Whittingham and Temple began to inch their way across the ice. It cracked loudly and Whittingham slipped over, but Temple continued to crawl towards the hole in the ice and got into the water. Suddenly, he disappeared beneath the surface and the men, who had by now formed a human chain to the bank of the pool, believed that he was either seized with violent cramp, or that one of the two boys in the water grabbed him and pulled him down. His body was recovered later, as were the bodies of sixteen-year-old Joseph and fifteen-year-old Harold.

At the inquest, coroner Mr A.C. Skidmore hailed twenty-seven-year-old Temple as a hero, saying that he had forwarded his name for consideration for a bravery award.

Queen Square,
Wolverhampton.
(Author's collection)

27 JANUARY

1859 Shoemaker Mr Hands rented an upper-storey room from milliner Mr Paling at his premises in Queen Street, Wolverhampton. The room was occupied by three young women, who did the stitching on the shoes and boots.

During the day, the girls often had occasion to visit what the newspapers of the time referred to as 'the one storey house' in Mr Paling's back yard. However, Paling maintained that this was not part of the rental agreement and the girls in his employ resented sharing their facilities.

On 27 January, Mary Ann Gee went to use the toilet but found her way barred by Henry Riddle, a boy in Paling's employ, who was waving a large stick. Miss Gee was not about to be thwarted and she and one of the other girls boxed Henry's ears and disarmed him, before barging past him into the lavatory.

Hearing Henry's shouts, Paling left his breakfast and rushed into the yard. By that time, Miss Gee was enthroned in the outhouse with the door locked and resolutely ignored Paling's orders to come out. In a rage, Paling broke down the door and seized Miss Gee by the shoulders, forcing her out into the yard in a state of partial undress. He swore at her, called her a 'street walker' and threatened to knock her head off.

Miss Gee summoned Paling for assault and he was fined 1s plus costs.

28 JANUARY

1861 Sarah Neal of Rowley Regis was the daughter of a nail maker who forced the girl to make nails alongside him, and on 28 January 1861 her father beat her dreadfully because she wasn't working fast enough, leaving her with a black eye.

William Neal physically chastised his daughter again on 23 February, this time hitting her twice over the head with an iron bar, and on 27 February she stayed out all night, too afraid to go home because her father had threatened to kill her.

She was found by an old friend, who took her home with him and, appalled by her physical condition, began to ask questions. Sarah revealed that she worked every day from seven o'clock in the morning until ten o'clock at night, apart from Saturdays, when she was permitted to finish work at noon.

When William Neal appeared at the Petty Sessions on 6 March charged with assaulting Sarah on 28 January, the girl was so weak and exhausted that she had to be carried in and out of court. She was emaciated to the point of being skeletal and bore numerous marks of violence all over her body.

William Neal insisted that he had always been a good father to Sarah but the Bench didn't believe him. He was fined £1 plus costs and cautioned that any repeat offence would be dealt with much more severely.

29 JANUARY

1827 As five miners worked below ground at Mr Wightwick's Colliery in Tividale, Rowley Regis, there was a sudden fall of coal. Miraculously, one miner escaped with only a slight injury to his hip, but Daniel Sowden, Thomas Jones, William Paine and John Corbet Brookes died instantly, crushed beneath 25 tons of coal. All but one of the deceased left a wife and children.

There was no warning whatsoever that the roof was about to fall, and the jury at the inquest, held by coroner Henry Smith, returned four verdicts of 'accidental death' on the victims.

30 JANUARY

1860   Twenty-nine-year-old Henry Draper climbed into a brewer's vat at Ettingshall to clean it. He was soon in difficulties and although he was pulled out of the vat as quickly as possible, he emerged unconscious. A doctor was summoned and attempted to bleed him but to no avail – Draper had suffocated to death.

An inquest was held the next day at The Builder's Arms in Wolverhampton, and, on hearing that Draper went into the vat against the express orders of his employer, the inquest jury ruled that he alone was responsible for his death.

31 JANUARY

1916   During the First World War, on the night of 31 January/1 February, the Black Country suffered a heavy air raid. Attracted by the glow of the industrial furnaces, Zeppelins made two bombing raids on Tipton, Bradley, Wednesbury and Walsall, which resulted in the deaths of thirty-five people.

Among them were the Lady Mayoress of Walsall, Julia Slater, who died from septicaemia three weeks after the tramcar in which she had been travelling was hit by flying fragments of a bomb. In Tipton, Thomas Morris lost his wife, two children and his mother and father-in-law when a bomb fell on their house in Union Street, while a courting couple died on the banks of the Wolverhampton Union Canal at Lower Bradley.

Hearing the sound of explosions in Wednesbury, Mrs Smith went out into King Street to see what the noise was. Her house suffered a direct hit, killing her husband and three children.

Thirteen-year-old William Hyman Jones, who lost a leg in the air raid. (Author's collection)

Spring Vale furnaces by night, 1905. (Author's collection)

FEBRUARY

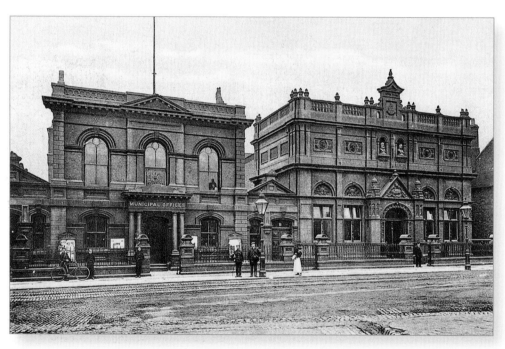

Wednesbury Art Gallery & Municipal Buildings, 1900s. (Author's collection)

1 FEBRUARY

1858 Licensed victualler Peter Harcourt was brewing beer for Mr Whitehouse at The Turk's Head Hotel, Wednesbury, when the cook heard groaning, which she traced to one of the inn's bedrooms. There she found Harcourt stretched out on the bed, fully clothed, with steam rising from his body.

The cook swiftly stripped off Harcourt's clothes and wrapped him in a sheet, while Whitehouse sent for a surgeon. However, Harcourt was scalded from head to toe and the surgeon was quick to point out that there was no hope whatsoever of his survival.

Harcourt died the following morning, but was able to tell Whitehouse that he had been sitting on the edge of the copper, waiting for the water to boil so that it could be added to the grain. Harcourt believed he dozed off and fell backwards into the copper, where he was completely immersed in near-boiling liquid. Somehow, he managed to climb out of the 5ft-deep vessel and walk upstairs to the bedroom, where he was found by the cook. He left a wife and several children.

The Market Place, Wednesbury, 1910. (Author's collection)

2 FEBRUARY

1859 Collier Thomas Williams of Wednesbury stored the gunpowder he used for his work in a can, which hung from a ceiling beam in his home.

On 2 February, Williams went to work, leaving behind his three children, who were soon joined by a neighbour's child, Anne Holland. Left unsupervised, twelve-year-old Sarah Williams reached down the tin containing around 3lbs of fine gunpowder and tipped some into a jug. It was the custom for miners to fill hollow lengths of straw with gunpowder to act as rudimentary fuses, and the children amused themselves by filling straws, which they lit at the fire. The resulting explosion blew out all of the cottage windows.

Sarah rushed out into the street with her clothes on fire. The flames were smothered by neighbours but Sarah was badly burned on her face, neck, arms and lower body, and succumbed two days later, having made a statement that she alone was responsible for taking down the can of gunpowder.

Coroner George Hinchcliffe held an inquest into Sarah's death at Wednesbury, at which the jury were of the opinion that Williams had been exceedingly negligent in leaving so dangerous a substance where it could be accessed by children. Even so, they did not find evidence of criminal negligence, returning a verdict of 'accidental death'.

3 FEBRUARY

1894   James and Elizabeth Hawkins appeared before magistrates at the Guildhall, Walsall, charged with having wilfully neglected their child, Jabez, in such a manner as to cause unnecessary suffering and injury to his health.

Five-month-old Jabez had recently died from 'consumption of the bowels' – inflammation and ulceration of the intestines from tubercular disease. Although he died from natural causes, at the time of his death he was filthy and emaciated, and the inquest jury recommended that proceedings should be initiated against his parents.

The Bench heard that Elizabeth was a drunkard, who spent all of her husband's income on alcohol, whereas James was a good husband and father, who tried to do his best for his family. Magistrates discharged James with a caution but sentenced Elizabeth to two months' imprisonment with hard labour.

4 FEBRUARY

1866   Thirteen-year-old George Edward Fox appeared at West Bromwich Police Court charged with assaulting Richard Phillips.

The two youths lived on the same street and on the night of 13 January, several fights took place between residents, including one between George and Richard's brothers. According to George's brother, Richard's brother did not fight fairly and tried to bite his nose off.

The two men were eventually separated and taken into their respective houses. Minutes later, George ran outside with a sharp piece of iron in his hand, which he threw at Richard in retaliation for his brother's unorthodox methods of combat. The metal struck Richard in the face and he was taken to the Birmingham General Hospital, where he stayed for three weeks. On his discharge, he was completely blind in his right eye and only partially sighted in his left.

Magistrates fined George £5 plus costs or two months' imprisonment, adding that if the fine were paid, it would be handed over to Richard's mother for her son's care. The contemporary newspapers do not record which option was chosen.

5 FEBRUARY

1878   When Amelia Harris's husband Joseph was taken into hospital in October 1876, her parents, Phoebe and James Jones, welcomed their daughter and their two granddaughters back into their Halesowen home. Joseph was transferred from the General Hospital in Birmingham to the Lunatic Asylum in Winson Green and, in March 1877, moved to Powick Asylum, where he was classed as a 'dangerous lunatic'. He was released on trial on 18 October 1877 then fully discharged as cured two weeks later, joining his wife and daughters, Alice (6) and Eve (3), at her parents' house.

Harris came to believe that Amelia had been unfaithful while he had been away and the thoughts tortured him. On 5 February, Phoebe left

Birmingham
General Hospital.
(Author's collection)

Powick Asylum, 1907.
(Author's collection)

the house with her husband's breakfast and when she returned thirty minutes later, Amelia was lying dead, with Eve's body beside her. Terrified, Phoebe picked up Eve and ran outside. Their neighbour, Samuel Harris, went back with her and they found Alice lying in bed in a pool of blood. Barely alive, she died the next morning.

Amelia and her daughters had terrible head injuries, inflicted with a hatchet. Joseph was quickly apprehended and gave two conflicting statements, first saying, 'It wasn't me that did it,' then explaining that his wife and mother-in-law had continually threatened to send him back to Powick.

Twenty-seven-year-old Harris was committed for trial at the Worcester Assizes in March 1878, where he faced charges relating only to his wife's murder. Although the surgeon at Winson Green Prison testified that Harris had shown no signs of insanity since the murders, his defence counsel called the superintendent of Powick Asylum, who persuaded the jury that Harris could have been insane at the time of the killings. The jury found him not guilty on the grounds of insanity and he was ordered to be detained at Her Majesty's pleasure.

6 FEBRUARY

1888 Magistrates at Dudley Police Court dealt with the case of twelve-year-old William Christman, who was charged with stabbing another child.

It was alleged that William had been bullying a much younger child and when eleven-year-old George Froggatt intervened to defend the youngster, William drew a pocketknife and stabbed Froggatt in the arm.

Magistrates ordered William to be handed over to his parents, to be punished as they saw fit. Meanwhile, his parents were forced to pay court costs, along with 10s 6d, which was to be handed over to Froggatt's parents, to cover the cost of their son's treatment by the surgeon.

7 FEBRUARY

1866 An explosion at Groveland Ironworks in Tividale claimed the lives of two men. A blocked tuyere – a pipe through which air was blown into the furnace to facilitate combustion – caused the furnace to burst, showering the men in molten metal. An inquest held by coroner Edwin Hooper into the deaths of Thomas Wallett and Thomas Pritchard heard that the tuyere was brand new and concluded that the explosion was a tragic accident.

Exactly two weeks later, the same furnace exploded again, in almost identical circumstances. Once again the explosion immediately claimed two lives, although a third man was badly injured and died on 2 March. The victims were Josiah Allbutt and Matthew and Abraham Wallett, the brothers of Thomas, who died in the first explosion.

8 FEBRUARY

1859 Former police constable Henry Handy appeared at Willenhall Police Court charged with murderously assaulting John Southwell.

Mr Southwell, the plaintiff, was a teetotal lay-preacher and, having attended the Wesleyan Chapel in Wolverhampton on 2 February, he dined with a member of the congregation before setting off to walk home to Willenhall.

On his way, he met Handy, who was so drunk that he was staggering. Afraid that the policeman would fall, Southwell went to help him and was sworn at. Then, as Southwell tried to pass, Handy attacked him with his fists and staff, banging Southwell's head against a wall.

After several minutes, Southwell managed to escape but Handy followed him and knocked him down. By then, Southwell's desperate cries of 'Murder!' had attracted the attention of people living in nearby houses. With Handy tagging behind them, one man accompanied Southwell to make a complaint at the police station. Once there, Southwell was examined by a police surgeon, who was so concerned by his condition that he ordered Handy to be locked up.

When Handy's superior officers heard the accusation against him, he was dismissed from the force. He admitted to being drunk before magistrates, but excused his violence by saying that Southwell had refused to let him examine the contents of a bag he was carrying, which Handy suspected contained contraband.

Magistrates commended the police authorities on dealing with Handy so quickly, and fined him £5 and costs (£2 of which was to go to Southwell), or three month's imprisonment with hard labour in default.

9 FEBRUARY

1882 Eighteen-year-old Emil Charles Hindelaing of Dudley asked his three younger brothers to go for a walk with him. Nine-year-old Lewis Benjamin and seven-year-old Francis Adlebert agreed to accompany him and so Emil took them along the canal at Tipton. There he threw both children into the water and waited until they had drowned, before handing himself in to police.

Tried for wilful murder at the Staffordshire Assizes on 28 April, Hindelaing was found insane and ordered to be detained at Her Majesty's pleasure. He was sent to Broadmoor Criminal Lunatic Asylum.

Dudley, 1926.
(Author's collection)

10 FEBRUARY

1865 Coroner Mr T.M. Phillips held an inquest in Wolverhampton into the death of shoemaker James Baynton.

Baynton was walking home to Bilston on 9 February when he came across a flood on the footpath. Rather than walk through the water, he climbed over the railings to cross the railway line.

He was seen standing stock still on the line by the driver of the express train from Wolverhampton and although Baynton could apparently see the train approaching, he didn't move. The driver was unable to avoid hitting him and he died from his injuries at Wolverhampton Hospital the following day.

The engine driver told the inquest that Baynton was leaning forwards slightly and clutching his stomach. He was known to suffer from fits and the coroner theorised that he had felt a seizure coming on and was unable to move out of the way. The jury returned a verdict of 'accidental death'.

11 FEBRUARY

1860 Coroner George Hinchcliffe held an inquest at Wednesbury into the death of an unidentified boy, said to be about twelve years old.

Colliers John Sheldon and Thomas Corser told the inquest that, at about 6 p.m. on 9 February, they saw the boy on the bank of the Blue Fly Pit at Mesty Croft Colliery. Both men then went down into the mine to work and later that night, heard the sound of something crashing down the shaft and landing heavily at the bottom. When they went to investigate, they found the boy with his head 'knocked in' and his leg broken.

The inquest heard that the boy went to one of the proprietors of the colliery to ask for work and, hearing that the child was an orphan, Mr Hammond took him into his house and gave him a meal. It was thought that, on leaving Hammond's house, the child accidentally wandered into the pit.

The jury concluded that the deceased died from injuries sustained from falling down the pit, but how he came to fall, there was no evidence to show.

12 FEBRUARY

1873 Frank Barnsley and Jonah Adams were sliding on ice on a pool in Brownhills when the ice broke. Fortunately, a young boy saw them fall into the water and raised the alarm at a nearby shop.

Grocer Mr Arblaster ran to the spot with a rope. Frank had already been rescued and was able to walk home, but eight-year-old Jonah had disappeared beneath the surface of the water and it took some time before Arblaster managed to find him and pull him to the bank, where surgeons Cook and Cooper were waiting to treat him. Sadly, they failed to resuscitate Jonah, who was pronounced dead at the scene.

The jury at an inquest held by coroner Edwin Hooper returned a verdict of accidental death, asking the coroner to communicate with the owners of the pool to have it fenced.

13 FEBRUARY

1860 Miner David Price lodged with a butty collier and his wife at Rowley Regis. On 13 February, when his landlord left for work, Price went into the bedroom where his landlady Louisa Pugh was dressing and threw her onto the bed. Fortunately for Mrs Pugh, her husband had forgotten something and returned to the house before Price could complete what was obviously intended to be rape. Mr Pugh walked into his bedroom to find his wife and his lodger grappling on his bed and, when he objected, Price attacked him.

Price was charged with felonious assault on the 'modest and well-behaved' mother of six and, at the Staffordshire Assizes, his defence counsel insisted that Louisa was a consenting party – a woman 'of light character', whose husband was well aware that she and Price engaged in frequent intercourse together. When the Pughs indignantly denied this, the defence changed tack, accusing them of concocting the whole allegation in order to provide Mr Pugh with grounds for divorce.

After much deliberation, the jury found David Price guilty. He had appeared before magistrates for minor offences more than twenty times, and, describing him as 'an incorrigible criminal', the judge sentenced him to ten years' penal servitude.

14 FEBRUARY

1877 Nail maker Thomas Lloyd appeared at Dudley Police Court charged with being drunk and incapable, having been found by PC Moore so intoxicated that he was unable to stand up. 'I'm guilty and I'm glad of it,' Lloyd told the Bench, going on to explain the circumstances of his arrest.

He told the magistrates that he had been off work for several weeks with a dislocated shoulder, unable to earn any money to support his wife and family. On the night of his arrest he met some friends, who sympathetically treated him to so much drink that he fell over several times. While rolling about on the floor, his shoulder clicked back into place and he was able to return to work.

Magistrates fined Lloyd 5s plus costs.

15 FEBRUARY

1928 An inquest in Wolverhampton concluded with verdicts of 'death from natural causes' on sisters Sarah Caroline and Hannah Marie Hodgetts. Fifty-eight-year-old Sarah and forty-nine-year-old Hannah lived together in absolute squalor, in a filthy house littered with stale food. When they became ill, the doctor called to treat them was told that the sisters had not been to bed for three years. He ordered their admission to hospital and called in a specialist to see them but, instead, the women went to the home of another sister, where they died within hours of each other.

Because the two deaths were so close together, it was initially suspected that the women had been poisoned but an analysis of their internal organs failed to reveal any traces of noxious substances and doctors gave the cause of both deaths as malnutrition and enteritis.

16 FEBRUARY

1862 Widow Phoebe Corfield of Bilston lived with miner Thomas Halford as man and wife. On 15 February, the couple went out for a drink and then visited a neighbour, Samuel Tonks.

As they were leaving their neighbour's house, Thomas made some remarks to Phoebe, indicating that he believed she was having an affair with Tonks. Phoebe denied any such thing but Thomas was far from convinced. 'You want hanging,' he told her angrily.

In the early hours of the morning of 16 February, Thomas took the rope that he used to hold up his trousers from round his waist and fashioned it into a noose. Before Phoebe could protest, he dropped the noose round her neck, hauled her off her feet and fastened the rope to a hook in the ceiling. He then sat down, laughing.

Phoebe's two sons were in the room, one of them sleeping. Fifteen-year-old William cried out but Thomas threatened to cut his throat if he interfered. William woke his older brother, Henry, who managed to break the rope before going to fetch a neighbour and a policeman.

Wellington Road, Bilston.
(Author's collection)

Thomas Halford was arrested and appeared at the Staffordshire Assizes before Mr Baron Channell charged with attempted murder. His defence argued that Phoebe wanted to commit suicide and, at her insistence, Halford gave her the rope from round his waist so that she could hang herself. Testimony from Louisa Higgison, the first neighbour to arrive on the scene, seemed to support Halford's explanation. However, Phoebe denied having tried to end her own life and neighbour Mary Ford supported her version of events.

The jury found Halford guilty of attempted murder and the judge sentenced him to twenty years' penal servitude.

17 FEBRUARY

1914 Fifty-year-old chimney sweep Charles Longmore from Walsall appeared at the Stafford Assizes charged with the wilful murder of his wife, Sarah Ann Longmore, on 31 January.

Sarah was an alcoholic, who spent all of her husband's earnings on drink. Longmore had tried everything he could think of to get her to stop drinking and, on 31 January, his patience was finally exhausted and he lashed out at her while holding a knife, stabbing her in the neck.

The jury found him guilty, although they recommended mercy on the grounds of what they termed the 'long-continued provocation' of Sarah's drinking. Longmore, who claimed throughout that he never intended to hurt his wife, fainted as Mr Justice Lush pronounced the death sentence.

The jury's recommendation was heeded and Longmore was later reprieved, his sentence commuted to one of life imprisonment.

18 FEBRUARY

1866 Joseph and Eliza Sayers (aka Phillips) appeared at West Bromwich Police Court charged with cruelly ill-treating Eliza's son by a former lover.

It was alleged that the four-year-old was regularly beaten and kicked by both defendants, was often kept without food, and locked in the house alone for hours on end. On one occasion, the child fell into the fire while at home alone and was severely burned.

Neighbours contacted the police after realising that the boy had been left alone for almost twenty-four hours. A concerned neighbour forced an entry into the house and removed the child, who was said to be covered in bruises and ravenously hungry. At the time, he weighed only 23lbs.

Magistrates discharged Joseph Sayers with a severe caution but sent Eliza to prison for six months, with hard labour. Her son was taken to the Workhouse.

19 FEBRUARY

1862 Coroner Mr T.M. Phillips held an inquest at Willenhall into the death of three-year-old George Hyde.

While out playing close to his home, George accidentally fell onto a limekiln adjacent to a canal. He was fatally burned and but for the efforts of a passing boatman, would have been entirely consumed by the flames.

The mouth of the limekiln was practically on the same level as a nearby footpath and, in returning a verdict of 'accidental death', the coroner severely censured the owners of the kiln for not having it securely fenced off. They were warned that if the kiln wasn't fenced, they would be liable for damages in the event of any future accidents.

20 FEBRUARY **1862** Edward Garvey appeared before magistrates at Stourbridge Police Court charged with assaulting his wife Barthenia by attempting to cut her throat.

Barthenia was a cripple, who walked with the aid of crutches, and her husband was described as 'a local pugilist' and 'an idle and brutish sort of fellow'. It was not his first appearance before magistrates for ill-treating his wife.

On 13 February, Garvey returned home to find his wife crying with hunger. He asked her why she was crying and, when she told him, he unleashed a torrent of abuse and threatened to give her something to cry about, adding that if she didn't shut up he would cut her throat. When Barthenia asked if she might share the bread and cheese he was eating, he made good on his threat.

Fortunately, the wound was only skin deep, but it was still serious enough to earn Garvey to six months' imprisonment with hard labour.

High Street, Stourbridge, 1946. (Author's collection)

21 FEBRUARY **1859** William Peace appeared at the Willenhall Petty Sessions charged with assaulting his seventeen-year-old wife, Patience.

Peace was more than double his wife's age and supposedly a staunch Methodist but, according to his wife, the assault with which he was now charged was the third such outrage perpetrated on her during their brief marriage. The couple separated only weeks after their wedding, when Peace objected to his wife spending 23s on a new black dress so that she could go into mourning for an uncle.

Patience was alone at her mother's house on 16 February when her husband walked in and asked if she meant to live with him again. Patience told him that she would not as she feared for her life, at which Peace told her that if she wouldn't live with him, she must have something else. With that, he knocked her over, pulled up her dress, grasped her throat with one hand and thrust his other hand into her vagina, pushing as far as possible into her body. Patience was left torn and bleeding, and, when her mother found out about the assault soon afterwards, she went to confront Peace and found his hand and shirt cuff still bloody.

Patience provided the magistrates with a doctor's certificate, confirming that her vagina was severely lacerated and that she had internal injuries following her husband's assault. According to Patience, he had done precisely the same twice before, leaving her unable to climb the stairs for a month afterwards.

Peace claimed that he had knocked Patience down in self-defence after she assaulted him and that her injuries were the result of normal marital relations. He made a counterclaim that Patience had thrown a half-brick at him, which she freely admitted doing after his vicious assault. Magistrates dismissed the charge against Patience then discharged her husband with a warning to keep the peace towards her.

22 FEBRUARY

1899 Fifteen-year-old Esther 'Ettie' Smith was ironing clothes when her thirteen-year-old brother arrived back at their Wolverhampton home. Unthinkingly, Samuel leaned against some of the freshly ironed clothes and Ettie shouted at him for his carelessness. Brother and sister began a loud argument, and their mother went to act as referee.

Samuel made a remark that so upset Ettie that she threw a fork at him. Furious, Samuel threatened to punch her, to which Ettie replied, 'You'll do no such thing,' and turned her back on him. Before anyone could stop him, Samuel picked up the breadknife and flung it at his sister.

The knife lodged in Ettie's back and she ran from the house screaming, the knife falling out as she did. 'Oh, Mrs Hill, our Sam has stabbed me in the back and I think I am dying,' she managed to say, before expiring in her neighbour's arms.

A doctor and the police were summoned, the former able to do no more than pronounce Ettie dead. Her brother was taken to the police station in a state of shock and could say nothing apart from, 'Are you going to hang me?'

At the inquest, the jury were told that the Smiths were a respectable, hard-working, church-going family and that Samuel was normally a well-behaved and even-tempered boy, who was extremely fond of his sister. The inquest jury determined that since Ettie threw a fork at her brother it constituted provocation and returned a verdict of 'homicide by misadventure'.

23 FEBRUARY

1820 Abel Hill and Mary Martin (or Malton) had lived together for six years and, although they weren't married, Abel acknowledged paternity of Mary's sixteen-month-old son, Thomas, and seemed quite fond of the boy. However, Mary was pregnant again and Hill was not keen to have a second child. Against Mary's wishes, he gave her medicine to induce a miscarriage, which didn't work.

On 23 February, Hill asked Mary to meet him at Bilston with Thomas, on the pretext of buying the boy some new clothes. Mary left home at about six o'clock in the evening and never returned. Her body, and that of her son, were found by a fisherman in the canal near Bilston on 3 March. Both bodies had bruises and fingernail marks, suggesting that violence had been used in drowning them.

Hill was the only suspect, especially since he had been seen by several witnesses on the night of 23 February, with his clothes soaked to the waist.

He was arrested and tried at the Staffordshire Assizes, where he treated the proceedings with disdain, confident of an acquittal.

His confidence was misplaced and he was found guilty and sentenced to hang. In the run up to his execution on 27 July, he refused to listen to the ministrations of the prison chaplain and continued to protest his innocence. He approached the gallows jauntily and joked with the hangman, asking to die without being hooded so that he could see the crowd. His body was given to surgeons for dissection and anatomisation.

24 FEBRUARY

1854   The body of thirty-six-year-old hawker Catherine Moore was found in the canal at Oldbury. Since she had been drinking, it was assumed that she had accidentally walked off the tow path and an inquest jury returned a verdict of 'found drowned'.

Towards the end of 1858, a man named William (or Joseph) Baker was drinking at The Seven Stars at Oldbury, near to where the body was found. As he grew more drunk, Baker began talking about Catherine's death, telling people that he had witnessed her murder by Mr Ballard and Mr Markwick. According to Baker, he came across the body in the water and tried to pull it out but was prevented from doing so by the murderers.

The police were notified and began making a few discreet enquiries. They discovered that, drunk and sober, Baker had been talking about the 'murder' to his family but had always refused to name the killers. Now, he claimed that his conscience would no longer allow him to keep quiet. Eventually, Baker was interviewed and told the police the same story.

Mr Markwick died in an accident on 10 October 1857, so it was left to James Ballard to defend himself before magistrates at Oldbury. Ballard was able to prove that he was in London at the time of Catherine Moore's demise and when Baker was questioned, he told magistrates, 'I have no remembrance of making such statements and, if I did, I must have been out of my senses.'

25 FEBRUARY

1870   Patrick and Catherine Jennings of Moseley Hole went to Wolverhampton Market, leaving their six children at home. During the day, they visited several public houses and by the time they headed home, both were drunk.

Late at night, Patrick was seen kicking Catherine and hitting her with a half-brick. When a passer-by remonstrated with him, he snapped, 'She is my own wife and it has nothing to do with anyone and if anybody interferes I will knock his brains out!'

St Peter's Church and Market Hall, Wolverhampton, 1907. (Author's collection)

Mr Justice Lush. (Author's collection)

Patrick arrived home alone at five o'clock the next morning and asked his fourteen-year-old son to help him with his mother. Catherine lay where she had fallen the night before, her features swollen and distorted from Patrick's ill-treatment. Barely alive, she died almost as soon as they got her home.

'It's me that killed her, it's to my grief,' Patrick sobbed over his wife's body.

He was charged with her wilful murder and appeared at the Staffordshire Assizes in March, where he claimed that Catherine collapsed in a drunken fit and that he had merely been kicking her in an attempt to rouse her. The jury found him guilty but, perhaps surprisingly, added a recommendation for mercy, on the grounds that they didn't believe that he intended to kill his wife. Even with the jury's recommendation, in sentencing Jennings to death, Mr Justice Lush warned him that he held not the slightest hope of mercy.

However, in April, the Home Secretary commuted the sentence to one of life imprisonment. Jennings was said to be most surprised and told the warder that he would really rather have been executed. He served his time in Portsea Prison, Hampshire.

26 FEBRUARY

1869 Seven-year-old Henry Cope of Darlaston was run over by a horse and cart and died within minutes.

The cart was driven by Joseph Lloyd, and people who witnessed the accident stated at the inquest that Lloyd was lagging behind the cart when the horse cut across the corner of the pavement and turned into Berry Street of its own volition. It knocked Henry over, the cart wheels passing over his abdomen, and he gasped once and died.

Lloyd explained that he had dismounted from his cart to answer an urgent call of nature and, as he stood behind his cart urinating, the horse

King Street, Darlaston, 1941. (Author's collection)

suddenly and unexpectedly moved off. Lloyd said that he saw several children playing on the road and shouted a warning and all moved out of the way except for Henry. Lloyd's employer gave him a good character reference as a careful and sober man and the inquest jury eventually returned a verdict of 'accidental death', although they added that Lloyd's conduct was 'blameable'.

The following day, Lloyd appeared at West Bromwich Police Court, having already been charged with causing death by dangerous driving. The police had a new witness, who stated that Lloyd habitually allowed his horse to walk around unattended near to where the child was killed, while he took a shortcut across a patch of wasteland and met up with it in Berry Street.

Hearing this, magistrates committed him for trial. He appeared at the Stafford Assizes on 9 March charged with manslaughter and, when found guilty, was sentenced to one month's imprisonment.

27 FEBRUARY

1862 At just before 6 a.m., a boiler exploded at Corbyn's Hall Iron Works, between Dudley and Brierley Hill. The boiler, which weighed 13 tons and supplied steam to a large hammer, was propelled through the roof of the boiler house, landing on an adjacent bank. Three men were killed instantly and several more were crushed or badly scalded, with a further three dying from their injuries later that day.

An inquest was held by coroner Mr T.M. Phillips into the deaths of Morris Christopher, Daniel Mason, Joseph Harper, Ezekiel Newman and brothers Thomas and George Hadley (or Hudley). It was thought that lack of water in the boiler or an excess of pressure caused the explosion, and that it was engineer Mark Simpson's responsibility to keep the boiler topped up and to release any excess of steam.

At the time of the explosion, Simpson was not at his post, and engineer Benjamin Stevens told the inquest that several times during the night of 26/27 February Simpson had been lying down on a bench, apparently asleep. Simpson argued that he may have laid down briefly but was not sleeping, adding that he had left the boiler in the charge of another man and was only absent from his duties for a very short time. Nevertheless, the inquest jury found that Simpson's neglect was the main cause of the explosion and returned a verdict of manslaughter against him.

Simpson did not have long to wait for his trial, which took place at the Staffordshire Assizes on 10 March. It emerged that the boiler was fitted with a warning whistle, which went off when the water levels were low. It was uncertain whether or not this whistle was working at the time of the explosion, and Judge Mr Baron Channell told the jury that without proof that the whistle was working, it would be unsafe to convict Simpson. Although the prosecution informed the jury that there was also a gauge showing water levels within the boiler, the jury felt that there was no need to continue with the prosecution and acquitted Simpson on the judge's advice.

28 FEBRUARY **1869** The mutilated body of Eliza Bowen was found at the side of a lane in Wednesbury, and a post-mortem examination showed that she had been raped, after which numerous pieces of furnace cinder and brick had been forced into her vagina and rectum, almost certainly while she was still alive.

Eliza was a drunkard, whose husband was serving a prison sentence for stealing fowl. On the night before her death, she was drinking with William Hall from Darlaston and, when the police searched his home, they found a torn muffler, which exactly matched a piece of cloth found at the murder scene.

Hall was arrested and remanded to Stafford Prison to await his trial at the Assizes. However, the inquest into Eliza Bowen's death had not yet concluded and, since the jury wished to return a verdict of 'wilful murder by William Hall', there was a legal requirement for him to be present. The inquest was adjourned again and again, while permission was sought from the Home Secretary to secure Hall's attendance, until finally on 27 May the jury was forced to return an open verdict. Thus, when the Grand Jury considered the case prior to Hall's trial at the Stafford Assizes, they found no bill and Hall was promptly released.

Although at least two people confessed to having murdered Eliza Bowen, they later withdrew their confessions and did not stand trial, leaving the murder unsolved.

29 FEBRUARY **1888** An inquest in Dudley concluded that Joseph and Ellen Russell and Elizabeth Christman died accidental deaths.

The key witness was Eliza Russell, the sole survivor of the fire that killed her brother and sister and their servant. Joseph ran a shoe shop on High Street, Dudley, and Eliza was visiting when, at 5 a.m. on 19 February, she awoke to the smell of burning and found the carpet in the living quarters over the shop on fire.

Eliza ran to the top floor to wake her sister and brother and Joseph went down with a jug of water, which he threw on the burning carpet. However, by that time the floorboards had caught fire and the flames spread rapidly.

High Street,
Dudley, 1950s.
(Author's collection)

Fighting the flames, 1905. (Author's collection)

The stairs leading to the ground floor and the street door were soon ablaze, forcing the occupants of the building upwards.

Eliza managed to climb through a window onto a water tank, from where she scrambled to the roof of an adjoining building, but the others were overcome by the suffocating smoke before they could follow. The police raised a ladder to the attic windows but were too late to prevent Eliza's siblings and their servant from perishing in the blaze and, by the time the fire brigade arrived, they could do no more than rescue Eliza from the roof.

The inquest jury were unable to determine the cause of the fire but remarked that the fire brigade's appliances seemed 'remarkably primitive' and suggested that the Town Council should purchase a portable fire escape, rather than rely on the jointed ladder used by the police to try and rescue the victims. The Council promised to do so at once.

MARCH

Oldbury, from Bury Hill. (Author's collection)

1 MARCH

1886 Heavy snow caused problems for the steam trams of the Birmingham and Midland Tramway Company, and one became stranded on Oldbury Road, Smethwick. The driver of the No. 10 engine shouted to the driver of another tram, and the driver of the No. 8 engine went to help him.

It was the responsibility of the conductor on the No. 10 car to couple the two engines together but, at the time, he was fetching water and coke. Consequently, fourteen-year-old Arthur George Wall went to help with the coupling but, just as the No. 8 engine approached, the coupling mechanism slipped and Wall was fatally crushed between the car steps and the engine.

Trams at Cape Hill, Smethwick. (Author's collection)

In a similar fashion, twenty-year-old Joseph Parnell lost his life on the same morning, when the coupling bar broke as he was coupling the No. 2 engine to its tramcar. It was thought that the iron may have been affected by the extremely cold weather.

Tragically, just ten days earlier, a decision was taken to fit all tramcars with an automatic coupling system and the entire fleet was currently being upgraded. At the inquests held in Smethwick by coroner Edwin Hooper, the jury returned two verdicts of 'accidental death', adding that they were of the opinion that youths should not be allowed to perform the coupling operation, and recommending the installation of some form of buffers to prevent further loss of life.

2 MARCH

1874 Sixty-seven-year-old widow Ellen Davies was strangled in her bedroom in Ettingshall. (A post-mortem examination was unable to determine whether or not she had also been raped.) There were clearly visible muddy footprints in the room and several drawers appeared to have been ransacked.

Mrs Davies was described by those who knew her as 'eccentric'. Her nephew went even further, saying that she was stupid, ill-tempered and often found fault with others, frequently accusing men of 'interfering' with her. However, the old woman did have an admirer – widower Thomas Matthews had made overtures of marriage towards her but she wanted nothing to do with him and threatened to 'give him the poker' if he offered marriage again.

When Matthews was interviewed by the police, he appeared to have fresh scratches on his nose and was promptly arrested on suspicion of having murdered Mrs Davies. Yet there was no evidence to connect him with the murder and, when he appeared before magistrates on 2 April, he was discharged.

A reward of £100 was offered for the apprehension of Mrs Davies's killer(s) but her murder went unsolved.

3 MARCH

1922 Trade at The Pheasant Inn in Bilston was poor and the landlord had to take a supplementary job, leaving the running of the pub to his wife, Alice Gertrude Pountney.

The pub took in lodgers and, rightly or wrongly, Elijah Pountney suspected Alice of getting a little too friendly with one of them, Edmund McCann. Physically, McCann was a large man, whereas Pountney was thin and puny and on 3 March, Pountney went to the police at Bilston and asked for their assistance in evicting McCann. However, the police refused to become involved in what they saw as a domestic matter.

Mr Justice Darling. (Author's collection)

On 16 April, after a night spent drinking, Elijah came downstairs to find his wife and McCann eating oysters together. Alice refused to get her husband's breakfast and Elijah seethed until lunchtime, when, in full view of a customer, he walked into the kitchen and cut Alice's throat. She bled to death almost instantly and, as the horrified customer summoned the police and a doctor, Elijah rushed from the pub and flung himself into a nearby canal. He was hauled out and taken to hospital. He was charged with his wife's wilful murder and, although it was alleged at his trial at the Stafford Assizes that Alice had provoked the attack, both by her shameful behaviour and by pointing a knife at her husband, he was found guilty and sentenced to death.

The sentence was challenged at the Court of Criminal Appeal on the grounds that the trial jury was not informed that Pountney had been drinking and that, owing to a previous head injury, he was unable to tolerate alcohol. Pountney's defence counsel also believed that the judge had made light of the provocation.

Mr Justice Darling delivered the verdict of the court of appeal, finding that Mr Justice Shearman had been meticulous with regard to his interpretation of provocation and that it was abundantly clear that Pountney had already made up his mind to kill his wife. With his appeal disallowed, Pountney was hanged by John Ellis at Winson Green Prison on 11 August 1922.

4 MARCH

1875   John Stoker appeared at Wolverhampton Borough Police Court charged with an aggravated assault on his sister-in-law, Mary Jane Goodman.

During the previous weekend, Stoker was drunkenly threatening his mother. Mary Goodman intervened on her mother-in-law's behalf, at which John seized her right hand and deliberately bit off the top of her third finger and swallowed it.

'Drink and Cannibalism' announced the *Birmingham Daily Post*, reporting that Stoker had been found guilty and sentenced to three months imprisonment with hard labour. Magistrates stated that the offence was down to intemperance and was as ferocious as would be committed by a wild beast.

5 MARCH

1896   At the Wolverhampton Union Workhouse, paralysed in-patient Thomas James Lovatt was taken for a bath. In spite of Lovatt's protests, he was lowered into a bath of what he later described as 'boiling water', by an attendant who refused to believe his complaints that the water was too hot and simply ignored his fearful screams of pain.

Forty-four-year-old Lovatt was eventually removed from the bath and later died from shock and scalding. At an inquest, the jury returned a verdict of 'accidental death', attributing no criminal responsibility to the attendant but suggesting that there should be more supervision over bathing at the institution in future.

6 MARCH

1922   People in Dudley Port heard a noise like a deafening clap of thunder, followed by terrible screams, and realised that something was amiss at the L.K. Knowles factory, managed by John Walter Knowles and owned by his wife, Louisa Kate. The factory had recently won a contract to break up live gun cartridges for their scrap metal value and employed twenty-four young girls to do the work by hand. Unfortunately, the shed in which they worked was heated by a coal-fired brazier, and it was thought that a stray spark ignited the gunpowder from the cartridges, causing a massive explosion.

The entire area was thick with choking smoke, and the badly burned girls were running round in a panic, their clothes on fire. People began ripping the burning garments away with their bare hands, while others tried to get into the shed where the girls had been working and where several now lay injured. They were hampered by the fact that the shed roof had collapsed and there were still bullets zipping around.

Sixteen girls died in the explosion, with the death toll rising to nineteen within the month. An inquest was opened on 8 March by coroner Mr R. Marshall into the deaths of Laura Dalloway (14), Nellie Kay (15), Annie Freeth (15), Violet May Franklin (15), Annie Elizabeth Florence Edwards (15), Priscilla Longmore (13), Annie Naylor (14), Elizabeth Williams (13), Edith Drew (15), Edith Richards (14), Elsie Fellows (15), Gladys May Bryant (14), Lizzie Griffiths (15), Mabel Weaver (14), Hannah Hubbard (16) and Margaret Burns (15). Elizabeth Aston (14), Edith Jukes (15) and Lucy Edwards (14) died later from their injuries.

John Walter Knowles and works manager Eber James Richard Chadwick faced charges of manslaughter after the tragedy, appearing at the Stafford Assizes in July 1922. The girls were young, inexperienced and untrained, and worked without any safety precautions whatsoever. The shed where they worked had a hard concrete floor and the girls wore ordinary boots, with nails that occasionally sparked. The room was also heated by an open fire and the factory had no licence to work with gunpowder.

Chadwick was acquitted but Knowles was found guilty and sentenced to five years' imprisonment. There were just five survivors of the explosion, all of whom were badly burned. A public appeal raised £10,000 and there were other more personal donations, such as that of Reverend G. Mortimore, who was the first to donate a square foot of skin for transplant. Part of the public subscription was used to construct a memorial to the victims at Tipton Cemetery.

7 MARCH

1858 When Mrs Taylor of West Bromwich developed a sore throat, she became convinced that the cause of the pain was a pin inside her throat. Although there was absolutely no logical reason for this supposition, nobody could persuade Mrs Taylor otherwise.

When her throat failed to get better after a couple of days, Mrs Taylor tried to remove the imaginary pin with a piece of copper wire and a mirror. In doing so, she damaged the tissues so much that, although a doctor was called, she died. The coroner was informed but decided not to hold an inquest on what was essentially a death from natural causes.

8 MARCH

1876 Ellen Thompson appeared before magistrates at the Guildhall, Walsall, charged with assaulting her husband.

Ellen was William Thompson's second wife and was much younger than her husband. According to William, as he was going to work on 4 March, Ellen first attacked him with a stick then pelted him with large stones when he refused to give her money.

William told magistrates that Ellen was addicted to drink and, over the past four months, had pawned most of the couple's belongings four or five times over to get money for alcohol. The Bench decided that the best place for Ellen was prison and, in the hope of curing her passion for drink, sent her to prison for two months with hard labour.

9 MARCH

Mr Justice Wright, 1900s. (Author's collection)

1896 Fifty-four-year-old widow Sarah Cocking appeared at the Staffordshire Assizes charged with the wilful murder of her daughter Sarah at Horseleyfields on 4 January.

The fourteen-year-old girl's tragic death occurred when her mother happened to go to sleep downstairs. Mrs Cocking was woken by her other daughter, Edith, who suggested that she went upstairs to bed. Irritably, Mrs Cocking threw a poker at Edith, which missed and hit Sarah, penetrating her skull.

Mrs Cocking's defence counsel insisted that she had never thrown the poker, but stated that the two sisters were larking about when Sarah fell, either against the door latch or onto a protruding nail.

Mr Justice Wright told the jury that, if the accused threw something at one person and hit another, she was guilty of murder in the eyes of the law. However, in this case, he did not believe that the jury would return a verdict on the capital offence and indeed they eventually found Mrs Cocking guilty of the lesser offence of manslaughter. Wright deferred sentencing, ultimately deciding on two months' imprisonment with hard labour.

10 MARCH

1860 At just after midnight, Mary Titley of Wednesfield cut her son's throat with her husband's razor, almost severing the three-year-old boy's head from his body. She afterwards stated that she intended to commit suicide but was prevented from doing so by her husband, who managed to snatch the razor from her hands.

An inquest returned a verdict of wilful murder against Mary and she was committed for trial. She had only six days to wait before the commencement of the next Stafford Assizes and, when called upon to plead, she stared vacantly at Mr Justice Keating and said, 'I certainly did murder my child.'

Mary had spent time in the County Asylum but was pronounced cured and discharged in May 1859. Now, the judge asked the jury whether or not they believed that she was capable of pleading and, when they found her incapable of understanding the difference between right and wrong, he ordered her to be detained at Her Majesty's pleasure.

11 MARCH

1839 Susannah Perry of Rowley Regis appeared at the Staffordshire Assizes charged with wilfully murdering her husband by poisoning him with arsenic.

Samuel Perry was a nail maker and on 10 July 1838, he complained of feeling unwell. He was unable to eat anything, sustaining himself by drinking brandy and gin brought to him by Susannah. Early the following morning, he was seized by agonising stomach pains but would not allow his wife to fetch a doctor. He grew weaker throughout the day and, in desperation, Susannah called in a neighbour and her mother-in-law but neither could persuade Samuel to seek medical assistance and he died on 12 July.

Because of the suddenness of Samuel's death an inquest was deemed necessary and, in spite of Susannah's objections, a post-mortem examination was carried out. Surgeon Mr Fereday found a quantity of gritty white powder in Samuel's stomach, which proved to be arsenic. When a packet of the poison was found in a cupboard at the Perrys' home, Susannah was arrested and charged with wilful murder. It was beyond any doubt that Samuel died from arsenic poisoning but, at Susannah's trial, the task for the jury was to decide if the poison was administered by his wife.

Susannah was suspected of consorting with another man, and when a chemist from Rowley Regis testified that she had bought a packet of arsenic from his shop, the case seemed as good as proven. However, the chemist described the woman who had bought arsenic from his shop as having worn a straw bonnet trimmed with blue ribbons and Susannah didn't own such a hat.

Her defence counsel pointed out that Susannah had tried over and over again to persuade her husband to consult a doctor, and had raised no objection to her house being searched by the police after her husband's death. The search was not conducted until several days after the post-mortem, which would have given Susannah ample time to dispose of the packet of arsenic had she wanted to.

It took the jury just five minutes to find her not guilty and she was discharged. The murder of Samuel Perry – if indeed it were murder – remains unsolved.

12 MARCH

1860 Forty-nine-year-old engine fitter John Andrews appeared at the Staffordshire Assizes charged with feloniously cutting and wounding Henry Churchyard with intent to kill and murder him at Wednesbury. There was a second indictment for the lesser offence of malicious wounding.

The court heard that Andrews and Churchyard lodged at the same house. Churchyard was a smoker and, on 21 January 1860, Andrews objected to him smoking in their shared bedroom and ordered him not to do so. Churchyard answered with a string of swear words and Andrews told him that if her persisted in using such 'obnoxious epithets' he would take him before the magistrates. This comment spurred Churchyard on to even fouler language and the two men squared up to each other, as if to fight.

Their landlady Mrs Stokes rushed between them and was knocked down. Churchyard picked her up but as he did so, Andrews stabbed him in the ear and throat. The two men grappled and it was left to a relative of the landlady to prize them apart. As he did so, he saw Andrews toss aside a small knife.

Andrews stated that he and Churchyard had a history of grievances and that Churchyard was always challenging him to fight. On the night in question, he was greatly provoked and stabbed Churchyard in self-defence, causing only minor injuries. Andrews insisted that, if his head were to be phrenologically examined, he would be found to be completely free of any signs of destructiveness and mischief.

Even so, the jury found him guilty of malicious wounding only and he was sentenced to nine months' imprisonment with hard labour.

13 MARCH

1854 Ellen Davis appeared at the Stafford Assizes before Mr Justice Wightman accused of the wilful murder of her four-week-old son, Isaiah.

On 17 December, Ellen's husband went to work as normal, leaving his wife looking after the couple's three children at their home in Wolverhampton. When he returned at midday, there was no sign of Isaiah and, when he asked where the baby was, Ellen replied, 'In the well'. The well was situated in the cellar of the house and Mr Davis fetched a neighbour, who helped him to retrieve his son's body. When Ellen was asked how the baby got into the well, she shrugged her shoulders and said simply, 'It fell in.'

At her trial, a doctor who had attended her during her first confinement testified that after the birth of her first child she had suffered from such severe puerperal mania that he had sent her to a lunatic asylum, where she had remained for several months. He believed that on the day of Isaiah's death, his mother was in the same mental state.

The jury acquitted Ellen on grounds of insanity and she was ordered to be confined as a criminal lunatic.

14 MARCH

1865 Twenty-year-old domestic servant Mary Smith was described in the contemporary newspapers as 'rather ordinary looking'. Nevertheless, she 'fell victim to the evil designs of a married man', her uncle Aaron Vaughan.

On 14 March, as Mary was walking across the Rowley Hills from Dudley to Rowley Regis, she suddenly went into labour and gave birth to twin boys. Leaving the babies on the hillside, she made her way to the nearest public house. There she sent for Vaughan, who stayed with her for just five minutes before saying that he could not help her and leaving.

Meanwhile, labourers Charles Archer and Reuben Wood were walking across Rowley Hills when their dog found what seemed to be freshly turned earth. Archer prodded the soil with his foot, scraping it back about an inch and revealing a child's leg. As Archer's foot touched the infant, it began crying.

Archer made no effort to extricate the baby but sent Wood for a policeman, who removed the infant from beneath its thin blanket of soil, finding a second baby underneath. One child was dead, the other still alive, although he died within minutes. Post-mortem examinations revealed no marks of violence on either child and surgeon Mr Cooper determined that the child found dead was killed by exposure to the cold, his brother dying from congestion of the lungs and exposure.

Mary Smith was quickly traced and charged with two counts of wilful murder. She appeared at the Stafford Assizes in July, where it was shown that she had prepared for her confinement and had made baby clothes. The defence insisted that when Mary gave birth, she was frightened, weak and in pain. The babies were not buried but merely lightly covered with soil and Mary admitted to leaving them, insisting that she had hurried as fast as she was physically able to the nearest pub for help. Although she had heard one of the children crying, she believed they were dead when she left them.

The jury found Mary not guilty and she was discharged from court. Mr Justice Byles expressed his regret that he could not punish Aaron Vaughan, who stated in court that he could not say whether or not he was the father of the children, and refused point blank to help a young woman in distress who, if not his lover, was indisputably his niece.

15 MARCH

1892 An inquest was held near Wolverhampton into the death of Delhi Montana, who worked as a lion tamer for Wombwell's Menagerie and Circus. Earlier that day, in front of a horrified audience, Montana went into a cage containing three bears and a hyena. Unfortunately, he stumbled and fell as he was entering the cage and the hyena attacked him.

To the consternation of the audience, the bears then began to worry him. The proprietor of the menagerie, Mr Bostock, went in to try and rescue Montana, but the animals were reluctant to leave him alone and by the time he was taken from the cage, he was very seriously injured. One of the spectators was a doctor, who rendered what assistance he could but Montana died within twenty minutes of the attack.

The inquest heard that the animals were the quietest in the show and that Montana was an experienced tamer of wild beasts, who had never before met with an accident. A verdict of 'accidental death' was returned by the inquest jury.

16 MARCH

1934 Builder Fred Parrish was driving on the Birmingham to Wolverhampton road when he was dazzled by the lights of an oncoming car. Parrish slowed down and extinguished his own headlights, as did the approaching driver. As the two vehicles drew level, Parrish put on his lights again and, as he did, the left side of his car windscreen shattered. Believing that the other vehicle had thrown up a stone, Parrish continued with his journey until he reached a junction, when he noticed that his steering felt wobbly. Only then did he check his car, to find a bicycle mounted on the front bumper, its lamp still burning.

Parrish placed the bicycle on the grass verge, before turning round and driving back the way he had come. He saw no trace of any accident so carried on with his journey, unfortunately failing to find John Clifford Davies. The twenty-one-year-old cyclist was later found lying dead on the roadside by another motorist, who reported his grim find to the police.

A radio broadcast was made, in which police appealed for the driver of the car who had run Davies down to come forward. However, it wasn't until the following day, when the case was reported in the newspapers, that Parrish and his three passengers went to the police. None of the occupants of Parrish's car had felt any impact and all claimed to be totally unaware that they had been involved in an accident. None had heard the radio appeal, although Parrish insisted that he would have come forward had he heard it.

An inquest was held on 21 March, at which the jury returned a verdict of 'accidental death', asking coroner Mr J.P. Hicks to severely censure the occupants of Parrish's car for their callous conduct in not trying to find out earlier what had happened. Hicks told the jury that it would be extremely difficult to prove a charge of manslaughter on what little evidence there was, and since it was a criminal offence not to report an accident, he preferred not to pass on the jury's comments.

17 MARCH

1860 Coroner Mr R. Docker held an inquest at The Angel Inn, Stourbridge, into the death of four-year-old Alice Crane.

Town centre, Stourbridge. (Author's collection)

Sarah Williams testified that on 15 March, she heard screams coming from the child's home. She went to the window and immediately realised that the house was full of smoke and, on opening the door, she found Alice lying on her back on the floor. All of the child's clothes had been burned off, with the exception of the waistband of her skirt.

Mrs Williams carried Alice to her grandmother's house next door, where she died within ten minutes from burns affecting most of her body. Alice was alone in the house when her clothes caught fire but there was no fire lit apart from a few smouldering ashes under the grate. When Mrs Williams questioned how Alice could possibly have set herself alight, Alice's mother indifferently revealed that she had been on fire twice before. Not only that but three months earlier, another child from the same family had burned to death.

Called to give evidence at the inquest, Alice's grandmother Mary Callighan insisted that she knew nothing. Alice's mother stated that she always left her children on their own while she went out to work. She conceded that she was a member of a burial club and admitted to receiving £2 10s from the club on the death of her first child but pointed out that she had to use that money to pay for its funeral. She now bemoaned the fact that the club was refusing to pay out for a second death.

Surprisingly, the inquest jury returned a verdict of 'accidentally burnt' on Alice, mainly because nobody could explain precisely how the child caught fire.

18 MARCH

1813 William Howe (aka John Wood) was hanged at Stafford Prison for the murder of farmer Benjamin Robbins (or Robins).

The victim was shot in the chest on 18 December 1812, as he made his way home from Stourbridge market. Having sold some sheep, Robbins had plenty of money and people recalled a man paying close attention to the farmer as he enjoyed a drink in The Nag's Head before setting off for home across Whittington Common. Others recalled seeing a man following Robbins, and all were struck by a distinctive waistcoat that the man was wearing.

Bow Street Runners managed to track the man with the waistcoat to London, where he was arrested. Tried at the Staffordshire Assizes, it took the jury only minutes to find thirty-two-year-old William Howe guilty, and he was executed forty-eight hours later.

His body was taken from Stafford and hanged in chains on Whittington Common, to serve as an example to other would-be criminals. Howe hung until his body disintegrated then was buried where he fell – his ghost is said to haunt the area to this day.

19 MARCH

1858 Sixteen-year-old Elizabeth Felton and her thirteen-year-old brother George quarrelled at the stone pit in Oldbury where they both worked, and quickly moved from trading insults to throwing dirt at each other and then physical violence. Elizabeth boxed her brother's ears and George retaliated by lashing at her with a whip that he was carrying, which Elizabeth snatched from him, pushing him to the ground and hitting him several times before walking off to carry on with her work.

In tears, George raised himself onto one elbow and picked up a small stone or a lump of clay, which he threw at Elizabeth, hitting her just below her left ear. Elizabeth stopped walking and turned to look at her brother before putting her hands to her head and slumping onto the ground.

George screamed for help and another worker, Philip Williams, knelt to check Elizabeth, who was dead. George went into hysterics, shouting, 'Oh, my sister is dead,' and begging, 'Oh, our Betsy, do rise!'

A post-mortem examination revealed a small, insignificant bruise on Elizabeth's right temple and another beneath her left ear. Under this second bruise, was a ruptured blood vessel, the blood from which had caused pressure on Elizabeth's brain, resulting in her death. At the inquest, surgeon Mr Cooper stated that he had never seen a more diseased brain than that of Elizabeth Felton. Under normal circumstances, the stone would have been highly unlikely to cause a ruptured blood vessel but Elizabeth's brain was so damaged that the mere excitement of arguing with her brother could have killed her.

The inquest jury returned a verdict of 'homicide by misadventure' but George still had to appear before magistrates, who, surprisingly, committed him for trial at the Worcestershire Assizes. When he was tried for manslaughter on 14 July 1858, the medical evidence, coupled with the fact that Elizabeth was believed to have provoked her brother, convinced the jury that he was not guilty and he was discharged.

20 MARCH   **1864**   Coroner Edwin Hooper concluded an inquest into the death of Edith Moore from West Bromwich.

The little girl died from a severe attack of diarrhoea and tests showed that it was caused by the water supply to her home. Water from the communal pump was strongly impregnated with sulphureted hydrogen gas, resulting from seepage of animal and vegetable matter into the well.

The owner of the property insisted that he was anxious to provide pure and wholesome drinking water for his tenants and promised to take immediate steps to rectify the supply.

21 MARCH   **1859**   Mrs Bridgen of Wednesfield left her three-month-old daughter, Sarah, at home while she ran an errand. Her husband was asleep by the fire, so as a precaution she tied Sarah around her waist to the chair, to prevent her falling off.

When Mrs Bridgen returned only minutes later, she found her house full of smoke. The back of the chair to which Sarah was tied was completely burned through and the baby was said to resemble a roast suckling pig in appearance. John Bridgen, who had been drinking, remained fast asleep as his daughter literally cooked alive.

22 MARCH   **1858**   Coroner William Robinson held an inquest at The Red Lion Inn, Dudley, into the death of miner Benjamin Ward, who died on 18 March at the coalmine at Saltwells. Another miner also died at the same time but the coroner argued that, since the evidence would be identical for both enquiries, there was no point in holding a separate inquest for Ward's workmate, John Baugh.

The only witness at the inquest was Richard Pearson, who was working with the two men at the time of their deaths, along with an unnamed boy. Pearson stated that around 6 or 7 tons of coal suddenly fell from the roof, burying Ward and Baugh. Fortunately, only a small amount of coal landed on Pearson and he was able to make his way to the bottom of the shaft.

There was nobody about and Pearson called for help and made a noise by banging on a skip, in which the coal was raised to the surface. After more than half an hour, Pearson heard a tentative voice and shouted up to the passing courting couple that there were men buried and he needed help.

The young man ran off but could not find the watchman, nor anyone else connected with the colliery. He eventually fetched butty James Bunn, who went with his sons to try and help. They in turn sent for the engineer and another butty, Mr Griffiths, and more than two hours after the accident, somebody finally went below ground to help Pearson dig out the two buried miners.

There should have been a watchman at the pit but for some reason there was nobody on duty that night. The coroner read a letter from the Government Inspector of Mines, who had inspected the scene of the accident and felt that the miners themselves were to blame for not using timbering to support the roof, instead relying on leaving some coal in place to take the weight. The Inspector was also shocked by the fact that there was nobody above ground at the time of the accident, leaving 'the living and the dead there together more than two hours before assistance came'. The Inspector felt unable to apportion any blame for the fall and, after considerable debate, the inquest jury returned two verdicts of 'accidental death'.

23 MARCH　　**1885** Fifty-two-year-old labourer Richard Bowering (or Bowring) appeared before magistrates at Wolverhampton Police Court charged with ill-treating his wife. Mrs Bowering was present in court and bore the horrific scars of her latest beating at the hands of her husband.

Magistrates were told that Bowering had made numerous appearances before the Bench for assaulting his wife, nine of which had resulted in convictions. They sentenced him to three months' imprisonment with hard labour and also granted a separation order to his wife, ordering Bowering to pay 10s a week towards her maintenance.

24 MARCH　　**1793** As well as being landlord of The Barley Mow Tavern in Wolverhampton, Henry Yates also worked as a carpenter and joiner. On 24 March, he rose early to finish some carpentry but when his wife went to fetch him for breakfast, she found him dead, his head almost severed from his body. Her screams brought neighbours running but nobody had seen anyone with Yates that morning, although footprints suggested that somebody had climbed over a wall at the rear of the premises.

At ten o'clock that morning, Ebenezer Colston was spotted by a jail keeper at the house of correction, enjoying a singsong in a pub. Colston had spots of what appeared to be fresh blood on his clothes and, when searched, was found to be in possession of Yates's watch.

Colston was the corporal for a recruiting party of the 31st Regiment of Young Buffs (Royal East Kent Regiment), who often helped Yates with his carpentry work. When questioned about the murder, he made a full confession, saying that while with Yates in the workshop on the morning of the murder, he had a sudden irresistible impulse to kill him. Colston hit Yates twice on the head with a hammer, before cutting his throat from ear to ear.

Tried at the Staffordshire Assizes on 31 July 1793, Colston was convicted and hanged on 17 August. He became the first person to hang at Stafford Gaol, previous executions having been carried out at Sandyford Meadow.

Note: Perhaps unsurprisingly given the date of this murder, there are some discrepancies between various accounts. The murderer is named Ebenezer or Ebenezar Colston, Coulson or Coulston and there is also some disagreement about the date of the murder, the most commonly reported dates being 24 and 25 March.

HM Prison Stafford.
(Author's collection)

25 MARCH

1859 John Corbett and his wife had been married for five years and had two children, the eldest of whom was six. The marriage was characterised by jealousy on both sides and in 1859, the couple separated, Mrs Corbett taking the children to her father's house.

At about 8.20 p.m. Mrs Corbett and her sister left the nail workshop at West Bromwich, where she worked after her separation. Suddenly, John Corbett leaped out at them and, putting his arm around his wife's neck, pulled her towards him and cut her throat. As his wife slumped to the ground with blood pumping from her wounds, Corbett ran off into the next street and cut his own throat.

Mrs Corbett bled to death within half an hour but her husband survived until 12 April, dying under police guard at his sister's house, where he had stayed since the night of his wife's murder. It was reported that Corbett worked in a pit and that, on the day of the murder, the pit boss repeatedly tormented him in front of the other colliers about his separation, even saying that he had been improperly intimate with

Corbett's wife earlier that week. After the inquest on Mrs Corbett, the man wrote to the local newspapers, vehemently denying the allegations against him.

Note: Mrs Corbett's forename is rarely mentioned in the contemporary newspaper accounts of her murder. It is believed to have been Mary Ann.

26 MARCH

1890 Sixteen-year-old William Ward was working as a grinder at malleable iron founders J. Hampton & Co., Smethwick, when his revolving emery wheel unexpectedly shattered. The pieces struck Ward on the head and abdomen, and he died in hospital from a fractured skull and internal injuries.

Factory Inspector Major Roe found no flaws in the wheel and noted that, at the time of the accident, it was revolving at less than its maximum speed. He observed that the wheel's fixings were somewhat smaller than normal, and suggested that all wheels should be stamped with the number of revolutions at which they might be safely run. The jury returned a verdict of 'accidental death', recommending that Roe's suggestions should be acted upon by all firms.

27 MARCH

1882 An inquest was held into the death of thirty-two-year-old William Clewitt, a foreman of the coal and cattle yards of the London and North Western Railway at Wolverhampton High Level Station.

Clewitt was loading some heavy timber on 25 March using a windlass – a lifting device turned by a hand crank, consisting of a cylinder onto which cable or rope is wound. All of a sudden, Clewitt lost his grip on the handle, which began to spin rapidly as the rope unravelled.

The handle hit Clewitt under the chin, knocking him clear over the top of a crane and onto the railway line 30ft below. Dreadfully injured, he was taken to Wolverhampton Hospital, where he died within hours.

The inquest recorded a verdict of 'accidental death' on Clewitt, who left a widow and three young children.

28 MARCH

1856 When Mary Aston of Tipton went into labour, her husband Edwin called in chemist and druggist Robert Dullum Tamlyn, who passed an opinion that she would not give birth for some time. He returned several hours later, by which time Mrs Aston had retired to bed. Tamlyn examined her and told her husband that she was in premature labour and was in no danger, although it was likely to be a long time before she finally gave birth.

When Mrs Aston died twelve hours later, the inquest jury reached the conclusion that her death was caused by unskillfulness and incompetence on the part of the person they referred to as 'the man midwife' and returned a verdict of manslaughter against Tamlyn. He was tried at the Staffordshire Assizes on 16 July but acquitted.

29 MARCH

1859 A charge and counter-charge of assault were heard at the Bilston Petty Sessions.

On 11 February, Sarah Granger of Coseley was about to give birth any day and was alone in the house when three bailiffs from Dudley County Court arrived unannounced to collect on a small debt owed by her husband.

Sarah asked the men to sit down for a moment while she got the money, but Bailiff James Morgan said it was too late and told his men to take everything they could find. They ransacked her cottage and, when Sarah protested that they had enough goods to offset the debt, Morgan knocked her down, hitting her several times, before handcuffing her and dragging her to the police station. Sarah felt faint and told the bailiffs, 'Oh, I shall die.'

'Die and be damned,' Morgan replied.

At the police station, Morgan seized Sarah by her hair and banged her head against the wall and, having lost the key to his handcuffs, tried to wrest them from her wrists using brute force.

Sarah was eventually released on her own recognisance and gave birth two days later. (Her baby was said to be very pale and to have a shocked expression when born, its hair standing on end.) She gave birth with difficulty, since the bailiffs had seized the only bed in the house as part of their haul.

Sarah summoned Morgan for assault and he counter-summoned her, saying that she had attacked him with a poker, adding that even so near to her confinement she had the strength of a young bullock.

Several witnesses supported Sarah's version of events, including James Penn, who was at the police station and described Morgan as acting 'like a man half mad', suggesting that he may have been drunk. Morgan didn't help by treating the case with levity and he was found guilty and fined £3 plus costs or one month's imprisonment with hard labour in default. The case against Sarah Granger was dismissed.

30 MARCH

1865 Mary Gibbons returned home from work to Darlaston and found her twenty-five-year-old daughter, Phoebe, unconscious on the bedroom floor, the dead body of a newborn baby boy at her side. When Phoebe

Town Hall and post office, Victoria Road, Darlaston. (Author's collection)

recovered consciousness, she told her mother that the child was stillborn. The baby wasn't due for another month but Phoebe had fallen downstairs three weeks earlier and hurt her side.

Coroner Edwin Hooper heard that Phoebe already had two illegitimate children, fathered by a married man. Hooper raged at Phoebe's morals, adding that he was astonished that Mary Gibbons permitted her daughter to engage in such a relationship. (Mary asked, quite reasonably, how the coroner expected her to stop it.)

When a doctor confirmed that there was no suspicion of foul play, Hooper asked the jury if they were satisfied or if they wished him to adjourn the inquest so that the baby's death could be investigated further. The jury were satisfied, returning an open verdict of 'found dead' on the baby boy.

31 MARCH

1858 Widow Rosannah Smith brought wealthy landowner William Coley to Dudley Public Office, charging him with fathering her illegitimate baby.

At the affiliation hearing, Coley's solicitor, Mr G.B. Lowe, asked Rosannah if she remembered consulting a woman named Lydia three or four months earlier. Lydia was well known in the area as a fortune teller and some called her a witch.

Lowe produced a witness who claimed to have accompanied Rosannah to see Lydia, saying that Rosannah beseeched the old woman to make the child's father marry her so that she was not forced into the Workhouse. According to the witness, Rosannah named the father as James Heath, at which Lydia pricked Rosannah's finger and dipped a pen nib in the blood. She wrote Heath's name on a piece of paper, surrounding it with a bloody heart. Then, having carefully pricked round the outline of the heart with a needle, Lydia told Rosannah to keep the paper in her stays and come back if Heath did not claim her.

Sadly, Heath was sent to prison the day after, so the spell failed. Mr Lowe then called Lydia into the hearing, who recalled that, with Heath out of the picture, Rosannah set her sights on ensnaring a Mr Swindell.

As William Coley appeared to be Rosannah's third choice in the matter of the paternity of her child, the affiliation case against him was dismissed.

APRIL

Dudley Town Hall. (Author's collection)

1 APRIL

1913 Thomas Fletcher and Lilian Wharton of Oldbury should have married on 26 March, yet as the wedding grew closer, Thomas seemed to have done nothing about preparing for his responsibilities and had not even arranged a home for himself and his bride. On the eve of the wedding, Lilian's mother suggested that the ceremony should be postponed and, to Thomas's dismay, Lilian agreed. Worse still, she seemed disinclined to set a new date.

Shire Hall,
Worcester.
(Author's collection)

Thomas brooded on his fiancée's apparent indifference for a few days before visiting a pawnbroker and purchasing a gun. On 1 April, he went to visit Lilian at The Fountain Inn, Brades, where she lived with her parents.

Lilian's mother served him with two glasses of brandy, before walking into the pub yard, leaving the couple alone. Moments later, Mrs Wharton heard a loud bang and Lilian staggered outside clutching her stomach, saying, 'Tom has shot me.' As Mrs Wharton rushed to her daughter's side, she heard a second bang as Fletcher turned his gun on himself.

While Lilian died seven days later from a gunshot wound in her abdomen, Fletcher survived to stand trial for her wilful murder, although he lost an eye. He appeared at the Worcestershire Assizes on 7 June, where his defence counsel tried, unsuccessfully, to convince the jury that Fletcher only intended to kill himself and that Elizabeth was shot accidentally as she tried to prevent him from doing so.

Fletcher was found guilty of wilful murder and sentenced to death. He was executed on 9 July at Worcester Prison by John Ellis, assisted by Thomas Pierrepoint.

2 APRIL

1860 Twenty-three-year-old William Trumper was coupling together empty goods wagons at the Great Western Railway Goods Station at Wolverhampton. The wagons were pushed into place by an engine and, as Trumper stepped between a moving wagon and a chain of stationery ones, with the aim of coupling the former to the latter, he was knocked over. A wheel from one of the moving wagons passed over him and the whole of the back of Trumper's head was sliced off.

At the time, it was thought that someone had stolen his watch and chain from his body. However, when coroner Mr T.M. Phillips conducted the inquest, he was pleased to be able to report that they had been found at Trumper's home.

3 APRIL

1872 John Bolton of Blackheath wished to invite some friends to his house to play dominoes but his sister refused to allow him to do so and, in a fit of temper, John slapped her face before storming out. Hearing the argument, John's brother Joseph ran after him and threw a pair of shears at his brother's back, causing a deep wound almost an inch long.

John contacted the police and PS Davies took him to a doctor before arresting Joseph, who subsequently appeared at the Police Court in Rowley Regis, charged with cutting and wounding his brother.

Joseph told the magistrates that he was very sorry for what he had done, admitting to being 'in a violent passion' when he threw the shears. Magistrates fined him £2 plus costs, or one month's imprisonment, warning both brothers about the dangers of losing their temper.

4 APRIL

1841 A pregnant ewe belonging to Mr E. Smith of Tipton was slaughtered in the field and butchered in what the contemporary newspapers described as 'a workmanlike manner'. It was the second such incident on Smith's farm, but on this occasion a note was left on what remained of the sheep: 'Dear Sir, I hope you will forgive me as I have a large family and in distress and a stranger to this sort of work but if I can I will pay you for it before long. So good by for this time.' [*sic*]

5 APRIL

1874 After Charles Lacy of Dudley drunkenly argued with his wife and daughter, he decided to obtain a little comfort from the family's lodger, Ann Lloyd.

He tried to force his way into her bedroom and when she protested that she had the body of her dead baby in her room awaiting burial and asked him to show some respect, he told her that he would 'throw the ******* corpse out of the window'. While Ann screamed for help, Lacy knocked her down and kicked her in the head several times until she lay unconscious.

When Lacy appeared before magistrates at the Dudley Police Court, his daughter and PC Harvey testified that he then rampaged through the streets for some time before he could be arrested. Lacy swore that this was the first time he had ever been in trouble but his daughter reminded him of the two occasions he had been summoned before, once for beating her and once for beating her mother.

Magistrates sentenced Lacy to one month's imprisonment, which the local newspaper at the time described as 'too light a sentence.'

6 APRIL

1859 Mary Ann Gregory of Willenhall was separated from her husband and, according to the contemporary newspapers, 'did not bear a strict moral character'. She was conducting an intimate relationship with George Vaughan, who went to her house on 6 April bearing a bottle of rum.

Vaughan persuaded Mary Ann to take a drink, pouring some rum into a glass. However, almost as soon as she had drunk it, Mary Ann was violently ill and it was suspected that she had been poisoned.

When her glass was tested by an analytical chemist, traces of cantharides were found. Cantharides, or 'Spanish Fly', was thought to heighten sexual pleasure and was also believed to cause abortions and, if ingested in sufficient quantity, was highly toxic. Precisely why Vaughan gave Mary Ann the drug was not made clear, but he was charged with administering cantharides with intent to murder and sent for trial at the Staffordshire Assizes.

At his trial, the presiding judge maintained that there was clearly no intent on Vaughan's behalf to murder Mary Ann Gregory, and unless the prosecution could demonstrate that there was an intention to do grievous bodily harm, the wording of the charge meant that Vaughan could not be found guilty. The prosecution were unable to prove any felonious intent and Vaughan was duly acquitted.

7 APRIL

1917 Sixty-year-old Frances 'Fanny' North was standing in the front garden of her home in Brewer Street, Walsall, when a plane suddenly fell out of the sky and landed on her. Fanny and her ten-month-old granddaughter, Edna Vass, died almost instantly.

The pilot, Flight Lieutenant Mann, an officer of the Royal Flying Corps, was taken to hospital suffering from shock and a cut face. (Some reports state that he also broke both legs.) Mann's bi-plane was written off, having crashed from a considerable height. It was said that he waved and shouted at the people below to get out of the way after experiencing an engine failure and losing control of his aircraft.

The inquest cleared Mann of any blame, deeming the deaths to be tragic accidents.

8 APRIL

1858 Richard Hodgkiss appeared at the Stourbridge Petty Sessions charged with beating his four-year-old daughter.

A policeman testified to apprehending Hodgkiss after seeing him carrying the child in his arms on 7 January and punching her with his fist several times, before throwing her down onto the street. On the same day another witness saw Hodgkiss beating the child with a plank of wood. Several people testified to the cruelty that Hodgkiss displayed to all of his children, who were often forced to sleep in pig stys and were always hungry and covered in bruises.

When summoned to appear before magistrates, Hodgkiss absconded and had only recently been re-arrested. He was sentenced to three months' imprisonment with hard labour.

9 APRIL

1874 Deputy-coroner Mr R.J. Watts held an inquest into the death of sixty-three-year-old Edward Finch Nayler of Dudley.

The inquest was told that Nayler suffered from a fear of choking and was afraid to go to bed in case he choked in his sleep. As a consequence of his phobia, he ate very little food, although he drank plenty of beer.

A frail, sickly man, Nayler had consulted a doctor who told him that all he needed was proper, nourishing food. However, Nayler was unable to bring himself to eat, even refusing broth. His last meal was a little lightly-salted boiled rice, washed down with two pints of beer.

The inquest concluded that he died from too much drink and too little food, returning a verdict of 'death from natural causes.'

10 APRIL

1860 Cooper Henry Cartwright and his fourteen-year-old son went to Birmingham to collect a load of staves. They were within half a mile of home at Cradley when Henry, who was leading the horse, remarked that he was tired. He tried to climb onto the front of the cart next to his son but slipped, touching the horse's behind as he did.

Cradley, 1944. (Author's collection)

The horse immediately broke into a rapid trot, throwing Henry under the wheels, which passed over his neck and the left-hand side of his body. Blood poured from his nose, ears and mouth and he died within minutes. Coroner Ralph Docker held an inquest on 12 April, recording a verdict of 'accidental death'.

11 APRIL

1845 Mrs Sarah Genever of Hagley took her daughters Jane, Emma and Sarah to Stourbridge chemist John Welch, who diagnosed ringworm and gave Mrs Genever some ointment to be rubbed onto the girls' scalps morning and night, and some powders to be taken every other night.

After a week, there did not seem to be any improvement and Mrs Genever took the girls back to Welch. The chemist thought their heads looked much better but gave her some more powders and told her to come back in a week.

On Mrs Genever's third visit, Welch mixed up a phial of lotion and told her to rub it on the children's heads to remove scurf. He warned her that it was poisonous and told her to take care that the children didn't drink it.

Mrs Genever did as she was instructed but when the liquid was applied the children complained of feeling unwell. They suffered from fever, sickness and diarrhoea and, when one girl developed blisters on her forehead, Mrs Genever sent for Welch. He didn't come, so the next day

Mrs Genever called out a doctor but in spite of his treatment, four-year-old Jane died in agony a few days later. Her death was followed by that of her twin sister, Emma.

The cause of the girls' deaths was absorption of mercury, from the lotion Welch had prescribed for their heads, exacerbated by the acid that the application also contained. Welch was charged with Jane's manslaughter and appeared at the Worcestershire Assizes on 16 July 1845.

His defence counsel convinced the jury that Welch's prescription was perfectly safe and that Mrs Genever, who was illiterate, had not understood his instructions and applied it wrongly. Welch was acquitted and a second charge of the manslaughter relating to Emma Genever was dropped.

12 APRIL

1864 Four children went to a colliery at Rowley Regis, where they played around the boiler for some time. Nine-year-old Samuel Portman was sitting down when a stone weighing 30lb fell off the boiler and landed on him. Twelve-year-old Joyce Siviter and another girl lifted the stone off Samuel but he was obviously very badly hurt and fainted from the pain. The two girls fetched him a drink of water then helped him home.

Later that day, Samuel complained of stiffness in his arms and legs. His mother assumed he had caught a cold but when he was still poorly the next morning, she consulted a doctor, who concluded that Samuel was suffering from internal injuries.

Samuel told his mother and the doctor, 'It's William Heath who has done this at me. I was sitting on the boiler side and he rolled a great big stone at me.' They were the last words he spoke, before dying on 16 April.

Coroner Edwin Hooper held an inquest at which fourteen-year-old William Heath denied touching the stone, saying that he had no idea how it fell. However, Joyce Siviter confirmed Samuel's story, swearing that she saw Heath push the stone off the boiler onto Samuel.

At the conclusion of the inquest, the coroner instructed the jury that there were only two possible verdicts open to them – accidental death or homicide by misadventure. The jury chose the latter option.

13 APRIL

1930 Most of the Blower family of Walsall fell ill after eating their Sunday tea of pork pie, bread and butter and pineapple. Thomas Blower and one of his children were the only ones who were not seized with violent sickness and diarrhoea, and Thomas quickly realised that they were the only two family members who had not eaten any pork pie. Mrs Blower, who ate only a small piece, was not seriously ill but the remaining seven children were all so poorly that they were admitted to the Walsall Manor Hospital.

Irene (10), Stanley (9) and Olive (4) subsequently died and a post-mortem examination determined that the cause of death was acute enteritis, most probably contracted from eating infected pork pie. The pie was bought from a reputable supplier and looked and tasted exactly as it should have done, although Mrs Blower did notice on 14 April that it was a strange colour and threw the leftovers to the chickens.

Hospital and Nurses' Home, Walsall.
(Author's collection)

An inquest was opened and adjourned on 16 April, and when it concluded on 25 April, the four children who were still in hospital were said to be 'progressing favourably.' The inquest determined that the deaths of the other three were due to acute enteritis, adding that nobody was in any way to blame.

14 APRIL

1887 Coroner Edwin Hooper concluded an inquest at Cradley Heath on the deaths of two-year-old Thomas Lot Bellingham (or Billingham) and four-year-old Lily Birch, who died after an explosion on 7 April. Several more children were badly hurt and Adam Bellingham (13) and his brother James (6) died after the conclusion of the inquest.

The tragedy occurred after ironmonger Henry Mould took delivery of 200lbs of gunpowder at his shop in High Street, Cradley. The powder was placed in a detached store behind Mould's shop but during delivery, a little of the gunpowder was spilled on the yard and the local children took great delight in scraping it into small heaps and setting light to them. Adam Bellingham was warned against doing this by at least two adults but he ignored their warnings. It appears that one patch of spilled gunpowder formed a trail to the barrels in the store since, when it was lit, the store suddenly exploded, showering the children with bricks and burying them in rubble.

Mould's premises were certified for the storage of gunpowder but an enquiry conducted by HM Inspector of Explosives Major Cundill found several irregularities in the way Mould and his apprentice handled the powder. Although the inquests found verdicts of 'accidental death' on all of the children apart from Adam Bellingham, whose demise was ruled 'death by misadventure', Mould was prosecuted and magistrates fined him a total of £12 3s 10d, including costs.

Cundill's report concluded that the children were killed by a combination of Adam Bellingham's actions and what Cundill called 'dangerous manipulation' of the gunpowder by Mould's seventeen-year-old apprentice, George Edward Millward. However, since Mould bore ultimate responsibility for the actions of his apprentice and had already been fined, no charges were pressed against Millward, who got away with a payment of 18s 6d costs at the court case against Mould.

15 APRIL

1846 When the Fire Clay Pit Colliery at Bilston re-opened after the Easter break, the first six men were lowered underground. The 'doggy', who managed the men, ordered them to wait for him at the bottom of the shaft but, although his colleagues told him not to, William Jones set off towards the coal face. He had travelled only a few yards when his candle ignited a pocket of sulphurous gas and there was a violent explosion.

Jones lost his life, as did Abraham Atkiss, Thomas Vinson, John Evans and Enoch Bettery. Jones and Atkiss left twelve children between them, and Thomas was only ten years old.

Coroner Mr T.M. Phillips held an inquest, at which the jury returned verdicts of 'accidental death'. It was indicated that, had Jones survived, he would probably have faced charges of manslaughter for disobeying orders.

16 APRIL

1920 At just after 7.30 p.m., St George's Hall in Garrick Street, Wolverhampton collapsed. Built in 1858, the building was used as a billiard hall, and it was feared that there were numerous people trapped inside and that countless passers-by were buried in the debris.

Early estimates suggested that up to 130 people might have died or be seriously injured but miraculously the final death toll was only two – Alfred Breakwell (or Brakewell) and Ernest Harry Plimmer. Fifteen people were taken to hospital, only three of whom were detained.

According to survivors, the first sign of trouble was a scraping noise, followed by masonry falling into Garrick Street. Seconds later, the roof fell in then the rest of the building collapsed, leaving only part of one wall standing. Some people managed to take cover under the billiard tables, an act that undoubtedly reduced the number of deaths and casualties.

At the inquest, Louis Reynolds, the husband of the proprietress, stated that Arthur William Grosvenor had repaired the roof three months earlier. However, there was still a slight leak and two hours before the collapse Reynolds and Grosvenor were in the roof space trying to locate the source.

Grosvenor found that a roof beam had shifted slightly and, although he assured Reynolds that there was no immediate danger, he sent for a carpenter as a matter of urgency. Unfortunately, the roof collapsed before the carpenter arrived and both the Borough Engineer and Grosvenor believed that decay of the principal beams was responsible for the collapse.

The inquest jury returned verdicts of 'accidental death' on Breakwell and Plimmer, finding no evidence of criminal neglect. Even so, they expressed an opinion that Reynolds should have rectified the leak earlier, and that the Corporation should have the power to inspect public buildings and places of amusement.

17 APRIL

1857 Mr Butler of Tipton was brewing some beer when his two-year-old son, Henry, toddled into the brew house. Butler picked the little boy up and was nursing him when the little boy suddenly twisted round, falling from his father's arms into a tub of boiling hot liquid. The little boy was severely scalded – as was his father, who plunged his arms into the wort to rescue his son – and in spite of treatment by a surgeon, Henry died the following day.

At the inquest the jury returned a verdict of 'accidental death'.

18 APRIL

1943 Four teenagers from Stourbridge were out looking for birds' nests in Hagley Wood when they happened to peek inside the trunk of a large wych elm tree and found the skeletal remains of a woman.

Professor James M. Webster of the Home Office Laboratory of Forensic Science determined that she had been dead around eighteen months, was around thirty-five and had probably borne at least one child. She was about 5ft tall, with mousey brown hair and irregular teeth in her lower jaw. She wore a mustard coloured skirt, a peach underskirt, a striped cardigan and blue, crepe-soled shoes. It was impossible to determine the cause of death but Webster guessed that the woman may have suffocated, since a piece of taffeta was stuffed deep into her mouth.

An inquest returned a verdict of murder by person or persons unknown and the woman remains unidentified, her murder a mystery. Her details were circulated throughout Britain, as were pictures of her distinctive teeth, yet nobody ever came forward with her name. It was suggested that she belonged to a Romany gypsy family, was a local prostitute or was associated with witchcraft and the black arts. After her discovery, local police were baffled by the appearance of graffiti, with messages like, 'Who put Lubella down the which-elm?' [sic] 'Hagley Wood Bella', and 'Who put Bella in the wych elm?'. All were neatly printed in capital letters and would have taken time to write but nobody ever saw the author at work.

In 1953, a local journalist advanced a theory that she was a female spy with the code name 'Clara', and in 1958, Professor Webster claimed on

An artist's impression of the victim. (Courtesy of the *Wolverhampton Express and Star*)

The old wych elm, where the body was found. (Courtesy of the *Wolverhampton Express and Star*)

television that the police had successfully identified 'Bella' but he refused to elaborate further on the matter, as did the police.

19 APRIL

1868 Rehearsals for a new show by a theatre company named the Lauri Family began at the Concert Hall, Wolverhampton. The show was to run for twelve nights and one of the performances was to be 'Love in a Tub', a seventeenth-century comedy.

On the first night, the proprietors of the hall took exception to one particular scene, in which an actor turned and showed the audience his posterior. Mr Brewster and Mr Lawson spoke to Edward Lauri and told him that he could not perform that particular piece again.

Lauri was happy to comply with the managers' request, although he felt that they were overreacting. However, the following night, Mr Lawson got up on stage and informed the audience that the Lauri Family would not be performing at all.

Lauri was furious and, believing that the reputation of his company was at stake, he took the hands of the other company members and they tried to walk onto the stage to explain what had happened. As they did, a waiter grabbed performer Eliza Sandford and manhandled her, giving her bruise. Lauri then went to complain to PC Hendricken, who, he later alleged, pushed him off the stage.

Lauri took the matter before magistrates, summoning the waiter for assaulting Miss Sandford, and PC Hendricken for assaulting him. The cases were heard on 24 April at Wolverhampton Police Court.

Magistrates reminded Lauri that the proprietors had every right to stop an objectionable performance. Lauri denied that there had been anything untoward, saying that Lawson and Brewster had mistakenly assumed that, after the actor had supposedly split his trousers by falling off a chair, a patch on the garment was meant to represent his bare flesh.

The magistrates ruled that the management were within their rights in stopping the performance, although they had probably used more force than necessary with Miss Sandford. Brewster and Lawson were ordered to pay her expenses, and the charges against the waiter and PC Hendricken were dismissed.

20 APRIL

1907 At the Jubilee Pit of the Sandwell Park Colliers' Company at West Bromwich, a piece of timber was being lowered down into the pit when the chain broke. The timber, which weighed several hundredweight, landed on a group of men working at the bottom of the pit. Two were killed outright, a third was so badly injured that he died later that day in hospital, and four more men were hurt, although not seriously. An inquest later returned a verdict of 'accidental death' on all three of the deceased – William Cooper, Matthew Copson and Thomas Ward, who were all married with children.

21 APRIL

1866 Coroner Mr A.A. Fletcher held an inquest into the death of five-year-old Thomas Doody.

The day before, wagoner George Bayliss was driving a two-horse cart in Walsall, when John Simmonds began frantically waving to attract his

High Street, Walsall.
(Author's collection)

attention and shouting at him to stop. When Bayliss climbed down from the cart to see what the problem was, he found Doody's body entangled with the spokes on the cart's rear wheel. The child was crushed and mangled, having been literally ground to death between the wheel and the body of the vehicle.

At the inquest, Simmonds stated that he had been watching the cart and had seen no children anywhere near it. His gaze was drawn to something else for a moment or two and, when he looked back, he spotted Doody and immediately drew the carter's attention to the child's plight.

The coroner theorised that Doody was trying to climb onto the moving cart when his feet were caught by the revolving spokes. The jury concurred, returning a verdict of 'accidental death' and stressing that no blame could be attached to Bayliss.

22 APRIL

1859 Forty-nine-year-old collier Abraham Duffield was ascending from the pit at Horseley Heath with three other men, when he suddenly fell out of the skip. The others tried to grab him but Duffield was a heavy man and they were forced to let go or be dragged out with him.

Duffield fell about 20 yards to the bottom of the shaft, bouncing off another skip as he landed. He was heard to say, 'O Lord! O Lord!' a couple of times before dying.

The inquest held by coroner George Hinchcliffe failed to solve the mystery of Duffield's death. He had not complained of feeling ill before falling and had been working as normal that morning. The other three men with him in the skip stated that it was travelling smoothly when Duffield fell and had not jerked or bumped against the sides of the shaft. Furthermore, the skip was fitted with a 'bonnet', which was supposed to act as a safety measure to prevent people falling out, and a government inspector had examined the mine since the accident and found no irregularities.

The jury returned a verdict of 'accidental death' on Duffield, who left a widow and six children.

23 APRIL

1861 Deputy-coroner Mr W.H. Phillips concluded an inquest at Coseley on the death of Walter Piper. On 25 March, Piper was walking home from Coseley to Bilston when he was waylaid by two men. One hit him hard on the forehead, while the second garrotted him.

The men rifled through Piper's pockets, stealing 3s 6d, a brass tobacco box, two handkerchiefs, an old cloth cap and all of Piper's groceries, before leaving him for dead. The muggers sprinted past miner Thomas Jones, who found Piper lying on the ground moments later.

Sixty-five-year-old Piper died on 2 April, although not before giving a deposition to a magistrate. A post-mortem examination showed that he had a fractured skull, beneath which his brain was inflamed and covered in blood and pus.

The inquest was adjourned to allow time for further enquiries and, when it resumed, Superintendent McCrea revealed that the police were still no closer to solving the case. The inquest jury returned a verdict of 'wilful murder against some person or persons unknown', and the coroner announced his intention of applying to the Home Secretary for a reward for information leading to the conviction of the killers. Although the sum of £100 was authorised, Piper's murder remains unsolved.

24 APRIL

1858   At Messrs Bradley & Co.'s Iron Works at Stourbridge, the men were preparing to cast a large iron crank wheel in the foundry yard. The mould for the wheel was placed on top of a specially excavated pit, covered by iron plates and sand.

As the molten metal was poured into the mould, the extreme heat caused the air in the pit to expand rapidly, suddenly forcing up the iron plates and tipping the mould over. Three labourers who were standing on the plates were plunged into the chamber below. One scrambled out, a second was pulled out with slight burns, but Joseph Roberts was left standing in the pit with molten metal up to his waist.

For a few moments, his fellow workers were paralysed with horror before one recovered his wits sufficiently to throw Roberts a rope, which he wrapped around his body. As he was pulled from the pit, his flesh peeled off from the abdomen downwards, leaving just blackened, charred bones.

Roberts was carried to his home where a doctor was called to attend him. Incredibly, he survived for two hours, remaining conscious almost to the end, during which time he muttered constant prayers asking God to have mercy on him.

25 APRIL

1871   Although forty-five-year-old William Wilcox was a married man, he lived with twenty-nine-year-old Mary Willetts at Dudley and on 25 April, after William had left for work, neighbours heard groaning coming from his cottage and found Mary lying insensible on the bedroom floor. She was taken to Dudley Workhouse, where she gave birth to a premature, stillborn baby, before dying on 30 April.

A post-mortem examination revealed more than thirty wounds and bruises on her body, eight of which were on her head. The cause of death was concussion of the brain, which surgeons believed resulted from blows received from a blunt instrument.

The inquest was told that the couple frequently quarrelled and that neighbours had heard them having a row on the night of 24/25 April. Wilcox accused Mary of 'spending his money among the Irish', calling her a drunken beast and other obscene names and threatening to murder her if she didn't give him some money. At one stage, neighbours saw Mary on the floor with William standing over her.

Wilcox was tried at the Staffordshire Assizes on 15 July, where he continued to protest his innocence, insisting that Mary had fallen over while drunk, hitting her head on the fender. He failed to convince the jury, who found him guilty of manslaughter, leading to a sentence of twelve years' penal servitude.

26 APRIL

1879 Twenty-three-year-old Robert Fosborough (or Fosbrey) Lines married his wife Emma in October 1878. The couple had known each other for four years and Emma had already given birth to Robert's stillborn baby, after which he left the area. However, they renewed their relationship in September 1878 and decided to get married, moving in with Emma's father in Walsall.

On 25 April 1879, Emma gave birth to a baby boy. Robert believed that he couldn't possibly be the child's father, since he was first intimate with Emma only seven and a half months earlier. He threatened to throw Emma and the baby out of the window, and, although Emma protested that she had not slept with anyone else, her husband went on a drinking spree. The next day, Robert took a chopper upstairs and began to hack at Emma as she lay in bed. Emma fought desperately and, when the candle which was lighting the room blew out, she managed to escape. The police were called and soon afterwards PS Alden met Robert walking out of his father-in-law's house.

'What's the matter?' asked Alden, to which Robert replied, 'I've killed the baby.'

An inquest was held on the infant's death but the jury were unable to agree, only seven of the thirteen in favour of a verdict of wilful murder against Lines. Coroner Mr A.A. Fletcher explained that if a person making a murderous attack on someone happened to kill someone else, that would be murder and after further deliberation, the jury agreed on a verdict of 'wilful murder'.

Lines appeared before Mr Justice Hawkins at the Staffordshire Assizes in July 1879. His defence counsel maintained that, such was their client's distress at his wife's deceit that he struck at her with a chopper. However, it was dark in the room and the baby was concealed in the bedclothes. Lines could not see the child and killed him accidentally, therefore the charge should be manslaughter rather than murder.

The jury disagreed and found Lines guilty of murder, although they recommended mercy, on the grounds that there were doubts about the baby's paternity. Hawkins passed the death sentence, telling Lines that he personally held out no hope that the jury's request would be heeded. However, after a petition to the Home Secretary attracted almost 6,000 signatures, Lines was respited and sent to Chatham Prison.

27 APRIL

1865 Thomas Augustus Frederick Brown appeared at Wednesbury Police Court charged with having unlawfully, maliciously and with intent to injure, aggrieve and annoy Eliza Griffiths by forcing her to take a noxious drug.

Eliza worked as a barmaid and, on 19 April, Brown offered her a lemon-coloured lozenge. As soon as she had eaten it, Brown began to laugh. After jokingly threatening to put a lozenge in the common water kettle, he gave her two more for her fellow barmaids, which they wisely refused to eat. Within twenty minutes, Eliza had excruciating stomach pains. A doctor was sent for eight hours later, by which time she had vomited several times and experienced between thirty and forty bouts of diarrhoea.

The lozenge was found to contain two grams of calomel, or mercurous chloride, a compound used both as a laxative and as an insecticide. Medical evidence suggested that some people would not be affected in the slightest by taking one lozenge, whereas it could make others seriously ill.

When Brown was arrested, he told police that he had cautioned Eliza not to eat the lozenge, which he described as 'a worm cake'. However, magistrates didn't believe him and committed him for trial at the next Staffordshire Assizes. He appeared on 20 July, charged with 'administering a noxious thing with intent to injure' but the Grand Jury found no bill against him and he was discharged without penalty.

28 APRIL

1858 At Groveland Colliery near Dudley Port, eleven-year-old Samuel Moore was hewing coal in an underground stall, which was 5 yards wide. As he bent down, around 2 tons of coal suddenly fell from the roof, burying the child alive. Although he was extricated as quickly as possible, his body was frightfully crushed and he was believed to have died instantly.

The area where Samuel was working had been examined only that morning and was judged to be perfectly safe. The fall was attributed to either the timber supports having been bumped or to a movement of the earth above the coal. No blame could be attached to anyone for Samuel's demise and coroner George Hinchcliffe recorded a verdict of 'accidental death'.

29 APRIL

1857 Eighteen-year-old Elizabeth Hopley left her uncle's house at Bilston at 9.30 p.m., without her bonnet or shawl. Eight hours later, she was found dead in the canal.

Almost a month passed before nightwatchman George Powell contacted the police to say that he saw a man named Philip Clare murdering Elizabeth at around midnight that night. Elizabeth had once worked for Clare and there was ill-feeling between them after she summoned him for non-payment of wages. Powell alleged that Clare had threatened to kill him too, if he revealed what he had seen.

When the inquest on Elizabeth's death resumed, Powell had left the area. Clare attended, along with someone who swore that Clare was with him at his house between midnight on 29 April and 2 a.m. on 30 April. That alibi was contradicted by a neighbour of Clare's, who was equally certain that she saw him arriving home at one o'clock. The inquest finally concluded with a verdict of wilful murder against Clare, who swore his innocence.

It took until September for the police to trace Powell, who was arrested for breaking windows at the Warwick Workhouse. Committed to Warwick Gaol, he was recognised and returned to Bilston.

Clare was tried at the Stafford Assizes, where the case against him hinged on the testimony of two witnesses. The first was Powell, the second was another watchman named Hawes, who saw nothing but heard a woman's voice shouting, 'Don't hit me. You said you would, but don't'. (This was remarkably similar to what Powell independently testified to having heard, which was, 'Don't kill me. You said you would, but don't'.)

Other than the testimony of Hawes and Powell, there was nothing to connect Clare to the murder, and some aspects of the evidence were contradictory. The medical evidence suggested that Elizabeth was conscious when she fell into the canal and struggled violently to try and save herself, whereas Powell, who claimed to have seen Clare putting her in the water, was adamant that 'she neither moved, nor groaned nor sighed.' The jury found Clare not guilty and he was discharged.

Note: In some reports of the trial, George Powell is alternatively named as Samuel Wall. Powell is the most frequently quoted name.

30 APRIL

1888 William Harper kept The Victoria Inn on Pountney Street, Wolverhampton, living in rooms over the pub with his wife and five sons, who were aged between ten and twenty-two years old. The eldest, Ernest, was known as a violent and passionate man, who served in the Navy but deserted after returning from a tour of duty in China. He was captured and served ninety days' imprisonment at Lewes Gaol, before being discharged from the service and returning to Wolverhampton.

Ernest got up very early on the morning of 30 April and went into his parents' bedroom. When they told him to go back to bed, he went downstairs and took a carving knife from a drawer, before returning to the bedroom he shared with his brothers.

As his seventeen-year-old brother Thomas slept, Ernest cut his throat. Thomas fell out of bed onto the floor, his lifeblood gushing from him. Nineteen-year-old John woke up and jumped at Ernest, trying to take the knife from him and although Ernest fought to kill, John managed to disarm him. As the boys' father rushed into the room, Ernest tore himself from his brother's grasp and, giving an animalistic howl, flung himself through the bedroom window.

Ernest's father managed to grab one of his feet but was unable to hold him and the young man fell 18ft onto the pavement, bouncing off some spiked railings and gouging out one of his eyes before hitting the ground. His father and brothers raced downstairs to find him badly injured but conscious. Asked why he stabbed Thomas, he could only say, 'I don't know,' before fainting.

A policeman happened to be passing and got Ernest to hospital, where his injuries were found to be severe but not life threatening. He survived to be charged with fratricide and stood trial at the Stafford Assizes on 24 July, where he was found guilty but insane and ordered to be securely detained at Her Majesty's pleasure. He was sent to Broadmoor Criminal Lunatic Asylum.

MAY

Town Hall, Walsall. (Author's collection)

1 MAY

1858 Sixty-year-old Thomas Nocton of West Bromwich slipped while walking downstairs, injuring his head so badly that he died three hours later. In reporting his death, the contemporary newspapers recalled that Nocton's entire life had been a chapter of accidents. He had been knocked over by an express train, luckily landing in the gap between the rails and emerging completely unscathed after the engine and five carriages passed over his prostrate body. He also survived numerous accidents in his job as a glass worker, the most recent of which involved a heavy box of glass that fell from a great height, fortunately just grazing one of his shoulders.

The newspaper commented on the irony that a man who had so often cheated death should die doing something as innocuous as walking downstairs.

2 MAY

1895 At eight o'clock in the morning, people heard screams coming from the house in West Bromwich occupied by travelling tailor James Stone and his servant Laura Williams.

Nobody investigated until early afternoon, when neighbours realised that there had been none of the usual signs of activity at the house. The police were called and, when there was no response to their knocks on the door, they forced an entry through the kitchen.

In the sitting room, the police found Laura's body on the sofa, a single gunshot wound beneath her right ear. The bullet had passed right through her head, through a pillow and embedded itself in the arm of the sofa. Mr Stone was sitting upright in a chair, with most of the front of his head blown away by a gunshot, and there was a recently fired military carbine on the floor nearby.

Although Stone was a married man, he had recently shown signs of mental derangement and his wife had left him. Earlier in the year, a doctor suggested that he was admitted to a lunatic asylum but he refused to go, and since nobody imagined that he was a danger either to himself or to others, he was not forced. Now an inquest jury returned a verdict of wilful murder against him in respect of his servant's death, followed by suicide whilst insane.

3 MAY

1948 A postwoman delivered a parcel to Captain Roy Alexander Farran at his home near Codsall, Wolverhampton. It was addressed to 'R. Farran' and when Captain Farran's twenty-five-year-old brother, Rex, opened the parcel it exploded, causing such severe wounds to his stomach that he died within two hours. Experts determined that the parcel contained a book, the middle section of which had been removed and the space filled with explosives.

Almost exactly a year earlier, Captain Farran was tried by court-martial in Jerusalem for the murder of a Jewish youth. He was acquitted but, after his trial, posters were pasted on walls in Tel Aviv by a militant organisation known as Lehi or the 'Stern Gang', stating, 'Captain Farran's time will come. We shall go after him to the end of the world.'

The inquest on twenty-five-year-old Rex Francis Farran returned a verdict that he was feloniously killed by some person or persons unknown. Later, intelligence suggested that the bomb was sent by a Lehi member in Britain.

4 MAY

1871 At Moxley, thirty-five-year-old William Lloyd slept all day after working a night shift, before rising at 8 p.m. and, completely without provocation, attacking his wife with a knife and a poker. Neighbours rushed to their house in response to her frantic screams to find Lloyd standing over his bleeding wife, while their fifteen-year-old son struggled to disarm him. The neighbours proved sufficient distraction for the boy to snatch the knife but not before his mother's throat had been cut.

Mrs Lloyd ran into the yard, while her husband waved the 2½ft-long poker at the neighbours and threatened to kill them. As the neighbours retreated, Lloyd caught up with his wife and began to batter her about the head, hitting her over and over again until her skull was smashed to fragments.

Then Lloyd charged towards the neighbours and people scattered in all directions, some taking refuge in a nearby beer house. Lloyd attacked the glass doors and, having broken the glass, jumped through the doors into the pub. He was met by the landlord, also wielding a poker, who dealt Lloyd a tremendous blow on the shoulder. Lloyd launched a savage attack on the landlord but was finally overcome and pinned to the ground. With difficulty, he was taken to the lock-up at Wednesbury, where he told police that he had killed his wife because of jealousy.

Charged with murder, Lloyd was tried at the Staffordshire Assizes on 20 July, where he was found not guilty by reason of insanity and ordered to be detained at Her Majesty's pleasure. He spent several years in Broadmoor Criminal Lunatic Asylum.

Broadmoor
Lunatic Asylum.
(Author's collection)

5 MAY

1859 William Baker appeared at the Wolverhampton Petty Sessions charged with leaving his wife chargeable to the parish. Mary Baker, who was described in the contemporary newspapers as 'an elderly and uncomely personage' was admitted to the Workhouse on 18 April, and her husband now owed the Union 7s 6d for her maintenance.

Mrs Baker stated that she was unable to support herself since her husband had broken her arm, an offence for which he served three months in prison (*see* 10 May). Since his release, he had contributed nothing towards her keep.

William Baker pleaded poverty, adding that his wife was a drunkard of very immoral habits. Baker called James Wood, who the newspapers described as 'almost half-witted but possessing a compensatory allowance of cunning', and, prompted by Baker, Wood admitted to having had 'improper intercourse' with Mrs Baker two years earlier. However, in the face of questioning by the Bench, Wood coyly refused to reveal any more details, obviously under the impression that he was protecting Mrs Baker's reputation. Baker also called witnesses to describe his wife's habitual drunkenness.

Other witnesses corroborated Baker's allegations about Mary's character and the Bench finally decided that they had heard enough and stopped what the chief magistrate referred to as a 'disgusting exhibition' by refusing to make an order compelling Baker to support his wife.

'What am I to do?' wailed Mary Baker and, when told that her husband was not bound to support her anymore, she declared that since he had a new woman, she was damned if she wouldn't find herself a new man.

6 MAY

1863 Fifty-two-year-old Maria Robinson cohabited with Joel Holloway for thirty years and, although the couple never married, they had nine children together, four of whom survived.

On 3 May, one of the couple's daughters came home late and Joel, who was known for his short temper, determined to punish her. The girl fled to the pantry, hoping that he would calm down but when she emerged, her father rushed at her. She evaded him and ran upstairs.

The following night, someone came into Joel's nail-making workshop in Rowley Regis and castigated him for his violent behaviour towards his family. Joel was furious that his business was being made 'public-house talk' and as Maria entered the room, he accused her of gossiping and threw a heavy lump hammer at her. It hit her on the lower stomach and she was in so much pain that she could barely move, although no doctor was called until after her death on 6 May.

An inquest returned a verdict of manslaughter against Holloway and when charged, he simply pointed to his neck and promised to sing as the rope was put round it. By the time his case reached the Stafford Assizes, Joel Holloway had lost some of his bravado. He pleaded guilty to the charge of manslaughter, prepared to accept that he was the cause of Maria's death but insisting that he never intended to kill her. He fell to his knees in the dock, sobbing and begging the judge to be merciful and was sentenced to six months' imprisonment.

7 MAY

1858 Butty collier Silvanus Ramsell was lent a horse and trap and, not knowing how to drive it, he asked clerk Thomas Hardy to take him out. As the trap was going down Goldthorn Hill in Wolverhampton, something startled the horse and it bolted.

Ramsell panicked and, even though he knew nothing about horses, he snatched the reins from Hardy and attempted to stop the animal, which galloped out of control until it reached the Penn toll bar. After colliding with the tollgate, the trap overturned and was smashed to pieces.

Ramsell and Hardy were thrown onto the road. Both men were knocked unconscious but while Hardy escaped with bruising and a broken arm, Ramsell's skull was fractured and he died that night in South Staffordshire Hospital. When Hardy regained consciousness, he could recall nothing after Ramsell seized the reins, but since numerous witnesses had seen the obviously inexperienced driver battling to control the horse, coroner W.H. Phillips recorded a verdict of accidental death.

8 MAY

1864 In the early hours of the morning, as PC William Lyons was patrolling his beat in Willenhall, he asked a member of the public, William Lowe, to stay with him for a little while, as there was going to be 'a row'.

Minutes later, brothers Thomas and George Lockley approached with some friends 'cursing and blasting' and Lyons warned them that if they didn't stop swearing, he would arrest them. He tried to handcuff George but John Edwards ran up and grabbed George's other arm. A tussle developed between Edwards and during which the policeman was punched and kicked.

Lowe tried to intervene but Thomas threw something at the policeman's head, which felled him. 'Oh, Lowe, they have killed me,' Lyons moaned as he lay on the ground. Eventually, another member of the public helped Lowe take Lyons into a nearby house, where his head wound was attended to. Lyons was well enough to accompany PCs Hampton, Hooper and Dutton to the Lockleys' house, where it was alleged that he was again hit on the head, this time with a poker.

The injury to Lyons's head was initially treated by doctors as a scalp wound but his condition deteriorated and he underwent surgery, from which he failed to recover. On his death, Thomas and George Lockley, John Edwards, Joshua Stanley and George Willetts were arrested and charged with his wilful murder.

The five stood trial at the Staffordshire Assizes in July before Mr Justice Shee, who was meticulous in summarising the case for the jury. Shee suggested that there was conflicting evidence regarding the extent of the involvement of Willetts and Stanley in the assault. The judge reminded the jury that initially, Edwards seemed to have done little more than try and persuade his drunken friend to go home. He and George were wrestling in the street and there was no doubt that, at the time, George had a knife in his hands – it was to his credit that he didn't use it. Shee also pointed out that when Lyons first tried to arrest George it seemed unlikely that he had actually done anything to warrant being arrested and a caution against using bad language might have been more appropriate.

The jury returned verdicts of manslaughter against Thomas and George Lockley, John Edwards and Joshua Stanley. Thomas was sentenced to eight years' imprisonment, George and Edwards to six years and Stanley to five. Willetts was found not guilty and discharged.

9 MAY

1864 Coroner Edwin Hooper held an inquest at The Star Inn, Horseley Heath, into the death of eight-year-old Sarah Ann Gary.

The chief witness was ten-year-old Hannah Fisher, who testified that on 6 May, she was walking along the canal towpath when she saw Sarah on the opposite side of the canal. There was a large fish floating on the surface of the water and, as Sarah tried to reach it, she overbalanced.

Hannah raced to a nearby bridge, crossed the canal and ran back to where Sarah was floundering. She managed to grab Sarah's hand but was unable to pull her out of the water and, finding herself being dragged into the canal, she was forced to ask Sarah to let go. As she did, Joshua Hall approached and Hannah appealed to him to help. Hall simply remarked that he couldn't swim and stood and watched Sarah's desperate struggles.

Workers from a nearby brickyard eventually heard Hannah's cries for help and raced to the canal side. Sadly, Sarah sank beneath the surface of the water as they arrived and even though they probed the water with rakes and dived to try and find her, by the time she was located in the murky water she had drowned.

Joshua Hall was universally condemned at the inquest for his inaction – the coroner remarked that, even if he couldn't swim, it was his duty to at least call for help. Sarah's father was particularly angry since he firmly believed that Hall could swim and could easily have saved his daughter. The inquest returned a verdict of 'accidental death' and the coroner remarked that it was a pity that there was no way in which the law could punish Hall's bad conduct.

10 MAY

1858   William Baker appeared at Wolverhampton Police Court charged with brutally assaulting his wife, who attended court swathed in bandages.

Mary Baker complained that, while drunk, her husband had jabbed her with his elbow, before deliberately breaking her arm in two places by sitting on it. A few days later, he got drunk again and knocked her off a stool, kicking her several times as she lay on the floor. A doctor listed her injuries as a three-inch long scalp wound to the bone, a broken arm, bruising to the face, nose and both thighs, two black eyes and a cut ear.

In his defence, Baker complained that it was Mary who was the drunkard, alleging that she didn't take care of him properly. After hearing witnesses for both sides, the magistrates found in Mary's favour, sentencing her husband to three months' imprisonment with hard labour. (*See* 5 May.)

11 MAY

1860   Prostitute Mary Ann Batley approached borough surveyor Mr Purnell in Wolverhampton and asked him to go home with her. When Purnell refused, she snatched his hat and ran off. Purnell chased her and managed to retrieve his hat but quickly realised that his watch and chain were missing. He ran after Mary Ann and the couple struggled, with Mary Ann screaming and raking Purnell's face with her fingernails.

Two men walked by and, thinking that Mary Ann was being attacked, rescued her from Purnell. Once freed, Mary Ann bolted but Police Sergeant Wardle had seen her following Purnell and, hearing a woman screaming, he ran back to investigate, finding Purnell lying flat on his back in the street, complaining of being robbed.

Mary Ann was well known to Wardle, who arrested her within the hour and took her to the police station, where she was searched by a female searcher. No watch and chain was found and the sergeant was on the verge of releasing her when, by the gaslight, he noticed something glinting at the back of her head. He asked Mary Ann what it was and she replied that it was just a hairpin, but when Wardle unrolled her hair he found a purse concealed in it, containing the stolen items.

Unable to argue with the sergeant's findings, Mary Ann Batley pleaded guilty to robbery at the Wolverhampton Petty Sessions and was sentenced to six months' imprisonment with hard labour.

12 MAY

1860 The northern express passed through Stourbridge Station at eleven o'clock every morning, only stopping if passengers had booked to join the train.

On 12 May, railway employee William Bowater left the goods shed and tried to cross the line. As he emerged from between two trucks, it was obvious to onlookers that he was about to step out in front of the express.

People shouted warnings but Bowater just stopped and looked round to see who was calling him. He eventually turned towards the approaching train but it was already upon him. The engine hurled his body into the air, propelling it forward several yards. Bowater's head was literally knocked off, leaving just his lips and chin, and both of his feet were amputated.

Nobody who witnessed the accident could understand how Bowater failed to notice the train. There were no bends in the line and the engine driver was blowing his whistle as he approached the station. There was no suggestion that Bowater was suicidal and the inquest later surmised that he was aware of the express but was unable to judge its speed and started crossing the line assuming that he had plenty of time to get clear.

13 MAY

1886 Heavy rains over a prolonged period caused catastrophic floods throughout the Black Country, not least at Walsall, where the station was inundated when the River Tame burst its banks. In Willenhall, six-

Flood at Walsall Station, 13 May 1886. (Author's collection)

year-old Clara Wolverson was playing outside, while her mother, who had recently given birth, watched through the bedroom window. Suddenly, Mrs Wolverson saw her daughter topple into a swollen stream. She raised the alarm but by the time anyone could get to where Clara fell into the water, she had long since been swept away by the current.

Later that day, Clara's parents were told that a little girl's body had been recovered at James Bridge. John Wolverson rushed to the scene but the dead child was not Clara. She was eventually identified as six-year-old Edith Wesson from Willenhall, who had slipped off a plank bridge earlier that afternoon.

Clara was found two-and-a-half miles from her home on 16 May, her body having been dumped in a field by the receding water.

14 MAY

1878 Neighbours heard screams from within the house in Walsall occupied by the Dalkins (or Dalkin) family. When they went to investigate, they found Elizabeth Dalkins crouching behind the bedroom door with her throat cut. Her two-year-old son Frederick was on the bed, his throat also cut, while Elizabeth's two other children lay stupefied by laudanum on the bedroom floor. All were rushed to hospital, where all fortunately survived.

Elizabeth had recently given birth to her third child and had been low and depressed since her confinement. When she was discharged from hospital, she was taken to Stafford Gaol, where the surgeon examined her and diagnosed puerperal mania – an acute mood disorder, characterised by severe manic reactions, experienced by women after giving birth. Even so, Elizabeth appeared before magistrates at the Guildhall in Walsall charged with the attempted murder of her son and also with attempting suicide.

The presiding magistrate stated that, even with the certificate from the doctor, the Bench had no choice but to forward the case for trial. When Elizabeth appeared at the Staffordshire Assizes in July, she was acquitted due to insanity, and records suggest that she returned to live with her husband and family in Walsall.

Birmingham Road, Walsall, 1913. (Author's collection)

15 MAY

1880 A calamitous boiler explosion occurred at Birchills Hall Iron Works, near Walsall, and forty of the firm's 200 employees were in close proximity to the boiler when it exploded. Large fragments of iron were blown sky high, landing on the yard and sheds of the adjacent Castle Iron Company and injuring several labourers there.

The boiler was one of three, and workers who courageously ran to open the safety valves on the others were met with a scene of absolute carnage. One man was completely cut in two, another's head was shattered and several people lost limbs in the blast. Many were terribly scalded and some were blown into the nearby canal. Twelve men died instantaneously and the final death toll was twenty-five.

Coroner Mr A.A. Fletcher opened an inquest at the Walsall Cottage Hospital, which didn't close until the end of June. The jury concluded that the boiler was corroded and weakened by frequent repairs, that the safety valve was too small and that the maximum safe steam pressure was regularly exceeded. They blamed the company for using a boiler in an unsafe condition but the coroner pointed out that there was a shared responsibility between the management of the Birchills Hall Works, the independent boiler-makers and the insurance company who undertook periodic inspections of the boiler. According to the coroner, although the owners of the Works were not blameless, the neglect attributed to them was not of a criminal character, thus the final verdict was twenty-five counts of 'accidental death'.

16 MAY

1830 Five-year-old Sally Chance of Lye Waste went out visiting with her mother Mary and her mother's husband-to-be, Charles Wall. While there, Sally asked if she could go out to play and, when she didn't return, her mother went looking for her. She searched through the night and, the following morning, went house to house asking if anyone had seen her daughter. One man replied that he had seen Sally alone with Wall, and throughout the day several more witnesses said the same.

Sally's body was found at the bottom of a limestone pit on 19 May and, since so many people claimed to have seen her with Wall, an inquest returned a verdict of wilful murder against him and he was committed for trial at the next Worcestershire Assizes.

For every witness called by the prosecution, the defence countered with a witness who had either seen Sally playing alone around the top of the unfenced mineshaft on the night of her disappearance, or who testified about the kindness shown by Wall to both of Mary Chance's illegitimate children.

Mr Justice Park told the jury that he personally could not see any possible motive that Wall might have for killing the little girl, reminding them that nobody had spoken of anything but kindness and fondness between Wall and his alleged victim. Nevertheless, the jury found Wall guilty, although they recommended mercy.

Charles Wall was hanged at Worcester Prison on 30 July 1830. Although the judge could see no motive for the murder, some sources report that Sally knew a little too much about some burglaries that Wall had committed and had to be silenced.

17 MAY

1893   Until 1887, fifty-seven-year-old Frederick Chriss of Wolverhampton worked in the goods department of the London and North Western Railway Company. Then he was knocked down by a train, severely injuring his spine. It was thought that he would die but after a long time in hospital, he was well enough to return home, although still too damaged to return to his job. As well as injuring him physically, the accident unhinged Chriss's mind and he was eventually admitted to Coton Hill Asylum in Stafford.

Coton Hill Asylum,
Stafford, 1907.
(Author's collection)

He was discharged on 17 May 1893, returning to live with his wife, Harriet, and five of the couple's eight children, the youngest of whom was twelve years old. Chriss's family found him far from cured. His speech was often incoherent and rambling and he constantly chided his family, 'Don't throw your sneers at me,' even when nobody had spoken. He also refused food and appeared strange in his manner.

On 20 May, Chriss rose early and prepared breakfast for two of his sons. He then went for a walk, returning at 10.30 a.m. in an apparently calm and peaceful state of mind. Yet he had hardly set foot in the house before he picked up a heavy meat cleaver and hit Harriet on the head.

Blood gushed from the injury and the couple's terrified twelve-year-old son Stephen bolted out of the house to fetch help. Meanwhile, Harriet ran into the yard, with her husband following. As his horrified neighbours watched, Chriss hacked at Harriet with the cleaver until she lay dead. He then began smashing windows, first his own, then those of his neighbours. Finally, Chriss returned to his own kitchen, where he took his razor from a drawer and cut his throat. Replacing the razor, he staggered outside, blood pumping from his throat and stooped to kiss Harriet's shattered face, before lying down next to her to die.

An inquest determined that Frederick Chriss murdered his wife while in a temporary fit of insanity, before committing suicide. According to Stephen, his mother did absolutely nothing to provoke her murder and not a single word passed between husband and wife before Frederick picked up the meat cleaver.

18 MAY   **1865**   Coroner Mr T.M. Phillips held an inquest into the death of thirty-seven-year-old steeplejack John McCann.

McCann was employed to work on a tall chimney at Wednesbury Oak Iron Works and the inquest heard that, having spent most of Sunday 14 May drinking, he decided to work that evening. Although several people tried to dissuade him, he somehow managed to climb the chimney and, on reaching the scaffold that had been erected at the top, he went to sleep.

People tried calling him from the ground but there was no answer for nearly an hour until finally, at half-past ten, McCann shouted that he was coming down.

He was seen lying on the scaffold with his head against the chimney and his feet dangling off the side, before hauling himself upright. He then stepped off the scaffold boards into space, tumbling through the air before finally plummeting through the roof of the building at the foot of the chimney.

The inquest jury returned a verdict of 'accidental death'.

19 MAY   **1879**   The funerals of William Thomas Baker (14), Frederick (or Alfred) Astbury (13), Arthur Etheridge (18) and John Mason (13) and his brother Joseph (15) took place at St Peter's Church, Walsall, with all five boys buried in a single grave. They were killed when a boiler exploded at the Walsall District Ironworks on 13 May (a sixth boy was badly injured).

The boiler was relatively new and made by a reputable manufacturer. At the time of the explosion, the man usually in charge of the boiler was at his supper, and it was suggested that the boiler became overheated and that water was being let into it when it exploded. However, an investigation found that the boiler had been made from poor quality iron that was unsuitable for boiler manufacture. It needed frequent repairs, which further weakened it and made it vulnerable to explosion.

At Walsall Cottage Hospital, coroner Mr Fletcher concluded the inquests shortly before the start of the funeral. The jury returned verdicts of 'accidental death due to explosion, caused by the poor quality of the iron and the injudicious way in which the boiler had been repaired.' Even so, they attached no blame to either the manufacturer or the factory.

20 MAY   **1865**   In the early hours of the morning, two colliers working the nightshift at Victoria Pit, West Bromwich heard something crashing down the pit shaft. The men took shelter and seconds later a policeman landed at the foot of the shaft, his body terribly mutilated.

Twenty-two-year-old John McHarg had served in the Staffordshire Constabulary for just seven months and was regarded as an exemplary officer. It was a very dark night and, although McHarg was patrolling his regular beat, part of the fencing around the shaft had been removed to allow coal to be removed from the pit. Coroner Edwin Hooper suggested that the policeman had just walked over the edge of the shaft and the inquest jury concurred, returning a verdict of 'accidental death'.

21 MAY

1884 Twenty-four-year-old Frederick William Dewen went with his sister, Agnes, to visit their parents in Wolverhampton. Their father was away on business but their mother, Sarah, was delighted to see her children and, as a special treat, bought a tin of salmon from the grocer.

Agnes barely touched her salmon, telling her mother that it tasted bitter, but Frederick and Sarah ate heartily. The following morning, after his usual breakfast of bacon and eggs, Frederick began to feel nauseous and giddy. He felt so poorly that he had to leave work and thought it prudent to visit his mother to check that she was all right. Finding his mother and sister terribly ill, he sent for a doctor then went to bed. Frederick was partially paralysed and had difficulty breathing and swallowing and died on 24 May. By that time, his sister had completely recovered but his mother was still very poorly and died later the same day.

An inquest was opened by coroner Mr W.H. Phillips and adjourned for post-mortem examinations and analysis of the remains of the salmon, which had been retrieved from the ash pit where they had been discarded. By the time the inquest concluded, tiny portions of the salmon had been fed to mice, which died within hours. It was concluded that the salmon was in a diseased state, probably due to a hole in the tin allowing air to enter. The inquest jury determined that 'the deceased persons died from poisoning arising from the decomposition of the food they had eaten.'

22 MAY

1870 When PC Riley saw lights on after hours at The Crown in Wednesbury, he went in and found Mr Wood with a jug of ale. Riley summoned landlady Jane Skidmore, for having her house open for the sale of ale during prohibited hours, and she subsequently appeared before magistrates at Wednesbury Police Court.

Her solicitor, Mr Ebsworth, asked Riley if the pub was a favourite haunt for policemen.

'Not in particular,' Riley replied.

'You, yourself have been sticking up to the widow, haven't you?' asked Ebsworth.

Riley smiled bashfully as Ebsworth suggested that he had proposed marriage to Mrs Skidmore and had told people that he would soon have his name over the pub door as licensee. When Ebsworth produced a photograph of a policeman in uniform, Riley blushingly admitted that it was him and that he had given it to Mrs Skidmore. He also conceded that he might have put his arm around her waist on occasions.

With the chief witness for the prosecution now an object of ridicule, Ebsworth pounced. He called Mr Wood, who said that he had been helping Mrs Skidmore and had consequently been given some ale, bread and cheese, which he was tucking into when Riley arrived. The front door of the pub was shut and Riley had to climb over a wall to gain entry. Furthermore, there was another police officer on the premises, who, at the time, was busy courting Mrs Skidmore's sister.

Ebsworth suggested that Riley had summoned Mrs Skidmore through jealousy, having seen her alone with Wood. The Bench dismissed the case against Mrs Skidmore, warning her to be a little more careful in future.

23 MAY

1869 William Hall and Richard Williams were working a night shift tending the furnaces at the Darlaston Steel and Iron Company, when labourer Thomas Evans heard a strange noise. He went to investigate and found that there had been a small explosion and that Hall and Williams had been very badly burned by liquid cinder blown from the furnace. The men's burns were dressed with oil at the factory before they were conveyed to the South Staffordshire Hospital, where both died within hours.

In order to produce iron, a mixture of iron ore, coke and limestone were fed into the top of the blast furnace, while heated air was blown into the bottom. The solid raw material gradually descended through the furnace over several hours, eventually ending up at the bottom as liquid cinder and liquid iron, which could then be separated.

A Black Country blast furnace. (Author's collection)

It was unusual to stop a blast furnace working but this one had recently been idle for three days and nights for maintenance. The consequent partial cooling of the contents could cause undermining of minerals, so that they formed unsupported 'shelves' within the furnace. On this occasion, solid material had suddenly dropped a distance of 9ft into the molten contents below, causing them to slop out of the furnace and burn the two men.

It was suggested at the inquest that furnace keeper Williams should have been aware that the material inside the furnace was overhanging, and that he could have remedied the situation by quickly raising and lowering a part of the furnace known as the 'baffler'. This would have brought the minerals down but Williams would have been some distance away and would thus have avoided being burned.

In recording verdicts of 'accidental death' on both men, coroner Mr T.M. Phillips suggested that the company placed printed notices close to the furnaces, reminding men to operate the baffler.

24 MAY

1893 Deputy-coroner Mr A.B. Smith held an inquest at Willenhall, into the death of fifty-two-year-old widow Mary Ann Baker.

On the previous day, Mary Ann was drinking with Ann (or Sarah) Downing and became so intoxicated that she was incapable of walking home. Thomas

Givney fetched a wheelbarrow intending to push her but as they trundled along Church Street, Givney wheeled the barrow into a horse and cart. The horse was startled and began to prance about and Mary Ann fell beneath its hoofs. She was picked up and taken home but died later that night.

Witnesses argued about whether or not Givney was drunk in charge of a wheelbarrow and Ann Downing insisted that Mary Ann wasn't drunk but had fallen and hurt herself earlier that day. With so much conflicting evidence, the coroner adjourned the inquest for a post-mortem examination to be carried out.

The examination showed only a small graze on Mary Ann's temple and revealed that the cause of death was a ruptured artery on the left side of her brain. The inquest jury returned a verdict in accordance with the medical evidence, finding that Mary Ann died from bleeding on the brain, with no evidence to show how that bleeding was caused.

25 MAY

1873 Philip Hayward of West Bromwich was looking for his son and heard that he had been seen with Charles Marris (or Morris) and Joseph Winwood, in a barn belonging to farmer Mr Darbey.

Hayward went to the barn but as he opened the door and went inside, he was jumped on by Marris and Winwood, who knocked him over. As Hayward lay helpless on the ground, the two farm labourers kicked him, and Marris deliberately tried to gouge Hayward's eye out with his fingers. Hayward screamed in agony and, when his wife came to his assistance, his two assailants ran off.

Marris and Winwood stated that Hayward was creeping about in the pitch darkness and they had believed that he was 'up to no good' and had merely tried to defend their master's property. Hayward accepted this but wanted compensation for his injured eye, suggesting that he would settle the matter out of court for £3.

When the two men refused, they were taken before magistrates at West Bromwich Police Court, where the chief magistrate stated that this was one of the most horrible offences ever to come before him. Although the two defendants had a just right to protect their master's property, they were guilty of a gross excess of punishment and he intended to fine them heavily – Marris was ordered to pay £5 including costs and Winwood £3 plus costs.

26 MAY

1866 Coroner Edwin Hooper held an inquest at Cradley Heath into the deaths of John Merriman (18) and James Elcome (17).

Jethro Nicholson Laley told the inquest that he was rowing on Cradley Pool when the two deceased asked him to row them around. However, Merriman refused to sit still and, in moving from the centre of the boat to the stern, caused it to capsize.

All three men were thrown into the water and Laley told Merriman and Elcome to cling to the upturned boat. Laley shouted for help but it was at least five minutes before anyone came to their aid. In the meantime, Merriman and Elcome made repeated attempts to grab Laley around the neck, and he was forced to dive to avoid their desperate clutches or be dragged under himself.

By the time help arrived, both Elcome and Merriman had sunk. The inquest jury concluded that they lost their lives through their own negligence and returned verdicts of 'accidentally drowned'.

27 MAY

1870 Brothers Noah and William Robinson came out of a pub at Wednesbury and made a beeline for a group of playing children. Noah singled out a boy of around six years old and gave him a cuff round the ear, knocking him down. He then picked him up and walloped him until the child screamed in pain.

Someone ran for the boy's father who, not surprisingly, objected to Noah's treatment of his son. When Edward Davis voiced his objections, the brothers turned on him and kicked and beat him senseless, before walking away.

The brothers were brought before magistrates at Wednesbury Police Court charged with assaulting Davis, while Noah was additionally charged with assaulting his son. In their defence, Noah stated that the boy had behaved indecently towards Noah's daughter, for which Noah 'moderately chastised' him, after which there had been 'a fair stand-up fight' between the men.

The magistrates chose to believe Edward Davis and fined each brother £2 plus costs, or one month's imprisonment in default.

28 MAY

1863 All that could be agreed upon was that on 28 May, Charles Birks had a woodpecker in his pocket.

PC Robinson arrested him and charged him under the Wild Birds' Protection Act with having the bird in his possession. When Birks appeared at West Bromwich Police Court on 1 June, Robinson told the magistrates that he saw Birks throw a stone at the bird and knock it down, after which he put it in his pocket. The policeman stated that he had some difficulty in taking the woodpecker from Birks and arresting him.

Birks was let off with a caution, although he was ordered to pay the court costs. The magistrates then turned their attention to the next case in the calendar, which was a charge by Birks that PC Robinson had assaulted him.

Birks produced a witness, Mr Asbury, who testified that he was walking with Birks at the time of the incident. According to Asbury, it was he who had spotted the woodpecker lying dead in the road. He picked it up and handed it to Birks, who put it in his pocket.

As the two men continued walking along the lane, PC Robinson suddenly pounced out of the hedge and seized Birks by the collar, demanding to know what he had in his pocket. Birks resented being grabbed and tried to twist out of Robinson's grip, at which point the policeman drew his staff and struck Birks several sharp blows about his head and neck.

The magistrates retired to discuss the case, returning to say that since the evidence was so conflicting, they intended to give the constable the benefit of the doubt and dismiss the case. Magistrate Mr Field wished it to be placed on record that he disagreed with the decision but since the three other magistrates were in agreement, the majority ruled.

29 MAY

1863   Richard Dorset went for a drink at The British Queen public house in Wolverhampton. He became rather rowdy and eventually the landlord asked another customer, George Gold, to help him throw Dorset out of the pub.

Almost as soon as he was ejected from the premises, Dorset returned. Furious, George Gold knocked him down and, while he was on the ground, Gold deliberately poked his thumb into Dorset's eye so violently that it burst his eyeball. Dorset was taken to the South Staffordshire Hospital, where he underwent treatment for a month but there was nothing that surgeons could do to save the sight in his damaged eye.

Gold was brought to the Staffordshire Midsummer Sessions in June, charged with unlawfully and maliciously inflicting grievous bodily harm on Richard Dorset. Found guilty, he was sentenced to nine months' imprisonment, and remarked that he sincerely hoped that Dorset would lose the other eye while he was in prison. He was ordered to keep the peace towards Dorset for twelve months at the expiration of his sentence.

30 MAY

1893   After his lunch break, Walsall schoolmaster William Hislop kissed his wife and children goodbye before returning to work. Just over an hour later, his six-year-old daughter Ethel came to fetch him at school, telling him that mama had taken something and was very ill.

William ran home as fast as he could to find his thirty-year-old wife, Alice, and the couple's six-month-old son, William Norman, unconscious. Mrs Hislop had also tried to poison Ethel, but the little girl refused to take any 'medicine' because it tasted nasty.

Doctors were unable to prevent mother and baby dying from ingestion of carbolic acid and, when coroner Mr T.H. Stanley held an inquest on 1 June, the Hislops' servant, Florence Stackhouse, stated that on 29 May, Mrs Hislop asked her to purchase some carbolic acid. Florence was sent for a second bottle on 30 May then given the afternoon off, as had been previously arranged.

When Mrs Hislop gave birth to baby William, Ethel was poorly with measles, and caring for a new baby and a sick child left Alice exhausted and suffering from depression, from which she never really recovered. Her behaviour after giving birth had been very strange but Mr Hislop told the inquest that his wife seemed much improved of late and that he had never heard her talk of destroying herself, although he had heard that she said something to her sister on the subject.

The inquest jury were reluctant to return a verdict of wilful murder against Alice Hislop and eventually decided 'that Mrs Hislop took poison while of unsound mind and that, while of unsound mind, she administered poison to the child also.'

31 MAY

1859   Coroner Ralph Docker opened an inquest in Oldbury, into the death of twelve-year-old John Forster. John and his three siblings lived with their parents, William and Hannah Forster, with all six of them sharing a bedroom.

On 29 May, the family retired to bed as normal, with the parents and the youngest child in one bed and the other three children in another.

At three o'clock in the morning of 30 May, William was woken by sixteen-year-old Eliza screaming and realised that Hannah had cut twelve-year-old John's throat. As William and Eliza watched in horror, Hannah slowly drew the razor across her own throat.

Her husband and daughter leaped at her and while Eliza wrested the razor from her mother, cutting her hand badly in the process, William grappled his wife to the floor, before running for help.

John was dead and Hannah was rushed to hospital, where she too was expected to die. The inquest eventually concluded that John died from the effects of a wound in his neck inflicted by his mother, who was not at the time in a sound state of mind.

Against all expectations, Hannah survived her attempted suicide but was never tried for the wilful murder of her son. When the case came to the assizes on 16 July, the gaol surgeon, who had treated Hannah since she was discharged to prison from hospital, stated that she was unfit to plead due to insanity. The court heard that Hannah was a loving wife and mother but that the recent death of her eldest daughter, Mary Ann, had unhinged her mind. Often delirious and delusional, she was prone to wandering uninvited into peoples' houses, and had commented to neighbours that two men appeared to her in a dream and urged her to 'do it'. On the night before the murder, she was walking around the house in a manner that so alarmed her husband that he only closed his eyes when she appeared to be sound asleep.

Note: Some accounts give the family name as Foster rather than Forster.

JUNE

Town Hall, Wolverhampton. (Author's collection)

1 JUNE

1868 One-year-old Edward Hunt of West Bromwich died from the effects of an accident on 23 May.

An inquest returned a verdict of 'accidental death', having heard that his mother had poured about four pints of boiling water into the ash hole beneath her fire in order to lay the dust and kill insects. Just as she finished, there was a knock on the door and she went to answer it, leaving Edward happily playing. Mrs Hunt was absent only momentarily but when she returned, Edward had fallen into the ash hole and was seriously scalded. In spite of the best possible medical attention, he died nine days later.

2 JUNE

1874 Henry Mitchell appeared at Wolverhampton Police Court charged with a criminal assault on a five-year-old girl.

Sarah Sankey told the Bench that on the previous day, she saw Mitchell entering the outside lavatory near her home. When eight-year-old Nellie Lisle reported that five-year-old Alice Walker was already in there, Mrs Sankey opened the door. She found Mitchell in a state of undress, holding Alice in his arms and sexually molesting her. Mrs Sankey asked Mitchell if he was ashamed of himself but Mitchell, who was very drunk, denied any wrongdoing.

Alice's mother took the little girl straight to a doctor and, when it was medically confirmed that she had been raped, Mitchell was arrested and charged. Magistrates committed him for trial at the next Staffordshire Assizes, where the evidence against him was overwhelming. He was found guilty and sentenced to seven years' penal servitude.

3 JUNE

1848 Shortly after 6 a.m., a boiler exploded at Hart's Hill Iron Works, near Dudley. So ferocious was the explosion that a fragment of the boiler weighing 26cwt was thrown almost a quarter of a mile and the body of one of the workers was blown more than 40 yards from the works. The blast was heard several miles away, and even the lamps in the area's coalfields were extinguished, leaving miners underground in pitch darkness.

Incredibly, there had been a breakdown at the works and consequently most of the labourers had been sent home. Otherwise the death toll would undoubtedly have been much higher than it was, but even so, ten men were killed instantly and a further three badly injured. Two more received minor injuries and one escaped completely unscathed.

It was said locally that the boiler was a disaster waiting to happen and some people even avoided walking past the works for fear of just such a catastrophe. At the inquest, it was established that the boiler was almost new but that the metal plates from which it was constructed were literally red-hot through lack of water before the explosion. The boiler had a safety valve but it was thought to be ineffective.

The inquest jury determined 'that the deaths of the unfortunate men on whose bodies the inquest was held were caused by an accidental explosion, the plates of the boiler having become heated, owing to the escape of water; and the jury are of the opinion that the boiler was defective in the riveting and manufacture and that, had it been secure, the explosion would not have been so destructive in its effects.' The owner of the works, Mr Jefferies, lost his brother and two nephews to the explosion and was said to be prostrate with grief.

4 JUNE

1852 Mary Ann Robins (aka Richards) gave birth to a daughter at the Wolverhampton Workhouse. Lucy was a fine, healthy baby, although she suffered from mild convulsions on 18 June, from which she quickly recovered.

On 19 June, Mary Ann washed and dressed her baby and took her to visit her mother. She arrived without Lucy and four days later, a dead baby was found in standing water at the bottom of a 46ft deep fire clay pit near Stourbridge. A post-mortem examination revealed that the infant had terrible brain damage.

The police interviewed Mary Ann, who initially denied having given birth, before amending her statement to admit that she had given birth to a baby, who died from natural causes and was buried at Bilston. At that stage, the dead baby had not been positively identified but Mary Ann's conflicting statements aroused the suspicion of the investigating officers, who arranged for the Workhouse staff to view the body.

With the baby's identity confirmed, Mary Ann gave more conflicting statements. She told police that Lucy died from convulsions while she was feeding her and she disposed of her dead body by throwing it in the pit. However, when one of the Workhouse staff asked her, 'How could you be such a cruel mother?' She replied, 'The devil tempted me and I threw it in the pit.'

Mary Ann was tried at the Worcestershire Assizes on 21 July and found guilty of wilful murder. The jury recommended mercy on the grounds that they believed that she was of weak intellect, and her death sentence was eventually commuted to one of detention in a lunatic asylum at Her Majesty's pleasure.

5 JUNE

1939 In the early hours of the morning, the Grand Theatre at Walsall caught fire and, once the blaze was finally extinguished, only the outer shell remained. It proved impossible to save the building, which dated from 1890.

Around twenty people were injured when part of the front wall crashed into the main street. Some were hospitalised and one man needed surgery but fortunately there were no fatalities. Thankfully, the current to the electric trolleybuses in the vicinity had been disconnected, otherwise the number of casualties would doubtless have been higher.

6 JUNE

1900 In the early hours of the morning, a woman's desperate screams were heard coming from a house in Wolverhampton. When neighbours went to see what was happening, they found widow Eliza Cooper with her throat cut and her lodger, Harry Slaughter, bending over her holding a razor.

Mrs Cooper was rushed to hospital, while twenty-five-year-old Slaughter was taken to the nearest police station and charged with her attempted murder. Fortunately, Mrs Cooper survived Slaughter's attack and was later to state that she had given her lodger notice to quit because of his quarrelsome conduct. He threatened her and, when she refused to change her mind, slashed her throat with his razor.

When Slaughter appeared before Mr Justice Bucknill at the Stafford Assizes on 27 July, he excused his actions by saying that he had been drinking all week. Bucknill told him that if a man chose to get into such a beastly state of drunkenness so that he became a ferocious animal, that was no excuse. The jury were slightly more tolerant, finding Slaughter guilty of the lesser offence of wounding with intent to do grievous bodily harm, and he was sentenced to nine months' hard labour.

7 JUNE

1862 Mary Ann Stringer was apprenticed to milliner Mrs Bostock of Wolverhampton. Twenty-one-year-old Mary Ann normally went home to her parents' house at Wednesfield at night, but on the evening of 6 June she complained of feeling ill and Mrs Bostock allowed her to stay the night in a room shared by two domestic servants. Mary Ann was still unwell the following morning and was allowed to stay in bed. When she finally got up at around midday, she insisted on walking home.

When Mary Ann returned to work on Monday 9 June, she was limping and told Mrs Bostock that she had fallen over. Nothing more was said until the body of a new born baby boy was found in the canal about half a mile from Mary Ann's parents' house. The baby had been wrapped in a duster with a stone so that it sank, but gases released as the body decomposed had brought it to the surface, where it was found by a boatman and handed to the police.

A post-mortem examination suggested that the baby had breathed independently and that his death was caused by strangulation. Several women in the area were suspected of having given birth but when a reward of £50 was offered, William Done and his wife came forward to say that they had noticed Mary Ann walking home and immediately come to the conclusion that she was about to become a mother. When the duster in which the baby was wrapped was found to belong to Mrs Bostock, Mary Ann was arrested and a medical examination confirmed that she had recently given birth.

Mary Ann Stringer was charged with the wilful murder of her illegitimate son and appeared before Mr Justice Blackburn at the Staffordshire Assizes in July. In spite of the testimony of two doctors to the contrary, Blackburn stated that he could see no evidence of murder and directed the jury to consider an alternative charge of concealment of birth. The jury found Mary Ann 'not guilty' of any offence and she was discharged.

8 JUNE

1868 Information reached the police at Wolverhampton that there was a child chained up in a house in Duke Street. PC Martin O'Donnell went to investigate and found nine-year-old John Wynn sitting on a chair, chained by the leg to the fire grate, where he claimed to have been for the last twenty-four hours. (There were two younger children in the room, a five-year-old and a two-year-old, but neither was tethered.) There was an old sofa nearby and although John could rest his head on it, he couldn't lie down unless he suspended his body across the gap between the chair and the sofa.

PC O'Donnell arrested John's father and charged him with assault. When James Wynn appeared before magistrates he explained that John's mother had died in April, leaving him with three young children to support, and since then John had become unruly and uncontrollable. He refused to help with his younger siblings, which would allow his father to work to earn the money to keep the family together, and ran away every morning, spending his days terrorising the neighbours.

The stipendiary magistrate told Wynn that even if John was a bad boy, he had been far too extreme in his method of punishment, adding that he wouldn't have been surprised if the child had gone quite mad under such torture. The magistrate maintained that in nine cases out of ten, bad character in such young children was the fault of the parents and the only reason that James Wynn was not being committed for trial at the assizes was that there were no marks of violence on John. James Wynn was sentenced to six months' imprisonment with hard labour, during which the magistrates hoped that he would repent. The sentence was met with boos from the spectators in court, some of whom shouted out, 'Hanging's too good for him,' as he was led away to start his sentence, while his children were sent to the Workhouse.

9 JUNE

1851 Catherine Morris was a prostitute and an alcoholic who lived as husband and wife with James Sones (or Jones) in Berry Street, Wolverhampton. James was determined to put a stop to Catherine's life as a woman of the streets but Catherine was equally determined to continue, a stalemate that led to frequent arguments.

On 9 June, the couple were seen arguing in the street and when passers-by intervened, fearful for Catherine's safety, James stormed off. Later that evening, as Catherine sat in a pub with two clients, James appeared and demanded his property back. Catherine flung a handkerchief at him but James wanted all of his possessions from their shared house. Eventually, Catherine consented to go back there with him but as they walked home together, James cut her throat with a clasp knife. He was arrested and the charge against him elevated to one of wilful murder when Catherine died on 11 June.

He was tried at the Stafford Assizes on 30 July 1851, where he was found guilty of the lesser charge of manslaughter and sentenced to be transported for life.

10 JUNE

1955 Having broken his leg in an accident at work two days earlier, fifty-seven-year-old Harold Millard of Coseley was told to visit the hospital daily to have the plaster checked.

On 10 June, Harold decided that he felt too ill to go, telling his sister Lydia that his leg was very painful. Lydia left her brother alone for ten minutes while she did some shopping, and returned to find him sawing at the plaster with a hacksaw trying to cut it off. What he didn't realise was that he had completely sawn through his own leg a few inches above his ankle!

Harold supposedly felt no pain and was so intent on removing his plaster that he was completely unaware of what he had done. The newspapers of 14 June reported that he was improving after emergency surgery.

11 JUNE

1909   An inquest heard that Benjamin Cole died when an electric tram car, on which he was travelling home from work, suddenly became live.

Cole boarded the tram between Wolverhampton and Dudley and went upstairs to sit on the top deck. He was the only other passenger there, and when the conductor went up to collect his fare, he found Cole dead.

It was established that the tram developed an electrical fault and when Cole placed his feet against an iron upright and rested his head against the iron rail he was electrocuted. The tram company accepted full liability for Cole's tragic death.

12 JUNE

1861   Eighteen-year-old James Jones worked as a delivery boy for grocers Reynolds & Co., in Digbeth, Walsall, and at 4 p.m. he was asked to ready the horse and cart for a delivery.

The cart was kept in a shed and James harnessed the horse and placed it between the shafts. However, as he drove the cart out of the shed, one of the wheel hubs made contact with a post. Unfortunately, the post was supporting the shed roof and when the cart wheel dislodged it, the roof fell in, burying James in rubble.

When found, he was bent double by the sheer force and weight of the fall of debris onto his body. He was still alive when he was extricated from the ruined building but had such severe head injuries that there was no hope of his survival. (According to one eyewitness, his brains were 'literally dashed out.') He was taken to his home but died on the journey there.

An inquest later returned a verdict of 'accidental death'.

13 JUNE

1894   Fifty-six-year-old building contractor Edwin Hassall woke his son, Major, for work at 6 a.m., but when Major returned to the house in West Bromwich four hours later, for his morning break, it seemed strangely quiet. The kitchen was in exactly the same state as it had been when he left and there was no sign of housekeeper Eliza Hall.

Major called his brother Albert and the two young men tried to get into the sitting room but the door from the kitchen was locked against them. Eventually, Major procured a ladder. Through a bedroom window he saw Mrs Hall lying senseless across the foot of her blood-soaked bed. The police were called and found Mrs Hall with her throat cut, while Edwin Hassall lay dead in his own bedroom, his throat also slashed.

Coroner Edwin Hooper opened an inquest on the two deaths, at which the main witness was twenty-year-old Major Hassall. The young man stated that his father had been 'very peculiar in his habits' following the recent death of Major's eighteen-year-old brother, Arthur. Edwin Hassall was injured by an explosion in his house in January 1893, which left him with an abscess in his neck requiring prolonged hospital treatment and, thirteen years earlier, had blown off one of his big toes in a gun accident. At the time of his death, he was despondent over Arthur's death and was also thought to be having business worries, but the catalyst for his actions was probably the fact that Mrs Hall was due to leave his employ, having handed in her notice because of his strange behaviour.

The night before his death, Edwin crept into his sons' bedroom and placed a sovereign and a watch in each of their trouser pockets. Major and Albert found them in the morning and gave them back to their father, who expressed surprise at what they had found. However, after their father's death, the boys found the articles in the pockets of their best suits.

Having heard all the evidence, the coroner recalled Major Hassall to ask why he had not thought it appropriate to have his father watched or treated. Major denied any concerns that his father might be a danger to himself or others. The inquest jury returned verdicts of wilful murder against Edwin Hassall for Eliza Hall's death and suicide while in a state of temporary insanity in respect of his own demise.

14 JUNE

1859 A group of children walking through the graveyard of St John's Church in Wolverhampton heard a thumping sound coming from deep within one of the vaults. There was a slightly displaced brick in the wall of the vault and one child peered through the hole, claiming to have seen a bright light, before someone or something within the vault threw a handful of grit into the curious child's face. Immediately afterwards, the knocking noises resumed, even more loudly than before. The news of the incident spread like wildfire and soon the crowd that gathered in the churchyard to try and see the phenomenon was so large that the police had to be called to control them.

A woman who lived opposite the vault was said to have been frightened into fits by a sepulchral voice intoning 'Let me out,' and it was also rumoured that when a policeman poked his staff through the hole in the vault, it emerged almost a foot shorter and covered in three-cornered teeth marks. People threw pieces of lighted paper into the vault and, on 22 June, the ghost supposedly communicated with spirit mediums that it would show itself later that day.

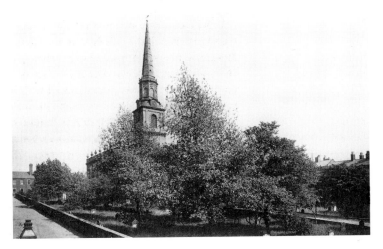

St John's Church, Wolverhampton. (Author's collection)

Nothing untoward was seen at the appointed time and the crowds gradually melted away. However, on 26 June, the body of a still-born baby boy was found in the graveyard, close to the vault. An inquest failed to identify the infant and returned an open verdict of 'found dead'.

15 JUNE

1879   Three-year-old Sarah Ann New died in Wolverhampton, having lain insensible for the past two days.

On 13 June, Sarah was at the home of a neighbour when there was a sudden storm and the chimney of the house was struck by lightning. The charge passed down the chimney into the room below, hitting Sarah and the neighbour, Mrs Morrison. Sarah instantly became unconscious and remained in that state until her death. Mrs Morrison was less dramatically affected but remained confined to bed at the time of Sarah's inquest.

The jury returned a verdict of 'death from burns caused by lightning'.

16 JUNE

1858   An inquest was held at Willenhall into the death of six-year-old Joseph Smith.

Joseph and his seven-year-old brother, Abraham, went into their father's workshop, climbed onto a bench and took down a gun, which they took into the yard to play with. Abraham pointed the gun at Joseph and pulled the trigger. Tragically, it was loaded and the bullet hit Joseph in the mouth, knocking out all but one of his teeth and severing his tongue.

Hearing the bang, an older brother went outside and found Joseph lying dead on the ground. Seventeen-year-old Samuel Smith later admitted at the inquest that it was he who had loaded the gun to shoot woodpigeons.

Samuel was severely reprimanded by the coroner for his carelessness but, in order to spare Abraham the stigma of having killed his brother, the jury returned a verdict that Joseph was 'found shot but the cause unknown.'

17 JUNE

1923   The Shakespeare family lived in a two-roomed tenement in Dudley and were so short of space that the two eldest children had to sleep at their grandmother's house.

On 17 June, Mrs Shakespeare bathed the two youngest children and put them to bed then, leaving her husband, Arthur, dozing in the kitchen, took the others to their grandparents' house. While she was gone, Arthur was awakened by the smell of burning and discovered that the clothes drying on the rack in front of the kitchen fire were smouldering.

Mr Shakespeare threw the clothes onto the kitchen table, forgetting that there was a paraffin lamp standing on it. The globe broke and he picked the lamp up, intending to throw it out into the back yard, but it exploded and he dropped it. Within seconds, the room was ablaze, making it impossible to reach the staircase to get to the bedroom where the two youngest children slept.

Mr Shakespeare rushed outside and made a valiant attempt to reach his children's bedroom window with a ladder but was beaten back by the ferocity of the flames. Clarice (5) and Reginald (1) perished in the blaze and were later found lying on the floor of their bedroom by firemen.

The inquest recorded two verdicts of 'accidental death'.

18 JUNE

1861 The morning after complaining of an excruciating headache, twenty-year-old Rachel Bradley died at the Workhouse in Walsall. A post-mortem examination revealed the presence of four *cysticercus cellulosae* – the sacs formed by larval tapeworms – in the spinal marrow, where her spinal cord joined her head.

Dr Burton confirmed that the 'hydratid sacs' were tapeworm eggs and that Rachel had undoubtedly ingested the worm through eating improperly cooked pork sausages. Once the worm was in the body, it forced its way into various organs such as the liver, head, eyes and brain, and laid its eggs.

The eggs then migrated to the part of the body where it could gain the most nourishment, in this case, Rachel's brain. Death ensued from pressure on the brain by the hydratid sacs, explained the doctor, and, when Rachel's brother confirmed that she had suffered from convulsions a couple of weeks earlier and that she often ate sausages, the inquest jury determined that she died of 'disease of the brain.'

19 JUNE

1853 Butcher Thomas Price was returning to his home in Wolverhampton when he saw a woman and child being beaten by a small group of men. Unwilling to stand by and watch the woman being ill-used, Price went to her defence, at which her three attackers turned their attention to Price and beat him. He begged for his life and the men let him go but followed him home and, before he could get safely indoors, they attacked him again.

He was found on his doorstep, his clothes saturated with blood. His jaw was broken, his right eye completely destroyed and he had a bad cut on the back of his head, as well as cuts and bruises all over his body. Price survived until 8 August before succumbing to his injuries and was able to give a full description of his attackers.

The description matched an Irishman named Thomas Quarlter, who had been reported for assaulting a woman on the night of the attack on Price. Quarlter fled Wolverhampton immediately after Price was attacked, but was arrested on 11 August and charged with assaulting Jane Rowden. The inquest on Price had already returned a verdict of manslaughter by person or persons unknown but magistrates determined that Quarlter, who denied all knowledge of either offence, should stand trial for wilful murder.

When he appeared before Mr Justice Wightman at the Stafford Assizes on 15 March 1854, the statements made by Price before his death formed the principal evidence against Quarlter. In fact, apart from two witnesses who had seen Quarlter arguing with somebody in the general area of the murder on the night in question, they were the only evidence.

Mr Justice Wightman was asked to rule on the admissibility of Price's statements and decided that they were inadmissible. Without Price's testimony, the case against Quarlter collapsed and the jury had no option but to acquit him. He immediately faced charges of assaulting Jane Rowden on the same night but there was insufficient evidence for the jury, who also acquitted him on the second charge.

20 JUNE

1856 At Number 20 Pit at Old Park, Dudley, eight miners were being brought to the surface when the chain bearing the skip suddenly broke, sending it crashing to the bottom of the pit. Six were killed instantly, the other two dying within hours.

The dead were named as brothers Stephen (20), John (18) and William (13) Crewe, Jesse Hawsthorn (18), Henry Fletcher (14), J. Jones (20), Henry Glaze (13) and Joseph Plant (15).

At the subsequent inquest, the focus for coroner W. Robinson's jury was the question of what caused the chain to break. The skip was supported by two types of chain – a flat one at the top and a round one at the bottom. It was a link in the round chain that had given way and a closer inspection of what remained of this chain showed that several links appeared worn.

There was a weekly inspection of the chains and the notebook kept by the chain inspector indicated that there were no problems at the inspection prior to the accident. The inquest jury deliberated for almost two hours before returning verdicts of 'accidental death' on all eight victims. They censured the pit manager for not having inspected the chains carefully enough, and recommended the discontinuation of round link chains, which were more likely to kink than the flat ones.

21 JUNE

1890 Susan Jones of West Bromwich carried her two-and-a-half-year-old son William downstairs and laid him on the floor in front of the fire while she went to fill the kettle. Although the fire was guarded, when Susan returned William's nightclothes were burning. Susan beat out the flames with her bare hands, sustaining severe burns in the process. She and a neighbour, Hannah Cornfield, rushed William to hospital but he died that afternoon.

Dr Lockwood promised Susan that he would inform the police of the death and that she would be notified when the inquest was held. However, after four days, Susan had heard nothing and went back to the hospital, where Dr Lockwood admitted that he had completely forgotten about the little boy lying dead in the hospital mortuary. When Hannah Cornfield

West Bromwich
District Hospital, 1911.
(Author's collection)

tried to question him on her distraught neighbour's behalf, he accused her of being impudent and told her that he was master there and that the situation was none of her business. Eventually, Susan and Hannah notified the police of William's death themselves.

When the inquest was finally held on 27 June, William Lockwood faced coroner Edwin Hooper's wrath. Lockwood first refused to give evidence until he had been allowed time to review his notes, although even when he had done so he actually said very little. 'It is a great scandal to this borough and I shall not overlook it but report it to the board of management' Hooper fumed, chiding Lockwood for his negligence and his 'great dereliction of duty.'

The jury returned a verdict of 'accidental death' on the toddler, joining the coroner in asking that Dr Lockwood should be officially censured for his lackadaisical attitude.

22 JUNE

1910 William Hodgetts and Frederick Pitcock worked at Wednesbury, where they spent their days at a furnace, heating pieces of metal known as tags.

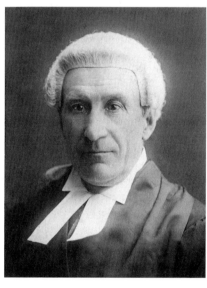

On 22 June, a man named Wilcox, who was straightening tubes nearby, turned round and accidentally hit Hodgetts on the head. Pitcock began to giggle and when Hodgetts turned round to see what had hit him, he saw Pitcock laughing and assumed that he was responsible. Without thinking, he threw the red-hot piece of metal he was working on and it pierced Pitcock's side, causing his death.

Sixteen-year-old Hodgetts was charged with manslaughter and appeared before Mr Justice Lawrence at the Staffordshire Assizes on 13 July. Lawrence recognised that Pitcock's death was the result of an unthinking act and that the defendant had no intention of killing or even hurting his work mate. The fact that Pitcock's death would be on his conscience for as long as he lived would be sufficient punishment for Hodgetts, said Lawrence, and bound him over in the sum of £5 to come up for judgement if called upon to do so in future.

Mr Justice Lawrence. (Author's collection)

23 JUNE

1887 At midnight, Joseph Southall went to work at Messrs Walker Brothers Galvanisers at Walsall. While waiting for another workman to arrive, Southall lay down beside a pickling bath, which was being heated by a coke fire. Soon afterwards, he was found unconscious. He was taken home and a doctor called to attend him but he died later that night without ever regaining consciousness.

A post-mortem examination showed that he had been overcome by the fumes from the coke oven – had he remained standing or even seated, rather than lying down, he would most probably have survived. The inquest jury returned a verdict of 'accidental death'.

24 JUNE **1887** An adjourned inquest resumed at Wolverhampton into the death of thirty-six-year-old Joseph Key, who worked at Messrs Jones Works at Monmore Green. The inquest was told that on 10 June, Key went inside a boiler to repair it and was taken ill shortly afterwards. One of the main symptoms of his illness was that his skin changed colour; that on his body being dark green while his face turned almost black.

When Key died on 11 June, the coroner opened and then adjourned the inquest so that a post-mortem examination could be made. Surgeon Mr J.W. Scott could find no trace of any natural disease or anything that might have accounted for Key's death, but another surgeon also examined Key's body and noted some slight changes to the appearance of the liver. It was surmised that Key had died from inhaling 'arseniuretted hydrogen', which might have been generated in the boiler. This was a rare form of poisoning and, at the time, only nine or ten previous incidences had been recorded. The inquest jury returned a verdict of 'accidental death'.

25 JUNE **1871** Isaac Blocksidge went into one of the hovels at Hall End Pit at West Bromwich and found Joseph 'Lame Joe' Marshall dead on the floor. Marshall's head had been battered, after which burning coals had been deliberately heaped on the old man's body, parts of which were charred and blackened.

Blocksidge fetched the police, who determined that Marshall had been hit with a hammer and two rakes, the latter having then been used to rake coals from the fireplace onto the body. Before his death, Marshall had been drinking in The Hall End Tavern with labourer, John Higginson, and the two were then seen quarrelling and fighting on a lane near the pit hovel. Higginson was seen returning to his lodgings at half-past three on the morning of 25 June by his fellow lodger. On hearing of Marshall's death, the lodger tried to persuade Higginson to go and see the body but Higginson was squeamish. 'I shan't like to see him,' he demurred.

When the police interviewed Higginson as part of their enquiries, he was found to have fresh blood on his boots, which had been washed. He was arrested and tried for wilful murder at the Staffordshire Assizes, where he was found guilty of the lesser offence of manslaughter and sentenced to penal servitude for life, serving his sentence at Portland Prison in Dorset.

Marshall was said to be cross-eyed. Anecdotal evidence suggests that Higginson was afraid that Marshall had 'put the evil eye on him' and consulted a wizard about getting the curse lifted. The wizard allegedly told Higginson that the only way to be relieved of the curse was for the perpetrator to be burned.

26 JUNE **1902** After twelve years as a policeman, William Lane worked on the railways, before becoming a private detective.

When John William Dyson suspected that his wife Eliza (or Elizabeth) was cheating, he asked Lane to keep her under surveillance, but the

Mr Justice Walton, 1903. (Author's collection)

business arrangement backfired when Lane and Eliza began an affair and left their partners. When Lane expressed his intention of evicting his wife from their home and moving Eliza in instead, Mrs Lane put her foot down, and so Lane and Eliza began travelling throughout the Black Country.

Both enjoyed a drink and, on 26 June, visited several public houses when they apparently quarrelled. People living near Gipsy Lane, Tividale, heard a woman screaming and found Lane kneeling over Eliza's body with a knife in his hand. Her throat had been cut and she bled to death on the roadside before medical assistance could reach her.

Lane could hardly deny having killed Eliza but maintained that her death had been part of a suicide pact and that he had lost his nerve and was unable to kill himself after slashing her throat. Tried at the Stafford Assizes on 22 July, before Mr Justice Walton, Lane initially pleaded guilty. Walton persuaded him to change his plea to not guilty and the trial went ahead, with Lane's defence team relying on trying to prove his insanity at the time of the offence.

The jury was not convinced, finding him guilty of wilful murder and he was hanged at Stafford by William and John Billington on 12 August 1902.

27 JUNE

1856 Nail making was extremely hot work and Elizabeth Millward passed a jug of water to her daughter, Eliza, who drank her fill then passed it on to a ten-year-old girl. She took a drink and passed the jug to her uncle, John Phipson, who was the brother of the owner of the nail shop at Lye Waste.

Elizabeth Millward was not happy for Phipson to drink from her jug and snatched up a handful of coal slack, which she threw into his face. The slack contained countless tiny fragments of metal from the nail-making process and, when it hit Phipson, it smarted. He retaliated by throwing a handful of slack at Elizabeth, who threw a second handful back. Furious, Phipson drew an iron bar from the furnace and threw it at Elizabeth. It hit her on the side and burned into her body, before clattering to the floor.

Elizabeth screamed and dropped like a stone. Several other nail workers carefully carried her outside and brought water to try and revive her but she died within minutes and a post-mortem examination showed that she had a deep wound on the left-hand side of her chest. Her left lung was burned and there was a large hole in a major blood vessel of her heart, from which she had bled to death. Surgeon Mr Harding surmised that the iron must have been white hot and thrown with considerable force, since it penetrated four inches into Elizabeth's chest.

An inquest returned a verdict of manslaughter against Phipson but magistrates committed him to the Stafford Assizes to be tried for wilful murder.

It was shown at his trial that the dust thrown at Phipson by the deceased would have caused him intolerable pain if it got into his eyes, and when the surgeon testified, he stated that the degree of damage to the victim was unprecedented. Normally, the white-hot iron would have caused serious injury but the fact that it proved fatal on this occasion was extremely unlucky.

Hearing this, Mr Justice Wightman instructed the jury to consider only the charge of manslaughter and, when they found Phipson guilty, Wightman took the view that he had 'momentarily yielded to passion, with unexpected but catastrophic ill effects.' Wightman sentenced Phipson to two weeks' imprisonment in solitary confinement, so that he might reflect on the consequences of his actions.

28 JUNE

1887 Coroner Edwin Hooper held an inquest at Wednesbury into the death of twenty-year-old Henry Roberts.

Henry was in perfect health when he left home on 25 June for his job at the Brunswick Wheelworks of the Patent Shaft and Axle Company. Furnace man John Yates had a conversation with Henry twenty-five minutes later about the fact that some water had run into the ash hole beneath the furnace overnight. Yates then left him alone for five minutes and, when he returned, found Henry lying on his back in the ash pit, his head, arms and body very badly burned.

Yates seized Henry's legs and pulled him out from beneath the furnace. He appeared lifeless but a doctor was summoned just in case and confirmed that he had burned to death.

At the inquest, coroner Edwin Hooper expressed surprise that Roberts had suffered such severe injuries, given that he was only alone for five minutes. He was told that the furnace had been cleared only a couple of hours earlier and was thus burning very fiercely.

The inquest was told that Roberts had worked at the Brunswick Works for about two years. Shortly after taking the job, he fainted on duty and the works manager was dubious about keeping him on for safety reasons. However, the fainting was apparently caused by a lack of food and the manager gave him the benefit of the doubt.

Yates told the coroner that he believed that Roberts fell backwards under the furnace after getting into the ash hole to clear out the water. He conceded that it was possible that Roberts may have been overcome by fumes but said that he had never heard of such a case. The inquest jury returned a verdict of 'accidental death'.

29 JUNE

1877 Henry Rogers walked into a police station at Wolverhampton and told the officers on duty, 'I have come to give myself up for murdering my wife ... She has got half her head cut off.' Rogers was handcuffed and led police to a field, where Sarah Jane Rogers lay dead near a haystack, the couple's eighteen-month-old baby sleeping peacefully next to her.

Rogers told police that he killed his wife because he had seen her with other men and believed she had been unfaithful. An inquest was held on Sarah Jane's death, at which Rogers violently argued with most of the witnesses. After his father testified that Rogers stole his razor to kill his wife, Rogers exploded. 'Don't tell any more lies, liar that you are, infernal liar,' he railed. 'But you always were the same to me and it is you and those belonging to you that have brought me to what I am. Wretched villains that you are, my murderers. The curse of God on all of you. My curse forever go with the lot. I have owned it myself and shall and I can die happy.' [*sic*]

The inquest found a verdict of wilful murder against Rogers and he was committed for trial at the Stafford Assizes. Although his defence was one of insanity, the jury found him guilty with no concession towards his mental state and he was sentenced to death.

On 31 July, Rogers calmly mounted the scaffold at Stafford Gaol, kissed his crucifix and faced his executioner, George Incher (or Insher). This time, there was no arguing and Rogers is said to have died quietly.

30 JUNE

1900 Charles Taylor of Darlaston came home drunk at 6 p.m. He lay down on the sofa and slept for three hours before waking up and accusing his wife, Rachel, of taking money from his pockets while he slept. Rachel denied having done any such thing but Charles jumped up and punched her.

Mr Justice Channell, 1897. (Author's collection)

Rachel ran for safety, passing her nine-year-old daughter Annie in the doorway. As she bolted, Rachel heard Charles pick up the poker from the fireplace, after which she heard it bounce off the wall behind her. There was a scream and Rachel turned just in time to see Annie fall to the ground, the poker stuck in her head.

Rachel carried Annie back into the house and a doctor was summoned but the little girl died soon afterwards. Coroner Mr H.A. Pearson held an inquest at the Town Hall, where Rachel sobbed that, when he was sober, there was no better father on earth than her husband.

The inquest jury accepted that thirty-four-year-old Taylor had not intended to harm either his wife or his daughter but still found a verdict of manslaughter against him and he was committed for trial at the assizes on the coroner's warrant. He didn't have long to wait, appearing before Mr Justice Channell on 24 July.

Channell blamed the entire incident on alcohol, saying that he wished people would learn to stop drinking when they had had enough and urging the passing of laws to prevent alcohol being served to intoxicated persons. When the jury found Taylor guilty of manslaughter, he was sentenced to twelve months' imprisonment with hard labour.

JULY

Church Street, Bilston, 1924. (Author's collection)

1 JULY

1925   Forty-one-year-old Alexander Pelan and thirty-five-year-old Dorothy Mary Henshaw appeared at the Staffordshire Assizes charged with conspiring to murder Mrs Henshaw's husband, George. Pelan was additionally charged with soliciting Mrs Henshaw to murder George, while she was also charged with administering poison or another unknown destructive substance.

Pelan lodged with the Henshaws at their home in Bilston between 1921 and 1924, during which time he and Mrs Henshaw had a passionate affair. When Pelan returned to his native Ireland, the couple continued to write.

At the time, letters from Northern Ireland were often opened on arrival in England, and the correspondence between Pelan and his mistress was photographed. Pelan repeatedly wrote that he would not return from Ireland to marry her until Mrs Henshaw had removed the obstruction of her husband.

Several bottles of toxic substances were found at the Henshaws' home and Mrs Henshaw replied that she hoped to get rid of him soon, saying that she had put the 'stuff' Pelan sent her in George's beer. 'He is torture to us both,' wrote Pelan. 'Use laudanum, laundry bleach or gas.'

In a dramatic twist at the trial, George Henshaw was called to the witness box but refused to testify against his wife. Pelan and Mrs Henshaw both testified. Pelan said that he was so desperately in love with Mrs Henshaw that he hardly knew what he was doing. He denied sending her anything apart from whisky and Izal disinfectant. Mrs Henshaw called the letters 'foolishness', saying that the only poisonous chemicals in her home were liniment for her husband's arm and some mouse poison.

The jury eventually found her not guilty of administering poison but found both defendants guilty of conspiracy to murder, and Pelan guilty of soliciting Mrs Henshaw to murder. Both were sentenced to imprisonment with hard labour, Pelan to fifteen calendar months and Mrs Henshaw to nine.

2 JULY

1877   The interment of murder victim Sarah Jane Rogers (*see* 29 June) took place at Wolverhampton, where the funeral procession was watched by an estimated crowd of more than 10,000 people.

The ceremony took place on a Monday morning, following the victim's brutal murder during the previous Thursday night/Friday morning, at which time she sustained numerous facial injuries and her head was almost severed from her body with a cut-throat razor. Her body was returned to her home and, until police intervened to prevent it, the dead woman's relatives were charging people a few coppers to view the mutilated corpse in her coffin.

3 JULY

1894   Deputy-coroner Mr A.B. Smith held an inquest at Bilston, into the death of sixteen-year-old labourer Charles Palmer.

On 2 July, Charles was asked to go to an upper stock room at the Atlas Bedstead Works and lower some bedsteads through a trap door to the floor below.

When he hadn't returned half an hour later, another employee went to check on him and found that a stack of bedsteads that had been leaning against a pillar had fallen over, landing on Palmer's neck and pinning him to the floor. Although a doctor was summoned, he was unable to revive the youth, who died from suffocation.

The inquest jury returned a verdict of 'accidental death'.

4 JULY

1906 A boiler exploded at the Providence Iron Works at Cradley Heath, sending huge chunks of metal flying sky high. One dropped into the garden of a nearby house and bounced onto the kitchen, completely demolishing it. A second flew almost 100 yards into a chain manufacturer's premises, while a third landed on a house adjoining the Iron Works.

Fortunately, many of the workmen were eating their breakfast at the time of the explosion and so were not near the boiler. However, John Penn, who was working in the boiler house, was blown to pieces, while a child named Gwendoline Pearson was struck by a flying brick as she played near her home and died soon afterwards from a fractured skull. Another child, who had brought her father's breakfast to the factory, was badly scalded, and several employees of the Iron Works and the chain factory were injured. The Iron Works was almost razed to the ground and a 60ft chimney collapsed when a piece of the boiler cut through its base.

An inquiry by the Board of Trade came to the conclusion that the accident was entirely preventable and was down to gross negligence, particularly by two officials of the Scottish Boiler Insurance Company, who were said to have signed incorrect information when issuing the company's Factory Act certificates. The insurance company was fined £50, with fines of £120 for one of the official inspectors and £20 for his colleague. Providence Iron Works were fined £50.

5 JULY

1890 Thomas Maloney, Charles Moore, William Carpenter, Alfred Bowers and Joseph Willows (or Williams) appeared at the Worcestershire Assizes charged with the manslaughter of Thomas Cartwright at Dudley on 3 May. (Another suspect named Probert had managed to evade capture.) The five defendants were also charged with assault.

The men, who were all in their late teens, attended a performance at The Coliseum Theatre in Dudley. There was an argument, which culminated in Cartwright leaving after the first act and going to a nearby public house. In due course, the others followed and a fight broke out, during which Cartwright was kicked in the lower abdomen.

Dr Brown sent Cartwright to Dudley Guest Hospital, where he was operated on for a rupture on 7 July. Unfortunately, he died from peritonitis the next day, having given a deposition stating that he did not know who had kicked him. When the police interviewed the youths, Bowers said that he spat on Cartwright, and Moore admitted to kicking him once only. The other youths denied taking any part in the fight.

Judge Mr Justice Cave advised the jury that there was little evidence against any of the youths other than Moore's own confession. All except

Moore were, therefore, discharged, whereas Moore was found guilty of assault and sentenced to nine months' imprisonment. He was most peeved, arguing that the others were all as bad as he and he didn't see why he alone should take all the blame.

6 JULY

1885 Coroner Edwin Hooper held an inquest into the death of thirteen-year-old Caroline Rotchell of Darlaston.

Along with a number of other children, Caroline was swinging on a gin at Wood's Bank Colliery. She climbed inside the drum and the other children pushed her, as if she were on a roundabout. However, Caroline decided to put her head through a hole in the top of the drum and her neck was broken by the main supporting beam.

The coroner noted the inquest jury's verdict of 'accidental death' before suggesting that the apparatus should be secured to prevent children playing on it. The colliery informed him that it usually was but the children always managed to bypass any security measures that they put in place.

A colliery gin, 1830s. (By kind permission of Dennis Neale)

7 JULY

1845 Eleven-year-old Joseph Slater was working underground with two other young men at a pit owned by Lord Ward at Rowley Regis. The three were working in a remote part of the mine and it was supposed that, while hacking at the coal with picks, the boys opened a pocket of foul air. The boys were working with candles and there was an immediate explosion of firedamp and Joseph was burned to death. His two companions, who were the sons of the mine manager, were also badly injured but are believed to have survived.

An inquest heard that the area had been checked for gas earlier that day and recorded a verdict of 'accidental death', attaching no blame to the mine manager.

8 JULY

1932 Mr and Mrs Hodgkinson of Brinton Kennels in Streetly, Walsall went to Brighton for the weekend, leaving the business in charge of kennel maid Ethel Corey and kennel boy Harold Hayward Wilkins. On 11 July, sixteen-year-old Wilkins contacted the police and informed them that there had been a burglary. Officers arrived to find Ethel bound and gagged in a bathroom. She was dead.

Harold's account of the burglary didn't quite ring true and he was arrested and charged with wilful murder, appearing at the Staffordshire Assizes in November 1932. The prosecution suggested that Harold left his bed in the garage and entered the house, tying a ligature around Miss Corey's neck and asphyxiating her, before staging a robbery as a cover. The defence contended that the youth, who was known as a practical joker, intended only to jump out at Miss Corey and give her a fright. His prank backfired when she dropped dead and, when he was unable to revive her, he bound and gagged her and ransacked the house to divert suspicion from himself. Medical evidence suggested that Miss Corey died from 'mental shock and concussion', and that the ligature around her neck appeared to have been placed there after death.

The jury took just thirty-five minutes of deliberation to find Wilkins guilty, although they recommended mercy on account of his youth. Significantly, Mr Justice MacKinnon didn't don the traditional black cap to pronounce the death sentence and, as was widely expected, Wilkins was reprieved a week later. At that time, the Children Act was undergoing revisions and in April 1933, an amendment was introduced forbidding the death penalty for persons under the age of eighteen.

9 JULY

1872 Eleven-year-old Richard Woolley was fascinated by trams and was a familiar sight around the West Bromwich tramways, where he pestered the drivers relentlessly. Very occasionally, they allowed him to ride alongside them.

On 9 July, he was riding with the driver when he suddenly jumped off the tram in West Bromwich High Street while it was in motion. He stumbled on landing and fell onto the rails, where one of the tram wheels ran over his head, killing him instantly.

Coroner Edwin Hooper held an inquest, at which Richard's parents stated that they had warned him time and time again about riding on trams and, only the afternoon before his death, his mother kept him indoors as a punishment for disobeying her instructions not to get onto them.

The inquest jury returned a verdict of 'accidental death' and, when Hooper expressed surprise at the common practice of jumping on and off trams while they were moving, some members of the jury pointed out that the drivers often refused to wait. The coroner asked the manager of the tram company to speak to all of its drivers on the matter and to get some printed notices forbidding passengers from embarking or disembarking while the trams were in motion. Hooper also stated his intention of talking to the police on the subject, so that they were looking out for any transgressions.

Victorian memorial card.
(Author's collection)

10 JULY

1872 Furnace labourer Charles Bocquet appeared at Dudley Police Court charged with assaulting John Hall on 29 May.

Hall was described as a 'boat steerer' and was quietly steering a boat along the canal at Pear Tree Lane, Dudley, when Bocquet suddenly jumped onto the vessel and threw Hall overboard. Hall was unable to swim and was rescued, with some difficulty, on the point of drowning.

The two men were strangers and Hall told magistrates that he had done absolutely nothing to provoke Bocquet into attacking him. Bocquet's defence was that he was simply having a joke with Hall but unfortunately for Bocquet, neither Hall nor the magistrates found his actions remotely funny. He was sentenced to two months' imprisonment with hard labour.

11 JULY

1866 Mine deputy John Hubbard inspected one of the pits at the Coppy Hall Coal and Iron Company, before sending two miners down to carry out some repairs on the No. 3 Road. One of them, William Long, asked if the pit was 'all right for gas' and Hubbard assured him that he had found no problems but gave Long a safety lamp and advised him to check for himself.

Hubbard checked on Long and his companion John Woodhouse frequently, and was told that Long had found no gas at all and had consequently abandoned the safety lamp and was now working with candles.

Several hours later, there was an explosion underground and when Hubbard went towards it he met Long and Woodhouse walking away. Both were badly burned and were taken to the bailiff's house, where their burns were dressed with oil. Long was well enough to walk home, while Woodhouse was taken in a cab. However, both men subsequently died from the effects of their burns.

Coroner Edwin Hooper held an inquest, which closed on 20 August. In summing up the evidence for his jury, Hooper remarked that it was a shame that Long and Woodhouse had been too ill to make depositions before their deaths. Hooper viewed Hubbard with some suspicion, suggesting that because he was so persistent in checking on the two deceased and asking if they had found any gas, he may well have suspected the presence of gas all along. The colliery rules quite clearly stated that safety lamps should be used whenever firedamp was expected and, since Hubbard had originally given Long a safety lamp, he should have made sure that he continued to use it.

The jury returned two verdicts of 'accidental death' and asked the coroner to admonish Hubbard. Hooper told the deputy that, in his opinion, he had been grossly negligent in allowing the men to work with naked flames, adding that he must have been suspicious otherwise he would not have asked so many questions on the subject. Hooper reminded Hubbard that, had it been possible to prove the presence of gas that morning, he would have faced charges of manslaughter.

12 JULY

1860 When the goods train from London arrived at Queen Street Station, Wolverhampton, goods foreman William Heywood ran across to meet it, eager to see if an urgent order placed by one of the local tradesmen had arrived.

Without waiting for the train to stop, he tried to leap into one of the trucks. Unfortunately, he missed his footing and fell onto the railway line, where four carriages passed over him.

Heywood was dreadfully cut and one arm and a leg were crushed. Every effort was made to stem the bleeding while he was rushed to the South Staffordshire Hospital but by the time he arrived, his pulse was almost non-existent. The administration of stimulants bought him only an extra couple of hours of life, before he died in agony, leaving a wife and five children.

Heywood had been in the service of the London and North-Western Railway Company for twenty years. Only three months earlier, his brother, who worked for the same company, died in a gas explosion at Birmingham Station.

13 JULY

1908 An inquest at Wolverhampton returned verdicts of 'accidental death' on steeplejacks, Tom Prendergast and John Thomas Sheen, who fell 100ft to their deaths from a chimney stack that they were in the process of dismantling.

One of the key witnesses at the inquest was Prendergast's father, also a steeplejack of many years' experience. Prendergast senior told the inquest that he had seen the stack erected forty years earlier and had always considered it unsafe, due to the way in which it was constructed. Because of this, he had pleaded with his son to turn down the contract for demolishing the stack.

14 JULY

1908 Three men named Griffiths, Jones and Beebee appeared at the Staffordshire Assizes charged with causing the death of David Pearson.

The court was told that the three accused met Pearson in a pub in Tipton and surreptitiously added two packets of jalap to his drinks. The jalap acted as a strong laxative and shortly after leaving the pub, Pearson

Mr Justice Ridley, 1897. (Author's collection)

was found in a state of exhaustion. He was taken to the Workhouse Infirmary, where he subsequently died of hypercatharis – excessive and frequent defecation.

The normal medicinal dose of jalap as a laxative was between five and twenty grains and the contents of the packets added to Pearson's stout and whisky totalled 120 grains. However, Pearson was a chronic alcoholic and, when his body was exhumed for analysis, no traces of jalap were found in his remains.

Mr Justice Ridley remarked that he supposed that the majority of people would not know the correct dose of jalap, nor realise that an excess could prove fatal. Ridley advised the jury that, although this was a regrettable occurrence, which the defendants would likely rue until their dying days, there was insufficient evidence of recklessness or gross negligence to secure a conviction of manslaughter. The jury accordingly returned verdicts of 'not guilty' and the three men were discharged.

15 JULY

1874 Seven-year-old George Edward Daniells of Wednesbury returned from playing outside and complained that his head, chest and bowels hurt. He was given a powder and later taken to a surgeon, Mr W.C. Garman, who examined him and could find very little wrong.

Two days later, George told his parents that some boys had knocked him down while they were playing and kicked him in the chest, causing him to spit up blood. The boy's mother took him back to Garman, who could find no marks of violence on him and she also spoke to the accused boys, who denied ever having touched George.

When George died, coroner Edwin Hooper demanded a post-mortem examination, which revealed that George had extensive inflammation of his right lung, liver, kidneys and intestines and his brain was congested. Garman gave the cause of death as pleurisy, saying that he believed that George had caught a serious cold, which had passed unnoticed. Although death did not directly result from violence, as George was ill, any violence or excitement might have accelerated his demise.

Two of the child's playmates testified that they hadn't seen anybody kicking or kneeling on George, although he had been fighting with two boys, who had thrown a stone that accidentally hit him on the back. The inquest jury returned a verdict of 'natural death'.

16 JULY **1881** Twelve-year-old errand boy James Hall was sent to Bilston with a message. On his way there, he made an unscheduled detour to see some of his friends who worked at the Bradley Boiler Works.

When James arrived at the works, a punching machine, which was not being used, was idling at about half normal speed. Workmen suddenly heard it stop and when someone went to see why, they found Hall entangled in the machinery with his head completely crushed.

Since Hall shouldn't have been in the factory in the first place, an inquest judged his death to be nobody's fault other than his own and returned a verdict of 'accidental death'.

17 JULY **1891** Reuben Ward walked past the boilers at Messrs W. Cross & Sons Iron Foundry at West Bromwich at 6 a.m. on his way to his place of work and noticed nothing unusual, but an hour later there was a sudden deluge of water on the roof of his workshop. The yard outside was strewn with bricks and other rubble and Ward realised that a boiler had exploded.

Birmingham Road, West Bromwich, 1950s. (Author's collection)

Enoch Price (67), Harry Taylor (14) and John Bristow (19) were killed and an inquest was held on the three deaths by coroner Edwin Hooper. The boiler was more than twenty years old and appeared to have been constructed from iron of an inferior quality. It had been repeatedly patched and there was also a faulty gauge, which gave rise to inaccurate pressure readings. (It was explained, for example, that when the boiler was working at 60lb pressure, the gauge read 37lbs.)

The boilers were inspected regularly and the proprietors of the works spent a lot of money on their maintenance, with safety as their main priority. According to witnesses at the inquest, owner Mr Cross and his son spent almost every day at the plant and their office was within 10 yards of the boilers, so it was highly unlikely that they had any concerns whatsoever about them.

The inquest jury found that all three men met their deaths accidentally, adding that they believed that inferior iron and the faulty steam gauge brought about the explosion that killed them. They attached no blame to Cross & Sons, or to the engineer in charge of the boiler.

18 JULY

1881 Labourers at the Eagle Edge Tool Company in Monmore Green, Wolverhampton, were moving some large grindstones, each weighing between 2 and 3 tons. Three had already been safely moved to their intended position and a group of seven men were moving the last by rolling it along on its edge.

As they passed through a narrow passage, the 5ft 9in-diameter stone suddenly overbalanced, pinning John Webb and John Thompson to the wall. Thompson suffered several broken ribs, while Webb had a broken arm and his chest was very badly crushed. He later died in hospital, leaving a wife and two children.

As the inquest recorded a verdict of 'accidental death' on Webb, the contemporary newspapers reported that, although badly hurt, Thompson was expected to recover.

19 JULY

1869 Fanny Frances Maud (or Maria) Oliver of Dudley appeared at the Worcestershire Assizes charged with wilfully murdering her husband by poisoning him with arsenic.

Joseph Oliver had some money saved but his wife had been surreptitiously withdrawing the money from his account until there was none left. Not only that, but Fanny was believed to be enjoying an intimate relationship with another man, leaving her poor husband surplus to requirements.

It was shown in court that Fanny had purchased arsenic, giving the druggist a false name and address. The poison was then mixed with some tapioca pudding and a servant who tasted it became ill and was told that Fanny had put vermin powder in it to kill mice.

Found guilty, Fanny was asked if there was any reason why sentence of death should not be passed. She immediately launched into a long, rambling speech asserting her innocence, raising her eyes to heaven and asking God to strike her dead if she told an untruth.

When presiding judge Mr Baron Piggott could finally get a word in edgewise, he pronounced the death sentence, at which twenty-seven-year-old Fanny began to sing a hymn with the words 'Though in the path of death I stand ... '. She was hustled from court, giving a cheery wave and saying, 'Farewell to you all, my dear friends' as she left. In the event, her death sentence was commuted to one of life imprisonment, the majority of which was served at Knaphill Female Convict Prison in Surrey.

20 JULY

1859 At the Stafford Assizes, pub landlord William Worsey of West Bromwich was found guilty of the wilful murder of his wife on 11 June, by stabbing her in the throat with a carving knife. The knife, which was over a foot long, was produced in court and the jury heard that it had passed completely through Sarah Ann Worsey's throat, severing her jugular vein and carotid artery and causing her to bleed to death within minutes.

Worsey told the court that he hadn't stabbed his wife but had merely thrown the knife while the couple were engaged in a heated argument, and a number of witnesses testified in court that Sarah had provoked her husband. Nevertheless, in his summary of the case for the jury, Mr Justice Byles stated that, even supposing Worsey threw the knife rather than stabbing his wife, and meant only to do her grievous bodily rather than killing her, he was guilty of a felony. By law, if a person committing a felony took away a life, that was murder.

The jury seemed far from happy. After deliberating for half an hour, they returned to court to say that, according to the definition of murder imposed by the judge, they felt duty bound to find the defendant guilty, but they strongly recommended mercy as they believed that there were extenuating circumstances, including provocation and the fact that Worsey did not intend to kill his wife.

Worsey was given the mandatory death sentence, which was later commuted to one of transportation for life. He sailed for Western Australia on board *Palmerston* on 8 November 1860.

21 JULY

1856 Joseph Chivers appeared before Mr Justice Wightman at the Stafford Assizes charged with the wilful murder of David Taylor at Quarry Bank.

Taylor was found lying in the road by a family returning home from a night out. He looked as though he had been in a fight but had died from a single stab wound that pierced his heart, killing him instantaneously.

When the news of Taylor's death was publicised, a witness came forward to say that he saw the deceased with four other men earlier on the night of his death. The witness was able to name two of Taylor's companions and, when the police went to see them, they discovered that Taylor's death was the result of a prank that went terribly wrong. While on an evening out, Taylor and his friends saw a handcart on the street and decided that it would be fun to ram it against the door of a house.

The house belonged to the Chivers family and Lavinia Chivers had recently given birth. Seconds after the cart hit the door all of the men in the house spilled outside to take issue with the youths and a fight broke out, during which somebody fatally stabbed Taylor.

Witnesses suggested that the main protagonist was Lavinia's husband, Joseph Chivers, although Joseph vehemently denied having stabbed anyone. When the case was brought before magistrates, Joseph, his brother and father, Josiah and Josiah senior, his mother, Mary and Lavinia, were all charged with wilful murder. All but Joseph were discharged.

The jury at Joseph's trial found him guilty of the lesser offence of manslaughter, apparently viewing him as someone who tried to defend his frightened, recently confined wife against a gang of boisterous ruffians. Mr Justice Wightman seemed to disagree, saying that Joseph's offence was 'very little short of murder' and sentencing him to fifteen years' transportation.

Note: Mr Chivers senior is named as both Joseph and Josiah in various reports of the murder.

22 JULY

1889 At Oldbury, twenty-one-year-olds Joseph Harvey and Elizabeth Bates were very much in love. However, the couple's parents disapproved

of their courtship and tried their hardest to break the couple up. In despair, the couple tied themselves together with string, which they wrapped around their chests thirty times, before throwing themselves into the canal.

Each left a suicide note explaining their actions. Harvey blamed the fact that his father was trying to keep him from Miss Bates, while Elizabeth claimed to be unhappy at home, writing that if she couldn't have Joe in life, she would at least be sure of having him in death.

An inquest jury returned verdicts that Elizabeth and Joseph threw themselves into the canal in a premeditated act of suicide, adding that they believed that both were temporarily insane at the time.

A kiss. (Author's collection)

23 JULY

1860 Boatman Edward Humphreys (or Humphries) appeared at the Staffordshire Assizes charged with the manslaughter of his partner, Elizabeth Evans, at Wolverhampton. (He was originally indicted for wilful murder but the Grand Jury reduced the charge.)

The couple were drinking on 12 May – although not together – and when they met up, both were drunk. Humphreys went to buy another drink but Elizabeth told the landlord not to serve him, which sent him into a rage. Later that evening, as Elizabeth walked back to their boat with some female friends, Humphreys kicked and beat her to death, ignoring her pleas for mercy. Several people tried to intervene but Humphreys threatened them with similar violence. He eventually left Elizabeth for dead and returned to his boat, warning her that if he hadn't killed her, he would get her when she came home.

Once he had sobered up, Humphreys expressed great contrition, tearfully blaming his actions on drink. After pleading guilty to manslaughter, he was sentenced to eight years' penal servitude.

24 JULY

1901 Twenty-eight-year-old Hannah Johnson Cox appeared before Mr Justice Bigham at the Stafford Assizes charged with two counts of wilful murder.

Hannah gave birth to her seventh child on Christmas Day 1900, the birth leaving her weak and low in spirit. By June 1901, Hannah's husband had deserted her, after running up rent arrears of £17. Hannah

Mr Justice Bigham. (Author's collection)

was evicted and had to rely on the charity and kindness of neighbours to feed her family. She applied to enter the Workhouse with her children but her application was refused unless her husband went in with her.

Hannah sank into a deep despair and, on 14 June, she was seen on the banks of the canal at Coseley with her two youngest children, five-month-old Mary Madeleine and two-year-old Flora Jane. Soon afterwards, the girls were pulled from the water, dead.

Meanwhile, Hannah went to the nearest police station and told the officers there, 'I have just put my two children into the canal. I pushed them through the rails but I never heard them cry after I put them in. I shall be hung now and that will end it all.' The police and a doctor rushed to the canal but even though artificial respiration was attempted for more than half an hour, the little girls were beyond assistance.

Hannah was normally a devoted mother, who had gone without food herself and sold what few clothes she had to put food in her children's mouths. At her trial, a doctor testified that her mental condition after giving birth could have led to homicidal tendencies towards loved ones.

The surgeon from Stafford Gaol agreed that Hannah was weak and depressed on arriving at the prison, neither eating nor sleeping. Dr J.B. Spence, the medical superintendent at the Burntwood Asylum, found her nervous and tearful and, although he could not say that there was anything wrong with her mind, he thought that she believed she was doing the best for her children by drowning them.

Mr Justice Bigham told the jury that it was clear to him that the defendant had lost her reason through misery and he thought the jury would agree. Their verdict was one of 'guilty but insane', leading the judge to order Hannah to be detained as a criminal lunatic at His Majesty's pleasure. The jury expressed a desire to censure Hannah's husband but, since he had not been charged with an offence or heard as a witness, this was not possible.

25 JULY

1860   Mary Twigg of Bilston was sleeping peacefully when her husband Samuel came home. She got up to let him in, to find that he was accompanied by a stranger.

Mary had very few clothes on and quickly ran back upstairs to get dressed, while Samuel shouted drunkenly at her to cook some steak for himself and their guest or he would cut her throat from ear to ear. There was no steak in the house and Mary eventually managed to persuade the man to leave, by which time her husband had fallen into a stupor on the chair. Mary removed his boots and asked him to go to bed but he refused and went back to sleep.

Shortly afterwards, Samuel woke and began bellowing for his son to give him a light. Mary went and as soon as Samuel saw her he said, 'Give me a kiss,' before jumping up and stabbing her in the side with his pocketknife.

The knife penetrated her liver and, although a doctor was called, Mary died soon afterwards. However, she was able to make a statement and Samuel was arrested later that day. 'I know nothing about it. I was drunk at the time,' he initially told police, later telling PC John Moffat that his cousin had done it.

At Twigg's trial for wilful murder at the Staffordshire Assizes in December 1860, his defence counsel tried to get the charge reduced to manslaughter. Mr Motteram argued that there had been no malice or premeditation, so Mary Twigg's death could not have been wilful murder. He reminded the jury that Twigg had suffered two serious head injuries in the past, after which his character completely changed. Prior to being injured he was a kindly husband and father but afterwards became violent and abusive. He was also very badly affected by even the smallest quantity of alcohol after his injury.

The jury were not swayed by Motteram's arguments and, when Twigg was found guilty, he fell to his knees as the judge donned his black cap and pronounced the death sentence. He was hanged at Stafford Gaol on 5 January 1861.

26 JULY

1861   Martha Christy (aka Jane Clarke) was a New Yorker, once married to the Captain of an American ship. However, when he was imprisoned at the Liverpool Assizes for the manslaughter of some of his crew, she found herself alone and friendless in a foreign country.

She fell into a dissolute life and took up with Thomas Clarke, a pit sinker from Wolverhampton. Thomas beat her time and time again and, after one such attack on 26 July 1861, she became paralysed and complained of terrible pains in her head, telling people that she believed that he had permanently damaged her. Indeed, when Martha died soon afterwards, a post-mortem examination revealed a blood clot on her brain that weighed more than 2oz, having steadily oozed from a ruptured blood vessel.

Thomas Clarke was charged with her manslaughter. At the Staffordshire Assizes in December 1861, the court heard that he had continued to beat Martha even as she knelt before him, begging for mercy. When the jury found him guilty, Judge Mr Baron Martin told him that such 'barbaric treatment' was rarely heard in a court of justice and he sentenced Clarke to ten years' penal servitude.

27 JULY

1893 Robert Spencer and Sarah Clancey appeared at the Staffordshire Assizes charged with the wilful murder of Elizabeth Annie Evans at West Bromwich, on or about Good Friday 1885.

Elizabeth suddenly disappeared and nothing was known of her circumstances until March 1893, when the police arrested Clancey for practising as an abortionist. Clancey confessed that she had operated on Elizabeth, who later died. Her body was first buried in Clancey's garden, then later dug up and burned in the cellar of Clancey's home.

Spencer, who was the father of Elizabeth's unborn child, was now married to another woman. A respectable chemist and druggist, he had arranged Elizabeth's abortion, and Clancey's husband had blackmailed him for years after her death, extorting almost £200.

Mr Clancey was now dead and it was agreed by the prosecution that Mrs Clancey would plead guilty to performing an illegal operation. She was sentenced to fifteen years' penal servitude, while Spencer was found guilty of being an accessory after the fact and sentenced to two years with hard labour.

28 JULY

1855 Twenty-three-year-old Joseph Meadows was hanged at Worcester, having been found guilty of the wilful murder of his sweetheart, Mary Ann Mason.

Seventeen-year-old Mary Ann worked as a servant at The Sailor's Return pub at Dudley, where she was known as a quiet, hard-working girl. However, her employers noticed that whenever her brother visited the pub, Mary Ann would be very standoffish and would often ignore him completely.

On the morning of 12 May, Mary Ann's brother was in the pub at 7 a.m., watching her mopping the floor as he drank his ale. Mary Ann's employer, Mary Hunt, briefly left the couple alone together and, when she returned, she realised to her horror that the young man was pointing a rifle at his sister. There was a flash and a loud bang and Mary Ann dropped to the floor, shot in the face and neck. She bled to death within minutes

Another customer bravely grabbed her shooter, who had dropped the rifle and stood calmly waiting. 'I've done what I intended to do,' he told the police, admitting that he was not Mary Ann's brother but her sweetheart, Joseph Meadows. 'She should have given me an answer,' he continued, adding, 'I have had my revenge. I have heard them say revenge is sweet.'

Given that Joseph was seen shooting Mary Ann, his trial at the Worcester Assizes was a foregone conclusion and it took the jury less than five minutes to return a guilty verdict. 'Do it quickly,' Meadows asked executioner William Calcraft as he stood on the gallows and Calcraft duly obliged.

29 JULY

1872 Christopher Edwards was tried at the Staffordshire Assizes for the wilful murder of his wife, Rosannah, at Willenhall.

The couple had been married for seven years and had two children. Their marriage was far from happy and Edwards often beat his wife but on 30 April, things were relatively peaceful between them as they sat with their children around them, talking about horse racing. Less than half an hour later, Edwards ordered Rosannah upstairs and battered her to death with a poker.

The ghastly scene was enacted in silhouette on the window blinds and neighbours attracted by Rosannah's screams broke open the door to see Edwards walking calmly downstairs, his youngest child in his arms. 'What do you want – what's the matter?' he asked in surprise, replacing the poker on the kitchen fender. 'I am the man. She commenced on me and I finished on her,' he explained, adding, 'I don't think her's dead.'

At his trial, his defence counsel tried to argue that Edwards was provoked by jealousy and thus his crime was one of manslaughter rather than wilful murder. The jury were not convinced and Edwards was found guilty and hanged on 12 August 1872.

Note: Various sources give the trial date as 24 July, 27 July and 29 July.

30 JULY

1888 Six members of the Salvation Army appeared at Brierley Hill Police Court charged with obstructing the highway, having led a service in Pearson Street, which attracted around 200 spectators and completely blocked the street.

Salvation Army ladies.
(Author's collection)

Twenty-eight-year-old Emily Turberville was especially indignant at the charges against her, telling the magistrates that when she used to serve the Devil, the police would not leave her alone and now that she was trying to serve Jesus Christ, it was worse than ever.

The newly reformed Emily had previously served numerous prison sentences, most for violence. In July 1881, she appeared before magistrates for the fifteenth time, charged with assault and using obscene language. In 1883, she was a 'disorderly pauper', and in May 1884 she was sentenced to twelve month's imprisonment for larceny. In 1887, she received another twelve months' imprisonment for common assault.

Sadly, Emily's reformation did not last and by 1893 she was described as 'a terror to workhouse officials', after refusing to work and assaulting the porter and two policemen.

31 JULY

1920 Only eight months after their first meeting, twenty-four-year-old Lydia Vaughan married twenty-six-year-old Samuel Westwood. Having no home of their own, the couple moved in with his parents but Lydia struggled to get on with her in-laws, believing that they interfered and were over-critical of her efforts to care for their son. Only six weeks after her wedding, Lydia asked her parents if she could move back to their home in Willenhall. When they agreed, she packed her bags and left her marriage, resuming her old job as a varnisher in the lock trade.

On 11 September, Lydia went to Willenhall Wakes, even though she knew that Samuel would probably be there. She told her parents that she intended to talk things over with him and, although her father pleaded with her not to go, she was determined. Lydia's mother decided to accompany her daughter and, when they spotted Samuel, he linked arms with Lydia, asking her to come with him. Mrs Vaughan linked her arm with Lydia's free arm and refused to be left behind. Samuel seemed keen to patch up the marriage but Lydia refused to go back to his parents' house. Suddenly, Samuel raised his hand and stabbed his wife's throat. He threw away his knife and ran, while Mrs Vaughan cried out 'Murder!' and begged people to help her daughter.

Samuel got as far as the police station on Walsall Street, where he handed himself in. Meanwhile, two policeman carried Lydia to the same police station, where life was pronounced extinct.

Tried for wilful murder at the Staffordshire Assizes on 19 November, Westwood's defence counsel tried to prove that he was insane and that Lydia had provoked him. However, the medical officer at Winson Green Prison, where Westwood had been confined since the murder, stated that he had examined Westwood and found him completely sane. It took the jury just fifteen minutes to pronounce Westwood guilty of wilful murder and he was executed at Winson Green on 30 December 1920.

AUGUST

Victoria Street, Wolverhampton, 1950s. (Author's collection)

1 AUGUST

1890 Coroner Mr E. Docker held an inquest at Langley, Oldbury, on the death of ten-year-old Philip Cross. Philip's friend, Thomas Sheldon, testified that he and Philip were sitting on a steep embankment on the edge of a marlhole (clay quarry), when Philip suddenly slid down the bank into the water. Thomas tried unsuccessfully to reach him, as did a nearby resident, John Owen, who heard the boys' shouts for help.

The marlhole was close to a footpath and, with the exception of a wire fence to keep out animals, was totally unprotected. Owen called the quarry a death trap, saying that if anyone did fall in, the banks were so steep that it was impossible to get out without assistance. (The coroner recalled that a man and his horse had drowned there fairly recently.)

The inquest jury returned a verdict of 'accidentally drowned', asking the coroner to communicate with the Oldbury Local Board and the landowner, calling their attention to the dangerous state of the marlhole and requesting them to fence it off or fill it in immediately.

2 AUGUST

1864 A child's body was found by a dog in a cornfield at Coseley. It was so decomposed that it was impossible to even determine the child's sex, although she was assumed to be female, since girl's clothes were found on or near the body. It was also impossible to pinpoint the cause of the child's death, although a large amount of blood on the field, coupled with the fact that the bonnet strings were blood soaked, suggested that her throat had been cut.

The body was identified as that of eight-year-old Eliza Silletto, who was reported missing by her father on 20 July, and once the discovery was publicised, hairdresser John Jones came forward to say that he believed that he may have witnessed her murder. On 20 July, Jones saw a couple with a little girl in the field, pushing the child back and forth between them until the woman almost threw the girl at the man and then turned her back. The child began to cry, the sound ceasing abruptly as if she had choked. Jones told the police that he had never imagined for one moment that anyone would commit a murder in broad daylight, especially when they could clearly see that there was a witness, so had said nothing.

Eliza was the daughter of Richard Hale, who had recently served a prison sentence for the manslaughter of her mother by starving her and who now lived as man and wife with Cecilia Baker. Jones identified Hale and Baker as the couple with the little girl, and an inquest into Eliza's death returned a verdict of wilful murder against them.

They appeared at the Stafford Winter Assizes in December 1864, where both were found guilty and sentenced to death. Cecilia immediately pleaded pregnancy and a jury of matrons confirmed that she was with child. Her death sentence was stayed until after her child was delivered or until Her Majesty's further pleasure be known.

Thirty-year-old Richard Hale was hanged at Stafford Gaol on 27 December. Cecilia's death sentence was commuted and she served time at Knaphill Female Convict Prison in Surrey.

3 AUGUST

1895 The parents of four-year-old Lily Mary Shoot of Wolverhampton took her on a day trip to Portland. Unfortunately, while Lily's father was carrying her in his arms he stumbled and fell over, bumping the child's head against a piece of flint.

Initially, the injury didn't look too bad but, as a precaution, Lily's parents took her straight to hospital on their return to Wolverhampton, where the small cut on her head was treated. However, rather than healing normally, the wound became 'poisoned', with the tragic result that Lily died from septicaemia.

An inquest held by deputy coroner Mr G. Martin recorded a verdict of 'accidental death'.

4 AUGUST

1937 An inquest was held on the death of two-and-a-half-year-old Charles Cosnett. The boy's distraught mother told the inquest that Charles and his brother Billie were playing in the garden of their Warley home, while she was attending to the baby upstairs.

When Billie shouted to her that the kennel was on fire, she ran downstairs and found Charles lying in the corner. Although Mrs Cosnett tried to reach him, she was beaten back by the fierceness of the fire, which burned away most of her hair.

Her frantic screams brought her neighbours to her aid and the fire was extinguished. Sadly, although the two greyhounds that lived in the kennel survived, Charles perished from a combination of shock and asphyxiation. There was nothing to suggest the cause of the fire, although Charles was said to have a fascination for playing with matches.

The inquest returned a verdict of 'accidental death', the coroner adding that he was satisfied that the neighbours did everything possible to try and save Charles.

5 AUGUST

1890 At West Bromwich Borough Police Court, fifty-one-year-old John Wood was charged with being drunk on 30 July.

Magistrates were told that a policeman found Wood lying helplessly drunk on the pavement in the High Street and took him to the police station. After sobering up for a few hours, Wood was liberated on bail to appear at the Police Court at eleven o'clock the following morning.

Wood failed to appear and when the police went to his home, they found him fast asleep. His solicitor apologised to the magistrates saying that, after leaving the police station, Wood went home and went to bed, sleeping right through until the police woke him at 2 p.m.

The magistrates were far from sympathetic, ordering Wood to forfeit his bail of 20s for failing to appear and fining him a further 20s plus costs for drunkenness.

6 AUGUST

1900 William and Louisa Ann Lowe were appalled at the way that Richard Jones treated his wife – their daughter – and on 6 August, they went to his home in Wolverhampton to have it out with him.

When they arrived, their daughter was ill in bed upstairs and her husband was in the room with her. Richard Jones was not pleased to see his parents-in-law, especially when they began telling him off, and he told sixty-five-year-old William that, if he was not an old man, he would put him out of the house. Lowe replied that he might be old but he could still deal with Jones and the two men began scuffling.

Before long, Richard and his brother Edward, who were both drunk, picked up William between them and carried him to the front door. They pushed him out of the house and William fell backwards, hitting the back of his head against the kerb and knocking himself unconscious.

Richard and Edward tried three times to lift William from the pavement but they were so drunk that they dropped him and each time his head connected with the pavement. Eventually, a policeman came along and Richard Jones propped his father-in-law up against the door.

PC Fryer arranged for William to be taken to hospital, where he was treated and sent home. He continued to decline until 21 August, when he was admitted to hospital, where he died from a fractured skull.

Coroner Mr R.A. Willcock held an inquest, at which the jury returned a verdict in accordance with the medical evidence, passing no comment on how Lowe's fractured skull was caused. It would have been pointless to find either 'wilful murder' or 'manslaughter' against Richard Jones, who hanged himself when he realised the seriousness of Lowe's condition. Richard's brother, Edward, declined to give evidence at the inquest for fear of incriminating himself. The coroner told him that his conduct on 6 August was entirely down to drink and did not reflect well on him, either as a relative or as a man. In the coroner's opinion, Edward Jones would remember and rue the day for as long as he lived.

7 AUGUST

1893 Edward and Catherine Boylin appeared at Wednesbury Police Court charged with neglecting their children William (7), Mary Ann (3) and Elizabeth (18 months).

Although Edward earned 10s a week working in the market, Catherine spent most of his wages on drink. She kept a disgustingly dirty house and the children were mainly fed on dry bread, with an occasional scraping of treacle. They were inadequately dressed, filthy and crawling with vermin, and Mary Ann was still unable to walk or talk. When drunk – as she often was – Catherine beat her children mercilessly.

Magistrates heard that Edward had twice before been convicted of a similar offence and Catherine once. Commenting that if there was any further incidence of child neglect he would send the couple to the assizes, the Stipendiary Magistrate contended himself with sentencing both defendants to prison for three months, with hard labour.

8 AUGUST

1928 An inquest at Oldbury returned a verdict of wilful murder against Mrs Sarah Jane Bastable in respect of the deaths of her two children, eight-year-old Gladys and two-year-old John.

Thirty-three-year-old Mrs Bastable drowned her children and then herself in the canal, after first writing to the police and announcing her intentions. Her letter stated that allegations had been made about her fidelity and, although there was no truth in the gossip, her husband believed the lies about her and she couldn't stand the situation any longer.

The inquest determined that she committed suicide while temporarily insane.

9 AUGUST

1880 At Oldbury, labourer Edward Jordan argued with shoemaker Henry Parsons and the two men began fighting. Witnesses saw Jordan knock Parsons over and then kick him while he was down.

Parsons was taken to West Bromwich Infirmary, where he died the following day. A post-mortem examination revealed that he was suffering from very severe heart disease and that, if Jordan had kicked him, the kick had only accelerated Parsons's death rather than killed him.

When an inquest was held, the jury leniently returned a verdict of 'death from natural causes', but the police were not satisfied and charged Jordan with manslaughter. He was allowed bail until his trial at the Worcestershire Assizes on 19 January 1881, where he was acquitted.

10 AUGUST

1932 An inquest was held at Wolverhampton on the death of fifty-one-year-old Harriett Gertrude Flint, who died after a petrol explosion at her home at Oxley on 7 August.

Miss Flint was alone in her house at the time of the incident but it was known that she was planning to remove some marks from her silk dressing gown using refined petrol.

The jury returned a verdict of 'death by misadventure'. They were satisfied that Miss Flint died as a result of the injuries received in the explosion, however, they could find nothing to explain how the petrol had become ignited. It was suggested that the explosion was triggered by Miss Flint either lighting or smoking a cigarette, but Fire Inspector Mr Edwards suspected that the friction generated by rubbing the silk together may well have caused a spark.

11 AUGUST

1874 Joseph Petty, a labourer living and working at Darlaston, was scheduled to appear before magistrates at Wednesbury.

Petty was summoned by the Atherstone Board of Guardians in Warwickshire for failing to maintain his wife and children. Magistrates in Wednesbury were told that as a direct result of Petty's brutal treatment of his wife, she had become hopelessly insane and was now confined in a lunatic asylum at a cost of 19s a week.

It was alleged that Petty had beaten his wife and children unmercifully, frequently leaving them without food. On one occasion, Mrs Petty was so terrified that she jumped out of an upstairs window to escape her husband's violence.

Petty failed to appear in court but magistrates found him guilty in his absence and issued a warrant for his immediate arrest, sentencing him to two months' imprisonment with hard labour.

12 AUGUST

1903 Thirty-three-year-old James Cartwright lived in Bilston with Mary Ann Pumphrey, her eleven-year-old son, Alfred, and their own two children, Jeremiah and Mary Ann junior, aged nine and six.

On 12 August, Cartwright was diagnosed with inflammation of the lungs and was told to rest. When his doctor visited the following day, Cartwright's illness had worsened to pneumonia and, by the next day, he was delirious. It was decided to bring his bed downstairs so that Mary Ann could nurse him more easily and Cartwright's seventeen-year-old niece Hannah came to help.

In the early hours of 15 August, Mary Ann was dozing in a makeshift bed near Cartwright's when she suddenly became aware that he was standing at her bedside. When she sat up, Cartwright went back to his own bed, groaning fearfully. Hearing the noise, Hannah came downstairs and Mary Ann fetched Cartwright a glass of milk, which he drank and immediately vomited up.

'Fetch me a sharp drink,' he barked and as Mary Ann handed him a glass of lemonade, he attacked her. So great was his strength that he managed to tear off most of Mary Ann's clothes until his energy finally waned, and she and Hannah managed to escape the cottage, holding the door handle from the outside to prevent Cartwright from following.

Completely naked and covered in cuts and bruises, Mary Ann shouted to her children to run before rushing off with Hannah to get help. As they fled, the women could hear screams and shrieks and assumed that Cartwright was slaughtering the chickens in his gardens – sadly, he had turned on the three children, battering them to death as they lay in their bed.

It took police several hours to gain access to the house, where Cartwright was still ranting and raving. Seeing the unbelievable carnage upstairs one officer asked him sorrowfully, 'Well, Jim, what have you done this for?'

'It was only a bit of fun,' Cartwright replied.

At his trial at the Staffordshire Assizes, Cartwright insisted that he could recall nothing about the killings which, since his temperature was 103° Fahrenheit at the time, was perhaps not surprising. Normally a fond and loving father, Cartwright was found guilty of three counts of wilful murder, although the jury believed that he was not responsible for his actions due to his high fever, and Mr Justice Bigham ordered him to be detained at His Majesty's pleasure.

13 AUGUST

1856   There were two shafts at Ramrod Hall Colliery at Oldbury, which were controlled by father and son butties Richard and Thomas Baker (or Barker). It was part of the butty's duties to inspect the pit for gas every morning but on 13 August this wasn't done and the first eight miners descended into the pit with a lighted candle. The candle was seen to burn blue, indicating the presence of firedamp, and was quickly extinguished. The men shouted up the shaft to the next batch of men, telling them to bring safety lamps down with them. Thomas Baker sent someone for a safety lamp but, before it arrived, he made the decision that there was no gas in the workings and ordered a shovel of live coals to be placed in the skip, to light the miners' candles when they reached the bottom.

The skip had barely descended 20 yards when there was a massive explosion. The eight men already at the pit bottom were blown into what the contemporary newspapers ghoulishly described as 'almost one indiscriminate mass of mutilated flesh, bones, entrails and blood,' adding that 'some of the skulls were lying here and there as perfectly empty as eggshells deprived of their contents.'

Of the sixteen men who went down the mineshaft, only six survived, most of whom were badly injured. All sixteen were brought to the surface and the injured were taken to hospital, while the mutilated remains of the dead were taken to their homes. Some bodies were so unrecognisable that they were taken to the wrong houses, and in one instance a man's remains were delivered to his house, only for him to turn up alive twenty minutes later. In all, the explosion claimed eleven lives, leaving more than twenty children fatherless. The youngest victim, John Bryan, was only twelve years old.

Surprisingly, the inquest held by coroner George Hinchcliffe returned verdicts of 'accidental death', even though the Inspector of Mines believed that the mine had been inadequately ventilated. The coroner gave his opinion that, had Thomas Baker survived, he would have urged the jury to return a verdict of manslaughter against him for his dereliction of duty.

14 AUGUST

1866 The horse racing meeting at Wolverhampton Race Course was beset by a series of accidents. Eighteen people were injured by the collapse of a temporary grandstand, constructed from seven tiers of deal planks roped together and fastened to uprights. Almost 500 people were standing in the structure and, as the Wolverhampton Stakes reached its conclusion, they grew very excited, cheering, jumping up and down and waving their hats.

The entire structure fell with a tremendous crash and a later examination showed that several of the planks and most of the ropes had broken. The casualties were rushed to hospital in cabs and it was believed that at least two would not survive.

In a second accident during the same race, a large party of race-goers from Birmingham climbed onto the roof of a covered waggon for a better view. The roof collapsed, precipitating twenty people onto the ground, five of whom were seriously injured.

Finally, having assured himself that the horses had passed, twenty-two-year-old Joseph Smith ducked under the railings in order to cross the course. He failed to notice a straggler, who kicked him so hard in the head as it passed that he was knocked out of his boots. He too was taken to hospital.

Although reports in the contemporary newspapers state that several people were badly hurt and were expected to die, no reports of any deaths have been found.

15 AUGUST

1903 A stuntman who went by the name of Professor W. Finney was hired to entertain the crowds at the Bloxwich Fête and Gala. Finney dived 12 yards from a platform into a small tank containing 5ft of water but,

Bloxwich Church
and High Street.
(Author's collection)

having completed his dive, he seemed to be unconscious. He was pulled
from the water tank and taken to hospital, where he was found to be
completely paralysed due to a fractured spine.

After his death, an inquest on 29 August theorised that he had probably
struck the water at an awkward angle and a verdict of 'accidental death'
was returned.

16 AUGUST

1896 Thirteen-year-old Samuel Harvey was one of a group of children
searching for coal on a pit spoil heap. He and three girls had burrowed
some way beneath the surface, creating a large overhang, which suddenly
fell, completely burying the four children.

An alarm was raised and local residents rushed to the scene with spades
and began to dig frantically until they reached the children. Initially, all
four appeared dead but PC Harrison was able to give artificial respiration
and managed to revive the three girls, who are believed to have survived
their ordeal. Sadly, Samuel was beyond help.

A later inquest returned a verdict of 'accidental death', the jury
condemning the practice of sending children onto the pit mounds to
collect coal.

17 AUGUST

1849 In 1849, slum housing and a complete lack of any proper
sanitation led to an outbreak of cholera in Willenhall, the first registered
death from the epidemic taking place on 17 August. The number of
deaths meant that St Giles's Church was unable to cope with the sheer
volume of burials, and a portion of land at Doctor's Piece was set aside
as a Cholera Burial Ground. Over 290 people died in just fifty days, and
three times during that period there were more than fifteen burials in a
single day.

Records indicate that there were other major epidemics of cholera in
the Black Country, including a widespread epidemic in 1832, during
which more than nine and a half thousand cases were reported, almost
a quarter of which were fatal.

18 AUGUST — **1869** An inquest was held at Wolverhampton into the death of William John Smith, who died after being run down by a horse and cart.

The horse belonged to Mr Evans, who, on 16 August, left it tied to a post by its reins at Bushbury. However, a passing train frightened the horse and, when it pulled backwards, its bridle came off. The horse galloped off at top speed, ending up in Canal Street, where eight-year-old William was among a group of children playing.

Horse and cart. (Author's collection)

The inquest jury expressed surprise that the keepers of the tollgate at Bushbury hadn't stopped the horse by closing the toll gate when they saw it galloping towards them with no driver. They returned a verdict of 'accidental death', saying that even though they didn't attach any blame to Mr Evans, they hoped that he would be more careful about tying up his horses in future, and that he should do something for William's parents. The coroner added that he believed that some of the blame for the tragedy was due to William's mother for allowing her child to play in the street.

19 AUGUST — **1931** An inquest was held at Wolverhampton into the death of ten-year-old Robert Layton of Bilston.

The jury was told that a company was pulling a cable over an electric power pylon at Bilston on 17 August. The cables were drawn over pulley blocks at the top of the 72ft-high pylons by teams of horses, and, in spite of repeated warnings from the contractors, the local children kept grabbing the cables and hanging on, allowing themselves to be lifted into the air.

The children fell off one after the other, two of them receiving severe injuries, but Robert hung on until he was 70ft up before plummeting to his instant death.

The inquest jury returned a verdict of 'accidental death' and, although they found no evidence of criminal neglect, they believed that the cable company had taken insufficient precautions to safeguard the public.

20 AUGUST

1889 The new hot air stove being erected at Spring Vale Furnaces in Bilston had reached a height of about 60ft, and men were working on scaffolding both inside and outside the furnace.

Robert Probert was responsible for erecting the scaffolding and used brand new planks, tied together with stout cord and further secured by nails. But while Probert and three other men were working on the scaffold platform on 20 August they heard an ominous crack and realised to their horror that a plank had snapped.

The four men were precipitated off the scaffold – twenty-year-old Richard Colley dying instantly when he hit the ground. Thomas Judson and Thomas Bennett were both seriously injured and later died from their injuries, while Probert suffered a broken leg and ribs.

Coroner Mr W.H. Phillips opened and adjourned an inquest, to allow an inspection of the scaffolding by an independent contractor. When the inquest resumed, builder William Scott stated that he could see nothing wrong with the scaffold planks and no evidence of criminal negligence, although he pointed out that the scaffold boards were made from spruce, which was not the most reliable of timbers.

Probert was able to make a deposition about the incident and insisted that it was simply a tragic accident. Satisfied that the scaffold was fit for purpose, the inquest jury returned three verdicts of 'accidental death'.

21 AUGUST

1866 Twenty-two-year-old Mary Brown entered the Workhouse at Wolverhampton and within hours gave birth to an illegitimate baby girl. She stayed in the Workhouse until 3 September, when she left, taking her baby with her. The following morning, after being caught stealing fruit and vegetables from Wolverhampton market, she was arrested on a charge of larceny and taken to Stafford Gaol.

At the time, she had no baby with her and the police weren't aware that she had recently given birth. However, on 25 September, the decomposed body of a baby was found in a pile of stones and brick ends. A post-mortem examination revealed several skull fractures and concluded that the infant had been battered to death.

The baby girl was wearing clothes bearing the Workhouse stamp, and was quickly traced back to there and identified as Mary Brown's daughter.

Mary was charged with wilful murder and appeared at the Stafford Assizes, where she was found guilty and sentenced to death. The jury recommended mercy for Mary – whose execution was set for 18 December – and the Home Secretary subsequently commuted her death sentence to one of life imprisonment.

22 AUGUST

1919 Sixteen-year-old Muriel Robinson, the daughter of the owner of Fallings Park Hall near Wolverhampton, fired a gun at a blackbird perched in a very thick privet hedge. Sometime later, the Hall's sixty-year-old gardener, James Hodson, was found lying on the far side of the hedge with a bullet wound in his head. Although he was taken to hospital, he died from his injuries later that day.

Since there was no way that Miss Robinson could have known of the gardener's presence when she fired, the jury at the subsequent inquest recorded a verdict of 'accidental death'.

23 AUGUST

1858 A special offer of incredibly cheap fares led to a high demand for tickets on a railway excursion to Worcester. The railway decided to provide two trains, the first having twenty-nine carriages, the second having sixteen.

All went well until Round Oak Station, near Dudley, when a broken coupling caused the last sixteen carriages to become detached from the front train. They travelled backwards down the steep incline towards Brettell Lane Station and collided with the second train at speed, smashing several carriages from both trains into matchwood.

At least thirteen died in the crash and many more were seriously injured. An inquest was opened by Mr T.M. Phillips on 25 August. The foreman of the jury was Reverend Josephus Bailey, although his integrity as a juror was later challenged when it emerged that he had inadvertently been involved in a compensation claim against the railway by one of the victims.

It took seven sittings before the inquest jury reached the conclusion that, as well as the broken coupling, the guard of the front train should also bear some responsibility for not applying his brake quickly enough. There was another challenge to a juror's impartiality, since jury member James Wheeler was alleged to have been hostile to the railway, having had two lawsuits against them. In addition, five of the jury disagreed with the apportioning of blame.

Guard Frederick Cook was indicted for manslaughter and appeared at the Staffordshire Assizes on 29 November 1858. The Grand Jury found no bill against him and, given the disagreements at the inquest, there was some discussion about whether or not he should be tried on the coroner's warrant. Eventually he was, but the jury found him 'not guilty' and he was discharged.

24 AUGUST

1890 The Deepfields area of Wolverhampton was scandalised when a respectable mother of four eloped with a nineteen-year-old man. The deserted husband, John 'Jack' Wise, was left with three young children to care for – his wife having taken the youngest – and immediately began a frantic search for the errant couple.

Local gossip suggested that the runaways were heading for America and, after buying a revolver and six bullets from a pawn shop, Wise set off for Liverpool to try and intercept them at the docks. Having scoured the city without success he returned to Wolverhampton and went to James and Mary Davis, the parents of his wife's lover.

'It's your duty to find them,' Wise told James Davis in a state of agitation. Davis tried to calm Wise down, saying that nobody had any idea where to look and urging him to relax and let the police do their job.

'If I had caught 'em, I'd have served 'em like this,' Wise said, pulling the revolver from his pocket to show Mr and Mrs Davis. As he did, the

gun went off, shooting Mary, and as her husband assisted her out of the house to safety, he heard two more shots being fired. The police arrived minutes later to find Mary in a nearby pub and Wise in her house, having shot himself. Both were taken to hospital where they were expected to die. However, Wise survived and an inquest into Mary's death returned a verdict of wilful murder against him, although the jury made it clear that they believed that he had been driven to despair by his wife.

Wise appeared at the Staffordshire Assizes in December 1890. The court was told that he was a devoted husband and father, a hard-working and sober man, of exemplary character, who was placed in a frenzied state by his wife's behaviour. There were only three possible verdicts – to find Wise guilty of murder, or of manslaughter, or to find that the shooting was an accident. After hearing all the evidence, the jury found Wise guilty of manslaughter, strongly recommending that the judge was merciful in sentencing him, due to his previous good character and the great provocation. Since Wise had been incarcerated while awaiting his trial, Mr Justice Mathews sentenced him to a token six days' imprisonment, which allowed for his immediate release.

25 AUGUST

1890 Magistrates at the County Police Court in Wolverhampton struggled to decide how best to punish nine-year-old Frederick Griffiths of Tettenhall, after finding him guilty of unlawfully maiming cattle.

Frederick was seen by a farm bailiff to throw a billhook at a calf, which penetrated the animal's body to a depth of twelve inches. The boy then retrieved the billhook and threw it at a different calf, causing such severe injuries to its leg that it had to be put down.

The magistrates reasoned that Frederick was too young to be sent to prison and that, if he was fined, his parents would have to pay, which would not be a sufficient deterrent against future offending, since it would not affect Frederick personally. The Bench finally settled on ordering Frederick's parents to pay 14s costs and sentencing the boy to six strokes with a birch rod.

Old Hill, Tettenhall, 1921. (Author's collection)

26 AUGUST

1865 Charles Christopher Robinson and Harriet Seagar were both eighteen years old and lived with Josiah Fisher in Wolverhampton. Fisher had been Robinson's guardian for the past eight years, while Harriet was the sister of Josiah's son's wife, thus her position in the household was slightly above that of a domestic servant.

On 26 August, Robinson and a friend were in the garden, shooting sparrows with a small gun, when Robinson remarked, 'Harriet is crying but I don't know what for.' Other people were well aware why Harriet was distressed, for several had seen Robinson trying to kiss her a little earlier and, when she had resisted, he slapped her face hard.

The garden of Josiah Fisher's house backed onto the pub run by his son, Isaiah, and later that day, Isaiah's servant Emma Silleto heard a gunshot, followed by a man's voice shouting, 'Harriet is shot.' Emma rushed outside and saw Robinson carrying a bloody razor and, as she watched through the window, he stood before the mirror in the scullery and cut his throat three times.

Harriet Seagar was found dead in her bedroom and although a gun had been fired into the ceiling, the cause of death was a single cut severing all of the major blood vessels in her throat.

Robinson survived his suicide attempt and stood trial for Harriet's wilful murder at the Staffordshire Assizes. It emerged at the trial that the nature of Harriet's injury did not preclude it being self-inflicted and Robinson's defence counsel contended that, rather than killing Harriet, his client had been distraught to find her dead by her own hand. The defence also claimed that there was a history of insanity in Robinson's family and called several witnesses to testify to incidences of strange behaviour in his recent past. However, the prosecution called the chief of the Staffordshire County Lunatic Asylum, who told the court that he had examined Robinson twice and found no evidence of insanity.

The jury was not convinced by the defence's claims and found Robinson guilty of wilful murder. He was hanged at Stafford Gaol on 9 January 1866.

27 AUGUST

1931 Shortly before the start of the evening film screening, the proprietor of the Alexandra Picture House in Lower Gornal, Ernest Jones, heard a shout coming from the cinema's rewinding room. Finding that a fire had broken out in an adjoining room, Jones managed to grab projectionist Francis Harold Danks and drag him out into the street. Danks was taken to hospital but died shortly after admission.

An inquest was held on 31 August, at which the coroner heavily censured the cinema's rewinding room, believing it to be unfit for purpose. Open to other rooms, it was in a poorly ventilated passage, with a door that opened inwards to an awkward stairway. The inquest heard that while Danks was preparing the films for the evening show, workmen erecting a new sound apparatus in an adjoining room found a film on fire. Danks could easily have escaped the blaze but stayed to try and extinguish the flames and was eventually overcome by fumes. The inquest jury returned a verdict of 'accidental death'.

28 AUGUST

1911 Express train driver George Loake of Walsall had been a reliable railway employee for more than fifty years. A widower with nine children, George married divorcee Elizabeth Newitt in 1903, welcoming her two children into his brood, and the family lived very happily together until 1909, when George had an accident at work.

George's head swelled alarmingly but a doctor seemed to think that no treatment was necessary and sent him home to rest. Within hours, George was in such severe pain that he threw himself into the canal to try and make it stop. Although George's injuries gradually healed, his personality underwent a complete transformation after the accident. He became short-tempered and persistently used foul language but worst of all, he began drinking heavily, and in March 1911, he was caught leaving his train to go and buy drink.

He was sacked on the spot, losing not only his regular wage but also his future pension at a stroke. His family fell into financial difficulties and eventually, Elizabeth took her two children and left.

On 28 August, George appeared at his wife's lodgings to beg her to return to him. When she refused, George seized her and stabbed her repeatedly in the face and neck. He eventually left his wife mortally wounded and went outside where, just as he was about to cut his own throat, a passing policeman managed to relieve him of his knife.

At his trial at the Staffordshire Assizes on 20 November, Loake's defence team relied on an insanity defence, and although the jury were made aware of his head injury and consequent change of personality, they found him guilty. Sixty-four-year-old Loake was executed at Stafford on 28 December by Thomas Pierrepoint and William Willis.

29 AUGUST

1860 Coroner Mr T.M. Phillips concluded an inquest at Quarry Bank into the death of eleven-year-old Timothy Lawley, who died on 14 August.

Timothy was of weak intellect and suffered from fainting fits. He was unable to speak and, according to neighbours, was treated abominably by his parents. He was rarely fed or properly clothed and was beaten at every opportunity. Several of the neighbours risked the Lawleys' wrath by surreptitiously feeding the child, although some stated that they had seen Timothy's father take the food that they had given the boy and eat it himself.

If anyone complained, Mr and Mrs Lawley raged that they had the right to do whatever they wanted with their own child – this included locking or tying him up and beating him until he bled. Neighbours finally called the police on 7 March 1859 and Mr Lawley was brought before magistrates, while Timothy was taken to the Workhouse. However, Lawley escaped with a reprimand and Timothy was returned home after his parents promised to mend their ways.

When Timothy died, a post-mortem examination recorded that he weighed only 15lbs. and that the circumference of his calf had been 5½ inches. He was covered with cuts and bruises from head to toe, with a very recent wound on the top of his head, and the cause of death was given as 'exhaustion consequent upon the want of the necessities of life and general ill-treatment.'

Memorial card.
(Author's collection)

Mrs Lawley – who was her husband's niece as well as his wife – sobbed that she had done the best possible for Timothy, given what his father brought home. Mr Lawley said nothing. He was described in the contemporary newspapers as having 'a physiognomy that would induce the belief that he was a very hardened character and capable of heartless cruelty'.

The inquest jury returned verdicts of 'manslaughter through ill-treatment' against both parents, who were committed for trial at Staffordshire Assizes. When they appeared on 14 December 1860, Mary Lawley was acquitted, but her husband Thomas was found guilty and sentenced to fifteen years' imprisonment.

30 AUGUST

1860 When the last tenant of The Pig and Whistle public house in Sedgley moved out, after finding it impossible to make a living, nobody else was willing to take it on, as it had a reputation for being haunted. Eventually, the pub's owners decided to pull down the building and, on 30 August, in the course of the demolition, most of a human skeleton was discovered buried beneath the hearth.

A roadside inn, it was one of the few in the locality offering accommodation for travellers and it was supposed that one of them had met a gruesome end – some even put forward a possible name for the remains, suggesting that a man known as

Bull Ring, Sedgley, 1906.
(Author's collection)

'Old Short' used to be a regular at the pub, before disappearing from the area some years ago.

31 AUGUST

1912   An inquest took place at Bilston Coroner's Court into the death of five-year-old Arthur Edward Payne.

Arthur had climbed onto the parapet of a railway bridge to get a better view of a train and overbalanced, falling 40ft onto the line below. By a miracle, he seems to have escaped injury but moments after his fall, the Wolverhampton to London express train rounded a bend, travelling at nearly forty miles an hour.

The driver could see Arthur sitting on the line, waving to him, but was unable to stop the train quickly enough to avoid hitting him. The impact killed the child instantly.

The inquest returned a verdict of 'accidental death', attaching no blame for the tragedy to the distraught train driver.

SEPTEMBER

Farley Clock Tower, West Bromwich. (Author's collection)

1 SEPTEMBER **1906** In common with much of the United Kingdom, the Black Country sweltered in a heat wave, as an inquest at Rowley Regis returned a verdict of 'accidental death' on forty-five-year-old miner David Lester.

The jury were told that it was so hot underground at Stour Colliery, that Lester expressly disobeyed the orders of his manager by wandering off alone to try and find a cooler place to work. He accidentally disturbed some pit props and the resulting fall of 2 tons of coal from the roof buried him, killing him instantly.

2 SEPTEMBER **1929** At 5.30 a.m., a booking clerk noticed flames shooting out of the upper windows of two shops opposite Smethwick Railway Station. Although he immediately raised the alarm, it took just minutes for the premises to become an inferno.

The Lee family lived on the ground floor and were able to escape but the families living over the shops were not so fortunate. Alexander MacDonald (44), his wife Theresa (33) and their children Jean (6), Hilda (4), Hector (2) and Alexander junior (10 months) all perished in the fire, as did James and Mary Ann Jones and their son James junior. Mrs Mary Ann Aston (55) and her son David (33) also died, while David's sisters, Emily (23) and Lilian (15), his brother Arthur (17) and Selina Jones (23) were badly injured jumping out of windows.

An inquest into the eleven victims' deaths was opened and adjourned for three weeks in the hope that those in hospital would be able to attend. Meanwhile, the bodies of the dead were buried in a single grave – most were charred beyond all recognition.

When the inquest concluded on 25 September, the jury learned that the cause of the fire was a fault in the electrical wiring. Only one fire engine attended, the driver of the other being otherwise engaged in taking the victims to hospital in the ambulance. The fire engine had the wrong fittings for the nearby water hydrants and although the Chief Officer tried to get water from a tank, it proved impossible to open. Thus the job of extinguishing the fire was undertaken by a private firm's engine, which drew water from the canal.

The jury were told that the victims died very quickly from suffocation and returned verdicts of 'death by suffocation from inhalation of noxious fumes.' Although the inefficiency of the fire brigade was not a contributing factor, the jury found that there had been a lack of proper care, for which they blamed the Smethwick Corporation.

The coroner commended the bravery of David Aston. A cripple, he undoubtedly sacrificed his own life by going upstairs to alert his brother and sisters, since he was then physically unable to escape himself.

3 SEPTEMBER **1893** Coroner Edwin Hooper held an inquest at Tipton, into the death of Willie Law.

A few days earlier, Willie and his friends went to play cricket at Wednesbury Old Fields. As they walked home after the game, Willie climbed onto a brick dome, which capped a disused pit, and began singing and dancing.

Willie fell off the dome but scrambled back again to continue cavorting. The other cricketers had walked on ahead and Joseph Tuckley was just about to call them back to see Willie's antics when the brickwork suddenly gave way, sending Willie into the mineshaft.

Joseph was frozen to the spot with shock but eventually managed to run for help. PC Whiston was one of the first people on the scene and, after checking the condition of the air in the pit by letting down a safety lamp, he decided that it was unsafe for anyone to go down to rescue Willie because of the presence of 'chokedamp' (carbon dioxide). Willie's shattered body was eventually hauled to the surface with drags, where he was found to have died from head injuries.

The inquest jury took the view that Willie's untimely death was entirely his own fault and returned a verdict of 'accidental death'.

4 SEPTEMBER

1873 Thirteen-year-old William Vaux appeared before magistrates at West Bromwich charged with stealing apples from an orchard and, when found guilty, was ordered to pay a fine of 6s, plus 3d for the cost of the fruit.

William's mother tearfully told the magistrates that she was unable to pay. When she was told that her son would be sent to gaol in default, she begged magistrates not to imprison him as her husband had recently died and William and his sister were her only support.

Two of the magistrates took pity on Mrs Vaux and offered to pay the fine themselves. The very next case to come before the Bench was another charge of stealing apples. This time, the magistrates were not so generous and the two fifteen-year-old thieves were fined 12s each, including costs and 2d damages.

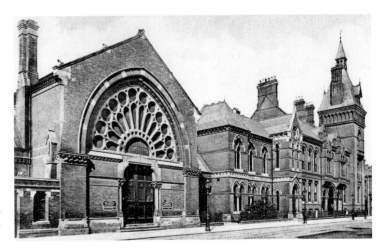

Municipal Buildings, West Bromwich. (Author's collection)

5 SEPTEMBER

1820 Before she ran off with another man, John Wright's wife had been away from their home in Wolverhampton for some months, caring for a sick relative. Wright knew nothing of his wife's affair until she left him but he tracked her down to Darlaston and brought her home. The couple slept together on the night of 3 September and were apparently reconciled but as soon as Wright left to go to work the following morning, his wife went back to her lover, leaving her husband alone with the couple's five-year-old son, James.

Wright was frantic and agitated. He slept with his son that night and, waking the boy early on 5 September, took him for a walk along the Wyrley Canal and threw him into the water. He immediately had second thoughts and jumped in and rescued his son. They went to a nearby cottage to get dry, where Wright was advised to take his son home and put him to bed. He promised to do so but shortly after leaving the cottage, he threw his child into the canal again – this time he didn't save him.

Wright returned to Wolverhampton alone and told two of his relations what he had done. Horrified, they accompanied him back to the canal, where one waded in and retrieved James's body. Wright was distraught at the sight of his dead son, cradling the child's body and kissing the boy affectionately.

An inquest held by coroner Henry Smith on 6 September returned a verdict of wilful murder against Wright, who was committed for trial at the Stafford Assizes in March 1821. He was found not guilty due to insanity and ordered to be detained as a criminal lunatic.

6 SEPTEMBER

1884 Hall End Colliery, between Wednesbury and West Bromwich, was considered a safe pit and, since there was no gas, the men were permitted to work with candles rather than safety lamps. Just before 5 p.m. on 6 September 1884, there was an explosion in an area where sixteen men were working a new seam of coal. The force of the explosion knocked the men over and blew out their candles but they were all able to make their way to the bottom of the shaft and were brought to the surface.

Many were severely burned and were sent straight to hospital. In all, eleven miners were seriously injured and on 9 September, Charles Darnell died. By 18 September, Edwin Hughes, William Birks, Charles Dancer, Joseph (or James) Broom, Benjamin Tranter and Edward Lawley had succumbed to their injuries.

An inquest returned seven verdicts of 'accidental death', although the jury believed that the colliery had not taken adequate precautions by not insisting on the use of safety lamps. 'As long as the law allows men to work in mines with naked lights, I am afraid such cases will continue to occur' concluded the coroner.

7 SEPTEMBER

1871 Coroner Edwin Hooper held an inquest at the Church Tavern, West Bromwich into the death of twenty-seven-year-old John Thomas Woolley.

Woolley left home on 4 September in excellent health. He was known to have called at the New Inn at 1 a.m. on 5 September, leaving there an hour later, when he was said to be perfectly sober. He was found dead close to his home just before 5 a.m., his head buried in a heap of manure.

The inquest theorised that Woolley had accidentally tripped over some palings, landing head first in the muck heap. His head sank so far into the soft manure that he suffocated before he could extricate himself.

8 SEPTEMBER **1887** As John Power was bedding down a cow belonging to a Bilston butcher the animal's foot became entangled in the pitchfork he was using to spread the straw. The cow kicked out frantically to try and free itself, and the handle of the pitchfork hit Power hard in the stomach. He was taken home in terrible pain and, in spite of the best efforts of a surgeon, died the next day from a ruptured intestine.

An inquest held on 11 September recorded a verdict of 'accidental death'.

9 SEPTEMBER **1855** John Cooper was keen to catch the Walsall train so, when his train from Stourport arrived at Dudley Station, he hurriedly disembarked. Carrying his four-year-old son, he stepped out of the carriage, falling between the edge of the platform and the still-moving train. By the time the train halted, Cooper had been dragged almost 30 yards, and his body was so tightly wedged against the platform that it was necessary to use levers to jack up the carriage to extricate him.

Cooper was dead but he was still tightly clutching his little boy in his arms and the child was alive. Although both of the boy's thighs were broken, his collarbone was dislocated and two of his fingers had been severed, he is believed to have survived the accident that killed his father.

At the inquest into Cooper's death, railway officials insisted that, in his haste, Cooper stepped from a moving train. However, other passengers swore that the train came to a complete halt and guards opened the doors, before the train began moving again.

The coroner adjourned the inquest for two weeks to allow further enquiries to be made and, when it resumed, one of the jurors became ill. Saying that he wished to keep the same jury, the coroner adjourned the inquest again.

There had been complaints that two of the jurors worked for the railway and should therefore be disqualified from serving. When the juror recovered and the inquest reopened, the coroner announced that he had written to the Home Secretary, Sir George Grey, about their eligibility and was told to use his own judgement and discretion.

The jury were unable to disentangle the conflicting evidence on whether or not the train stopped and restarted, in which case, the railway could be blamed for Cooper's death. They eventually returned a verdict of 'accidental death'.

10 SEPTEMBER **1870** Horse slaughterer John Nash of Bilston boiled down horseflesh in an open, eighty-gallon boiler prior to sending it to London. On 10 September, the boiler was full of flesh that was in the process of being rendered down. The boiler house quickly filled with foul-smelling steam and James Whitehouse decided to open a window.

Although he had lost a leg and normally hobbled around on crutches, Whitehouse scrambled up and balanced precariously on the greasy brickwork surrounding the boiler, but as he opened the window, his foot slipped and he fell. His desperate screams brought Nash running to his assistance and with considerable difficulty Whitehouse was pulled from the boiler and taken to Wolverhampton Hospital. He was scalded from head to foot and later died from his injuries.

The General Hospital,
Wolverhampton.
(Author's collection)

11 SEPTEMBER   **1889**   Alice and Thomas Westwood of Cradley Heath appeared before magistrates charged with neglecting their children, Edith and John Thomas. Magistrates were told that the Westwood family lived in squalid lodgings. There was water running down the walls, barely any furniture and the stench was so bad that the policeman who arrested the Westwoods found it almost impossible to stay in the house without vomiting.

The couple were found guilty of neglect and sent to prison – Thomas for one month and Alice for three. The children were taken to the Workhouse until Thomas had served his gaol sentence, when they were discharged into his custody. By mid-December, both children were dead and at a special petty session, their parents were charged with causing the deaths of two-year-old Edith and twenty-month-old John Thomas, both of whom died in suspicious circumstances. The proceedings were adjourned so that post-mortem examinations could take place.

Edith was found to weigh less than a third of the normal weight for a child of her age and John was similarly emaciated, although doctors believed that he died from inflammation of the lungs. An inquest returned a verdict of 'death from natural causes' on John, but one of manslaughter against both of her parents in respect of Edith's death.

At their trial at the Stafford Assizes, Mr Justice Hawkins stated that the medical evidence suggested that Edith had died from starvation, even though her father was in constant work. Edith died on 14 December, only three days after her mother's release from prison, thus it was inappropriate to charge Alice with manslaughter, since Edith had been waning for some time. The child had been consumptive since birth and, as well as finding it difficult to accept starvation as the sole cause of Edith's death, the court seemed to think that, in spending a month in prison, Thomas Westwood had already been punished for neglect and so both parents were discharged without further penalty.

12 SEPTEMBER   **1887**   Forty-nine-year-old labourer John Reed appeared at Tipton Police Court charged with an aggravated assault on his landlady, Eliza Noch.

Reed had a deformed foot and, as well as walking with a stick, he also wore specially adapted boots. On the day of the assault, he came home in a temper because his foot was hurting, eventually taking off his boot and hurling it on the fire. When Mrs Noch spoke to him, he exploded into a rage, hitting her over the head with his stick and knocking her unconscious. The blow was so hard that, for a couple of days, her life was in danger.

Magistrates were unsympathetic to Reed's pain and suffering and sent him to prison for one month with hard labour.

13 SEPTEMBER **1878** John Fellowes died at Lower Gornal and at the subsequent inquest on his death, coroner Mr W.H. Phillips apologised profusely to the jury, who would have to view the body.

Seventy-two-year-old Fellowes died at his home, which was an 8ft by 12ft hut in the middle of a field. He shared the shack with his wife, Susannah, his daughter Eliza Jane, who was described as an imbecile, Eliza's illegitimate baby and a pet cat. The hut had no sanitary arrangements and the only water available for drinking and washing came from an open sewer nearby. The only furniture was a bed frame, which had no mattress or bedclothes, and an old bench outside.

The deceased rested in a parish coffin on the floor and was naked. When the sheet covering him was peeled back for the jury to see the body, his skin was absolutely black with filth. Such was the smell emanating from the hut that several of the jury and a policeman rushed outside to vomit.

The inquest returned a verdict that Fellowes had 'died from natural causes', after hearing that he had been unwell for some time with a bad cough and dropsy. He was paid only 4s a week parish relief to keep his entire family and, at the time of his death, had not eaten for three days. Mrs Fellowes sobbed at the inquest and refused to go into the Workhouse, saying that she would rather live in the fields. The coroner tried to persuade her that she and her family could be clean, well-fed and comfortable there but she was adamant, 'I won't flinch an inch' she insisted, telling the coroner that she would cut her own throat before going into the Workhouse to be 'clemmed to death' (starved).

14 SEPTEMBER **1855** At about 2 p.m., a fire broke out at Messrs Booth and Vickers naphtha and creosote works in Wolverhampton. Initially, there was an explosion, which sent a huge fireball into the air, followed by a ferocious blaze as the highly inflammable chemicals ignited. Liquids leaked into the canal adjacent to the factory, the surface of which burned for more than 20 yards.

The flames reached houses near to the works and two of the inhabitants – a pregnant woman and a four-year-old child – were burned to death. Other residents were also badly burned and were taken to South Staffordshire Hospital.

The fire claimed one further life, that of labourer Bernard (or Barnard) Maley, who was the only person in the yard at the time of the explosion. He was seen making desperate attempts to escape the conflagration and eventually sought refuge in a shed. A hole was made in the roof with a boat hook but before a ladder could be brought, Maley burned to death.

The inquest jury returned a verdict that 'Maley came to his death in consequence of burns from an explosion and that such explosion originated in the misconstruction of the naphtha still, although in what particular there does not appear sufficient evidence to show.' An identical verdict was returned on the woman and child who also perished.

Note: The woman and child who died appear to have an unusual surname, which is cited in the contemporary newspapers as Garratty, Garotti, Garrotty, Garraghty, Guraughty and Gerratt. The forenames are given as Mary, Christina and Sarah. It has proved impossible to establish which is correct.

15 SEPTEMBER

1895 A much-adjourned inquest into the death of fifty-five-year-old Catherine Hill concluded at Wolverhampton.

Catherine's entire family suffered from sickness, diarrhoea and severe abdominal pain, but while her husband and son recovered, Catherine died. It was suspected that she might have been poisoned and, when several more people experienced the same symptoms it was noted that they had all consumed soup made by the wife of Reverend J.W. Morrison, who regularly distributed it among her husband's poorer parishioners.

In the hot summer weather, Catherine's body putrefied very quickly and a post-mortem examination failed to determine a cause of death. There was known to be typhoid in the neighbourhood but Catherine's symptoms were not consistent with that disease. It was also pointed out that the conditions in which the Hill family and their neighbours lived were far from sanitary.

Mrs Morrison's cook told the inquest that the soup was made on 8 August from both cooked and uncooked meats. There was leftover beef, which was roasted four days earlier, boiled chicken and fresh mutton. Once cooked, it was placed on the scullery floor to cool before being given away.

Home Office Analyst Dr Arthur Pearson Luff analysed Catherine Hill's viscera and found small amounts of an alkaloid poison known as ptomaine, but couldn't say whether this had arisen from the putrefaction of the remains or if it was present in the soup. The families who had received the soup all found it perfectly palatable but Catherine had heated the soup so that it was 'just nice for eating', rather than boiling it.

On balance, the medical witnesses seemed to think that the soup had somehow become contaminated and that, had Mrs Hill boiled it rather than warming it, the heat would have killed any germs.

The inquest jury returned a verdict of death resulting from accidental poisoning.

16 SEPTEMBER

1870 Twenty-one-year-old James Alsop worked at the Wyrley Cannock Colliery near Walsall. He was described as being 'of irregular habits' and continuously tried the patience of his supervisor, chief engineer John Farnall, with his bad attitude to his work. Nevertheless, Farnall wasn't about to give up on his young protégé and had more than once talked the management into reinstating Alsop after he had been sacked for some misdemeanour.

On 16 September, Alsop finally pushed Farnall too far. He was late for work and when Farnall reprimanded him, Alsop responded with a stream of obscenities. Farnall boxed Alsop's ears and Alsop kicked him in retaliation. As Farnall went to hit the young man a second time, Alsop stepped back a pace, pulled a pistol from his pocket and fired.

The bullet struck Farnall just above his liver and he fell to the ground. Other workers rushed to help, but when Alsop threatened to shoot them too, he was allowed to escape.

A doctor and the police were called and PC Lindop set off in pursuit of Alsop. Lindop caught up with him two miles away but when he challenged Alsop to stop, the young man shot at him. Fortunately for the policeman, the contents of the pistol only grazed his coat and he was able to apprehend Alsop before he could reload.

When Farnall died in hospital the following morning, after having given a deposition, Alsop was charged with his wilful murder. He treated the whole business with the utmost levity, telling the police that the pistol was loaded with a small piece of lead when he shot Farnall and a few small stones when he shot at PC Lindop. Tried at the Stafford Assizes on 3 December, Alsop was found guilty of the lesser offence of manslaughter and sentenced to ten years' imprisonment.

17 SEPTEMBER 1887 William Parkes of West Bromwich died in hospital a month after being terribly burned in a fire at his home. Conscious and lucid almost to the end, he insisted that he did not know how the blaze started. However, earlier on the day of the fire, his wife Sarah was heard to threaten to set light to the bed, so that her husband couldn't sleep in it, and the jury at the inquest into his death returned a verdict of wilful murder against her.

On 17 August, William arrived home drunk. He swore at Sarah and tried to hit her and when she fled in fear, Parkes went out again, returning at 11 p.m. and asking for supper. When it was placed before him, he complained that it wasn't good enough and demanded something else.

Sarah said there was nothing else, at which Parkes flew into a rage and tried to throw a lighted paraffin lamp at her. Sarah told him to go to bed and he eventually went upstairs. Sarah followed him soon afterwards and told him that she had no intention of sleeping with him while he was in such a temper. Five minutes later, William's desperate cries roused the whole household, and lodgers George and Emma Harrison ran into Parkes' bedroom, to find his bed on fire. The Harrisons beat out the flames and took William downstairs, where they sat him in an armchair. PC William Smith was called into the house and bandaged the severe burns on William's arms, chest and thighs before taking him to hospital.

Sarah Parkes was tried at the Stafford Assizes in November, appearing before Mr Justice Hawkins. The prosecution maintained that, having

Mr Justice Hawkins. (Author's collection)

threatened her husband, Sarah set light to his bed and was obstructive when people tried to douse the flames. There was also half a pint of lamp oil missing from a bottle on the kitchen table.

Yet Parkes, who suffered from gout, often rubbed his legs with paraffin and he was a pipe smoker – his pipe and matches were found in his waistcoat pocket after the fire. He was also drunk when he went to bed, and the prosecution's case wasn't helped by the fact that PC Smith had made no notes. Mr Justice Hawkins suggested to the jury that it was possible that, in trying to throw the lamp at his wife, Parkes spilled paraffin on his own legs and that his wife's threats were simply 'the angry exclamation of one who has been brutally used.' In the face of the judge's remarks, Mr Lawrence declined to offer any further evidence for the prosecution and Sarah Parkes was acquitted and discharged.

18 SEPTEMBER   **1871**   An inquest was held on the death of thirteen-year-old Henry Jones from Wolverhampton.

Two days earlier, Henry's father asked him to take their horse back to its field. It was a job that Henry had done many times before and, as usual, he climbed onto the horse's bare back, with just a halter to control the animal. One of his friends, Edward Cotton, sat behind Henry.

Henry and Edward were given a leg up by another boy, who then slapped the horse's rump with his hand and shouted 'giddy up'. This made the horse start and both boys slipped off. Edward was uninjured but Henry fell onto the kerb and the horse trod on his abdomen. He died from his injuries the next day.

The horse was an exceptionally quiet, steady animal and the inquest jury ruled that Henry had suffered an 'accidental death'.

19 SEPTEMBER   **1835**   The *Staffordshire Advertiser* reported on two unrelated inquests held by coroner Henry Smith in the Tipton area. The first, on 11 September, concerned the death of Charles Palmer, whose age was not recorded. The second was held three days later at Ocker Hill into the death of eight-year-old Enoch Powell.

Both boys had died remarkably similar deaths after falling down open shafts of old pit workings, while running backwards trying to launch kites. Smith referred to the practice of leaving old pits open and unprotected as 'reprehensible and inhuman' and, although verdicts of 'accidental death' were returned at both inquests, he advised parents to warn their children about the inherent dangers of not looking where they were going.

20 SEPTEMBER   **1926**   Twenty-eight-year-old Edward Leatherland of West Bromwich arrived home at just after midnight. His brother Joseph was dozing on the sofa and Edward woke him to ask where their mother and father were. When Joseph told Edward that their parents were in bed asleep, Edward opened the door at the bottom of the stairs and shouted, 'Mother, I've done Sally in!'

Joseph quickly slammed the door shut and, noticing that his brother's shirt was heavily bloodstained, he asked Edward to take him to Sally. The brothers set off for an area known as 'Hilly Piece' but Edward suddenly changed his mind and instead went to the police station, where he asked the duty sergeant to handcuff him as he had just committed murder.

Sally was Sarah Brookes, the Leatherheads' neighbour, who was a war widow with three children. Lately, she and Edward had been courting, but when Edward found out that she had given him a venereal disease, he battered her to death with two beer bottles and a large piece of furnace cinder.

Tried at the Stafford Assizes on 15 November, Edward insisted that he had only meant to tell Sarah that she had infected him. According to Edward, she treated the news with total indifference and, believing that she had ruined his life, he took a razor out of his pocket, intending to cut his own throat. Sarah knocked the razor out of his hands, at which point Edward said that he 'lost his head' and began to hit her.

Edward's defence counsel tried to show that the venereal disease may have affected Edward's sanity but the prosecution argued that it hadn't stopped him from deciding to confront Sarah, nor had it prevented him from handing himself in to the police, which showed that he knew right from wrong at the time of the killing.

The jury eventually found Edward guilty of the lesser offence of manslaughter, a verdict the judge described as merciful, saying that it was the most wicked, cruel manslaughter he had ever encountered. He sentenced Leatherland to fifteen years' penal servitude.

21 SEPTEMBER

1885 Coroner Edwin Hooper held an inquest in West Bromwich into the death of two-year-old Thomas Henry Bateman.

The inquest heard that on 16 September, Thomas was with his mother in the wash-house. As Mrs Bateman walked to the door to empty a tub of water, Thomas somehow managed to climb onto the sink, from where he fell headfirst into a boiler half full of boiling water. He died in hospital from severe scalding the following day.

It was noted that the boiler was fixed much lower than normal and that it had no lid, and after recording the jury's verdict of 'accidental death', the coroner promised to write to the owner of the property, pointing out the advisability of rectifying these matters.

22 SEPTEMBER

1863 Benjamin Holding sent his wife to collect some potatoes. Mrs Holding thought her husband looked a little strange and something made her suggest taking their two children with her. However, Benjamin objected and, soon after his wife left the house, he murdered them. Neighbours heard screams and rushed into the house to find four-year-old Mary Jane and fourteen-month-old Joseph Benjamin with their throats cut, their heads almost severed from their bodies.

What was remarkable was that Holding was normally an affectionate husband and a devoted father to his children. He was respectable, religious, hard-working and teetotal, and the only motive anyone could suggest for the murders was a sudden mental aberration.

Throughout the inquest, magistrates' hearings and his trial at the Staffordshire Winter Assizes for two counts of wilful murder, Holding seemed barely able to comprehend what he had done. At his trial, his mother revealed that he suffered from the disease *tic douloureux*, which was characterised by excruciating facial pain and prevented him from sleeping. Mrs Holding also revealed a family history of insanity and at the end of the trial it took the jury just ten minutes of deliberation to find Holding not guilty due to insanity and for the judge to order him to be detained at Her Majesty's pleasure.

Note: Benjamin Holding is also alternatively referred to as Benjamin Holden and William Holding in various contemporary newspapers. His daughter is named as Mary Jane and Sarah Jane.

23 SEPTEMBER

1865 William Roberts was plagued by boys stealing damsons and apples from his orchard and, on 23 September, he caught Luke and Joseph Cunnif in the act. Roberts fired his gun, intending to frighten the boys, but unfortunately misjudged the distance.

Roberts appeared at the West Bromwich Police Court on 30 September charged with maliciously firing a gun at two boys aged twelve and fourteen. Surgeon William Hopkins told the court that both boys were still under his charge, having been completely riddled with shot on the back of their heads, shoulders and necks. Police Sergeant Passey produced the caps and jackets worn by the boys, which were peppered with holes.

In his defence, Roberts told the court, 'I had no intention of shooting them,' and promised to compensate the boys' parents if the charges against him were dropped.

'If you had no intention of shooting them then you wouldn't have shot them at all,' retorted the chief magistrate, sending Roberts for trial.

Roberts appeared at the Staffordshire Quarter Sessions in October 1865 charged with two counts of assault, occasioning actual bodily harm. Found guilty, he was sentenced to three months' imprisonment.

24 SEPTEMBER

1860 Several people saw Ann Williams carrying her six-week-old baby at Willenhall but nobody was in the slightest bit concerned about the baby's welfare. Seth was Ann's fourth child and she was known as a good, kind mother. However, Ann had suffered from depression for the past eighteen months and had also complained of violent pains in her head.

When Ann returned home, she was almost catatonic and there was no sign of Seth. After persistent questioning, Ann admitted that she had thrown her baby into the canal. The police were informed and started dragging the Birmingham Canal at the Walsall Bridge and, on 28 September, they recovered Seth's body.

A post-mortem examination showed that he had drowned and Ann was charged with wilful murder, appearing at the Stafford Assizes in December 1860. A doctor who saw her on 25 September told the court that she appeared 'heavy and melancholy' and 'practically unconscious' and added that, at the time, he believed she was insane.

In summing up the case for the jury, the judge urged them to be cautious about the defence's claims that Ann was insane when she threw her baby into the canal. He reminded them that there was absolutely no proof whatsoever that she had thrown or placed her baby in the canal, apart from her own statements, made at a time when she was described as 'practically unconscious'. The jury decided that they were not satisfied that Ann Williams purposely threw her baby into the canal and found her not guilty. She was discharged without penalty.

25 SEPTEMBER 1891 Five-year-old Joseph Shelley of Bilston was in bed when his mother heard him screaming. She rushed upstairs to find her son writhing in agony on the floor, having drunk from a bottle of liniment that had been left on the mantelpiece. Joseph was rushed to a doctor but died before surgeon Mr Kennedy could treat him.

At the inquest held by coroner Mr W.H. Phillips, Mr Kennedy stated that he had prescribed the liniment for the Shelleys' lodger. It contained aconite, which was a deadly poison.

Mrs Shelley said that she wasn't aware that the liniment was poisonous and, when it was pointed out to her that the word 'poison' was clearly written on the label, she tearfully admitted that she could neither read or write.

The inquest jury returned a verdict of 'accidental death', adding a recommendation that doctors should label their medicines with some distinctive character, so that it would be obvious to all that bottles contained poison.

26 SEPTEMBER 1858 Coroner Mr A.A. Fletcher held an inquest at Walsall into the death of sixteen-year-old Ann Careless, who lost her life in an accident in a chain making factory.

Samuel Taylor, who witnessed the accident, told the inquest that when Ann bent down to pick up a basket of buckles, her long skirt caught in some machinery and she was dragged into the mechanism. Although Taylor immediately raised the alarm and the machine was stopped, Ann's body was crushed and one arm and one leg were almost severed.

Taylor told the inquest that Ann was perfectly aware of the dangers of going too close to the machinery, adding that if she had exercised proper caution the accident would not have happened.

The inquest jury found a verdict of 'accidental death' but recommended that Messrs Mills & Son either introduced a guard around the machine or prohibited females from approaching it, to prevent future accidents.

27 SEPTEMBER 1855 For some time, Joseph Budd of Wednesbury had regularly been giving his wife Mary small sums of money, asking her to put it safe for him until 27 September. Earlier in the week, Joseph reminded Mary that he would need the money soon and she assured him that she had it ready for him. However, unbeknown to her husband, Mary had actually spent the money and had nothing left to give him.

In desperation, she tried to borrow the sum from her neighbours but without success. Too afraid to admit to Joseph that the money was gone,

Mary kissed her two oldest children and picked up her youngest, two-year-old Mary Ann. The next day she was found drowned in the canal, her little girl still clutched tightly in her arms.

28 SEPTEMBER 1861 During the night of 28/29 September, somebody broke into the Bilston home of pawnbroker John Bagott (or Baggot), who was reputed to keep large sums of money on the premises. The house was ransacked and Bagott was killed. His pockets were ripped from his clothes and an attempt had been made to set the house on fire. Medical evidence showed that he died from asphyxiation, after someone compressed his chest, while forcing his nose and mouth closed.

The burglars, one of whom was thought to be David Brandrick, were seen leaving the premises early in the morning of 29 September. Policeman John Harrison was sent to watch Brandrick's father's house and saw him return there at about 4 a.m., with William Jones and William Maddocks. One man threw down a bundle of clothes and, when Jones came back to retrieve them, Harrison arrested him and charged him with stealing the garments. 'You did not see me carrying them,' Jones protested.

On 28 September, Jones and several companions were drinking with Bagott at The King's Arms in Bilston and offered to escort Bagott home, since he was intoxicated. Several witnesses had seen Thomas Jukes, Samuel Bills and William Maddocks in the area around the time of the murder, and stated that Maddocks had a pistol in his hand. Jones was wearing corduroy trousers with dirty knees, and there were corduroy impressions in the dirt on Bagott's cellar floor. Footprints matching the boots of Jones and Jukes were found near to Bagott's home and a box of stamps known to have belonged to the victim was found in Jones's pocket.

Eventually, all of the drinkers were charged with wilful murder and William Jones, David Brandrick, William Maddocks, Thomas Jukes, Samuel Bell, Ezekiah Webb and Thomas Lilley were tried at the Stafford Assizes on 20 December.

Charges against Webb, Bell, Jukes and Lilley were dropped due to lack of evidence against them, but Jones, Brandrick and Maddocks were found guilty and sentenced to death. Brandrick alone faced the hangman on 4 January 1862, Jones and Maddocks having been reprieved. Brandrick was unaware of this until he reached the scaffold and immediately began to protest, 'Why me? Why have I got to die alone?' Executioner George Smith turned a deaf ear to his protests.

29 SEPTEMBER 1908 Twenty-four-year-old former soldier Joseph Dainty was found stumbling along a lane in Wordsley with a horrific gash in his throat. The police were called and, before being taken to hospital, Dainty made some rambling remarks, saying that 'she' was in the canal.

A search of the area produced a bloody knife and a letter on the canal banks, and, soon afterwards, the lifeless body of a young woman was pulled from the water. She was identified as twenty-two-year-old Annabella Carter Davis of Stourbridge.

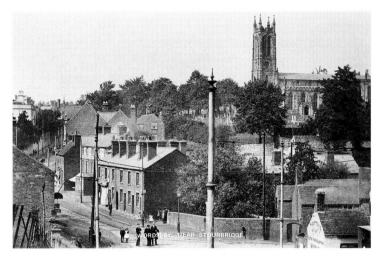

Wordsley, 1915.
(Author's collection)

An inquest was opened at the Stourbridge Workhouse and adjourned in the hope that Dainty would recover and be able to attend as a witness. When the proceedings finally closed on 16 December, the jury had heard that Dainty and the dead woman had been courting for eighteen months but, according to the letter found on the canal bank, had decided to end their lives in a suicide pact because her mother refused to permit them to marry.

The jury determined that Annabella had committed suicide and that she was sane at the time of her drowning. They also decided that Dainty was an accessory to her death and was thus guilty of wilful murder. He was committed for trial at the Staffordshire Assizes but acquitted.

30 SEPTEMBER **1859** Forty-six-year-old William Kilby and his son George lived in the same house in Wolverhampton. George had a workshop at the end of the garden and employed William Crump as an assistant wrench maker, while William had his own workshop a little further from the house.

Although George was a very religious man of exemplary character, he and his father didn't see eye to eye and George went out of his way to avoid him. On 30 September, George deliberately went for his lunch before his father, returning to his workshop at one o'clock and sending Crump for his break. George was heard singing at his work half an hour later but within minutes, the song was replaced by the sounds of two men quarrelling.

When Crump returned at two o'clock, he found George dead. His head was under a workbench, with his throat on the edge of a wooden box of iron filings, so that he lay face down in the box. George's hands were in his pocket, with a small amount of money clutched in one.

Crump raised the alarm and William Kilby rushed from the house to the workshop and began to cry when he saw his son. However, he was later charged with George's murder, when a witness told the coroner that he had seen him hurriedly leaving George's workshop about ten minutes before the body was found.

Mr Justice Willes. (Author's collection)

William Kilby appeared at the Staffordshire Assizes in December 1859. The prosecution pointed out that William was known to beat his son, and that whenever he did, George would deliberately put his hands in his pockets to stop himself from hitting his father back. Given that William had been seen leaving his son's workshop, the prosecution contended that he had beaten his son and knocked him down, before pressing his throat against the edge of the wooden box until he was asphyxiated. However, the two doctors who had performed the post-mortem examination pointed out that George may have just had a dizzy spell, accidentally falling and hitting his head and landing unconscious, with his throat on the box edge.

Since the witness who had seen William leaving the workshop was old, very deaf and somewhat confused in his testimony, and hearing that there was a possibility that George died a natural death, Mr Justice Willes asked the jury if they wished to hear any more evidence. The jury decided that they didn't and William Kilby was acquitted.

OCTOBER

Brierley Hill, 1910. (Author's collection)

1 OCTOBER

1855 William Russell of Bilston was awakened by screaming at 6 a.m. and, realising that his wife Ann was no longer in bed with him, he rushed next door to the bedroom shared by their four children. There he saw four-year-old Joseph with blood pumping from a wound in his throat and, as William entered the room, Ann drew a knife across her own throat and fell to the floor.

Surgeon Mr W.H. Hancox was quickly on the scene but Joseph bled to death. Ann, whose head was said to be almost severed from her body, was still alive, although she gesticulated that she wished to be allowed to die.

Ann lived for several days – long enough for an inquest into Joseph's death to return a verdict of wilful murder against her – but died without revealing why she had killed the boy.

She was said to have been a devoted mother, who sank into a deep depression when one of her children died a year earlier. Even so, she had never given anybody any cause to suppose that she posed a risk to her children and had recently seemed much improved. On the evening before killing Joseph, she attended church as normal and seemed in good spirits. It was supposed that she intended to murder all of the children but was prevented from doing so when Joseph's siblings awoke and began screaming.

2 OCTOBER

1930 An inquest was held at Tipton into the death of twenty-eight-year-old Daisy Irene Ball. Mrs Ball lived in a council house with her husband and had allowed large rent arrears to accumulate without his knowledge.

Eventually, the council decided to seize and sell the couple's furniture and had bills posted throughout the district advertising the sale. Realising that she could no longer keep her debts a secret, Mrs Ball wrote a letter to her husband informing him, 'I am a wicked woman,' and threw herself into the canal.

At the inquest on her death, the Coroner recorded a verdict of 'suicide while of unsound mind' and strongly criticised the council for not informing Mr Ball of the arrears, especially since he could quite easily have paid off the outstanding debt.

Dudley Road, Tipton, 1904. (Author's collection)

3 OCTOBER

1846 Twenty-five miners descended into the coal-pit near Lyttleton Hall, West Bromwich. As always, the pit manager tested the workings with a safety lamp for the presence of dangerous gas and, unusually, an accumulation was found.

The manager set the men to clearing the gas while he went to a different part of the coal seam and, within a few minutes, there was a terrible explosion. Those men in the vicinity of the pocket of gas were dreadfully burned and some parts of their bodies were literally roasted.

A skip bearing two men was descending into the pit at the time of the explosion and the rush of hot air carried the skip back up the shaft for several feet. The supporting rope became unhooked, plunging John Robinson and William Hadley 800ft to their deaths at the pit bottom.

Seventeen-year-old Joshua Cash was terribly burned in the explosion and died on 6 October. By that time, an inquest had already been held by coroner George Hinchcliffe on the deaths of Robinson and Hadley, at which the jury decided that there was no criminal negligence on the part of the pit managers and that the explosion which had claimed the men's lives was purely accidental. An inquest on Cash's death reached a similar conclusion. Six other men were badly burned in the incident but, at the time of the inquests, all were alive, although one was said to 'lie in a very dangerous state.'

4 OCTOBER

1858 Seven-year-old Charles Chance was playing in his garden at Stourbridge, when his father suddenly noticed that he had gone very quiet. He went to check on the boy and found him upside down in a tub containing about eighteen inches of water. His father immediately pulled Charles out but the boy was already dead and, although a doctor was sent for, nothing could bring him back to life.

The inquest suggested that Charles had leaned into the tub and, either accidentally or while trying to perform some acrobatic feat, his shoulders became wedged tight in the top, leaving him head down in the water and unable to get free.

South Road, Stourbridge.
(Author's collection)

5 OCTOBER

1864 Coroner Mr T.M. Phillips held an inquest into the death of three-year-old Walter Henry Gillis of Dudley Road, Wolverhampton.

The jury were told that, a few days earlier, a bottle of paraffin oil had broken and what remained of its contents were placed in a jug, which was then put in a cupboard. On 3 October, little Henry found the jug and took a long drink from it. He died within hours, after suffering from coughing and vomiting, followed by lethargy.

The coroner pointed out that the oil would have looked exactly like water to the little boy, and cautioned parents about the unsafe storage of such chemicals.

6 OCTOBER

1900 Henry Ledbrook walked into The Earl Grey public house in Walsall and called for a drink, before turning to Josiah Smith and William Adams and asking for a light.

Smith picked up a piece of paper and tried to light it at the fire but the flame wouldn't catch. Ledbrook complained that Smith wasn't quick enough, at which Smith threw the paper at him and told him to light it himself.

Ledbrook took his drink and went to sit at a table, and, soon afterwards, Smith and Adams left the premises. As they passed Ledbrook, Smith stopped. 'For old time's sake, I have had it in for you for a good while,' he told Ledbrook, punching him hard on his jaw, then again on his nose.

Ledbrook went to punch Smith back and missed. Adams told Smith, 'Out of the way, I'll soon polish him off.' He too took a swing at Ledbrook, who fell to his knees on the floor then rolled onto his back, turning blue in the face and dying within minutes. A post-mortem examination revealed that his neck had been dislocated and death was due to pressure of the displaced bone on his spinal cord.

Smith and Adams appeared before Mr Justice Lawrence at the Staffordshire Autumn Assizes, where both pleaded not guilty to manslaughter. Smith said that, as he left the pub, Ledbrook kicked him hard on the ankle, laughing when Smith asked him why he had done so. Smith swore that he had not threatened Ledbrook and had no quarrel with him. Adams also testified that he had neither struck nor threatened Ledbrook but had seen the deceased kicking Smith as he passed him.

The jury found both men guilty but recommended mercy on the grounds that the offence was not premeditated. Lawrence sentenced each man to twelve months' imprisonment with hard labour.

7 OCTOBER

1855 Young widow Mary McDonnell was discharged from Wolverhampton Union Workhouse with her fifteen-month-old child. She went straight to a disused coal pit, threw the child down a shaft and went off to look for work without a backward glance.

The following day, a young miner heard crying and, realising that the cries came from the pit, he volunteered to be let down by rope into the depths, from where he rescued the child, who was cold and ravenously hungry but miraculously unharmed. The child was taken to the Workhouse and was immediately recognised as Mary McDonnell's baby. The police began a search for her and she was found riddling ashes at Spring Vale Ironworks.

When questioned about her child, she first asked if it was alive or dead. Told that the baby had survived, she responded, 'The Lord forgive me, but I don't care if they'll let my mother have the child.' She admitted dropping the baby into the shaft, telling police that she had suckled it before kneeling at the edge of the pit, leaning as far as she could reach and letting the child drop.

Mary was charged with attempted murder and appeared at the Stafford Assizes on 1 December. Said to be of a sulky and petulant disposition, she showed no signs of mental derangement and could offer no explanation as to why she had thrown her child into what a policeman described as 'a most loathsome place, infested with venomous reptiles such as lizards and toads.' Found guilty, she was sentenced to two years' imprisonment.

8 OCTOBER

1895   William Evans had worked for shoe manufacturer Edward Allsop at Blackheath, Rowley Regis, for more than twenty years, apart from a brief period when Evans was committed to an asylum. However, Evans was released as cured and Allsop generously gave him his old job back.

On 8 October, Allsop had cause to criticise Evans's work. Evan's was furious, and when he met up with his employer on the street later that day, an argument began between them, which culminated in Allsop telling Evans that he was fired. In response, Evans flew at Allsop, biting off the end of his nose and also biting his thumb.

Evans was sent for trial at the Staffordshire Assizes, where he tried to persuade the jury that Allsop attacked him first and he acted only in self-defence. He was found guilty of unlawfully wounding without intent and sentenced to eighteen months' penal servitude with hard labour.

9 OCTOBER

1859   A group of youths spent the night of 8 October drinking in Sedgley. When the pub closed at midnight, they were reluctant to end their evening and go home. They had a whip round, each contributing 6*d* towards the cost of buying more beer, but were unable to find anywhere open. Eventually John Reynolds, who was holding the money, handed back all the contributions and the youths went their separate ways.

Seventeen-year-old Thomas Wilkes had not put any money into the kitty, having spent everything he had. Nevertheless, his workmate Beck had contributed and, since Beck was very drunk, Wilkes asked Reynolds to give him Beck's contribution for safekeeping. Reynolds refused but Wilkes was persistent, eventually holding out his hand to Reynolds and telling him that if Reynolds gave him a shilling, he would give him 6*d* change.

Reynolds put his hand in his pocket as if to fetch out a shilling, then laughingly handed Wilkes a piece of gun wadding. Wilkes was furious and told Reynolds that he wasn't about to be made a fool of. When Reynolds continued to refuse him, Wilkes raised his hand above his head and brought it down hard on Reynolds's breast. Nobody saw a knife in his hand but Reynolds dropped like a stone, dying almost instantly from a single stab wound to the heart.

An inquest returned a verdict of wilful murder against Wilkes, who was already in custody. On his arrest, he told PC James Fellows, 'It served him right and if I'd had an axe in my hand I would have cut the bastard's head off.'

When Wilkes came to trial at the Staffordshire Assizes, he pleaded not guilty, stating that he had only thrown a cinder at Reynolds, who might then have fallen on some workmen's tools that were lying by the roadside. The jury didn't believe Wilkes, especially since they had heard he was strongly attracted to Reynolds's girlfriend and was very jealous of him. Wilkes was found guilty of the lesser offence of manslaughter and was sentenced to ten years' penal servitude.

10 OCTOBER

1847   At just before 8 p.m., there was an explosion at St Matthew's Church, Walsall, causing around £1,000 worth of damage. The exquisite stained-glass windows were blown out, the ornamental plasterwork on the ceiling was badly damaged and the pews were, according to the contemporary newspapers, 'shivered to atoms.' More seriously, beadle James Lunn lost his life.

A few days earlier, the manager of the local gas works was notified about a strong smell of gas coming from beneath the floorboards. On investigation, it was found that the gas pipes had rusted but, according to the gas man, they were still sound enough to take ten times their normal working pressure. He removed the gas meter and took it away for repair, making sure that all of the connecting joints were perfectly safe.

The smell of gas permeated the church throughout the service on Sunday evening and Lunn went to try and find the source of the leak, taking with him a lighted candle. Fortunately, he waited until all the worshippers had left, otherwise the death toll would undoubtedly have been much higher.

The inquest jury returned a verdict of 'accidental death', adding a recommendation that 'scientific persons' should be employed to manage the gas in churches and chapels to prevent such catastrophes.

St Matthew's parish church, Walsall, 1904. (Author's collection)

11 OCTOBER

1886 William and Harriet Narrowmore of Wolverhampton were members of the Salvation Army. The couple had been married for three years, during which time Harriet's flighty behaviour drove William almost to distraction. She fought with members of his family, associated with other men and, more than once, her exasperated husband was heard to say that he would murder her one day. Yet in spite of the wretched life she led him, William loved Harriet far too much to harm her and wanted nothing more than to live happily with her.

Although the couple were officially separated, and Harriet had moved back to her mother's house, William was keen to reconcile and called for her on 11 October to see if she would go for a walk with him. In view of his previous threats towards Harriet, her sister Eliza followed the couple but eventually left them since they appeared to be getting on well together.

Harriet's body was found the next morning in the canal and an inquest returned a verdict of 'found drowned', finding that there was insufficient evidence to show how she came by her death. However, after his threats towards Harriet, magistrates committed William for trial for wilful murder at the next Staffordshire Assizes.

Although William initially denied having anything to do with Harriet's death, he made a full confession while he was in prison. He admitted to having pushed Harriet into the canal, although he was insistent that he had never intended to murder his wife and that his previous threats had been an attempt to frighten her into staying away from a man she was seeing. As they walked along the canal bank, Narrowmore asked Harriet to live with him again and, when she had refused and taunted him, he pushed her.

William Narrowmore was found guilty of wilful murder at the Assizes and sentenced to death. As he awaited his execution, a petition for clemency gained almost 10,000 signatures and his sentence commuted to one of life imprisonment, part of which Narrowmore served at Gillingham Prison.

12 OCTOBER

1859 Samuel Hawkins appeared at Wolverhampton Police Court charged with violently assaulting Sophia Bowen.

Both Hawkins and Sophia worked at The Cock and Cross Keys Inn, where he was a brewer and she a servant. On the previous afternoon, Hawkins called for half a pint of ale, which he wanted warming. However, when Sophia took it to him, he threw the ale in her face before smashing the tankard on her head. He then picked up a poker and hit her.

In his defence, Hawkins stated that he had been so drunk at the time that he couldn't remember hitting the servant. He described her as a lazy girl, who tried his patience by refusing to get up in the mornings. Sophia argued that the reason Hawkins had hit her was that she refused to allow him to rob their mistress.

The magistrates chose to believe Sophia's version and sentenced Hawkins to one month's imprisonment.

13 OCTOBER

1894 In response to concerns from neighbours, Inspector Hinde and Dr Higgs visited a house in Dudley. The following day, they returned to the property and removed a five-year-old child to the safety of the Workhouse.

Market Place, Dudley. (Author's collection)

The little girl was the illegitimate daughter of domestic servant Fanny Charlotte Mason. While she was at work in Wolverhampton, Fanny left her daughter with her stepmother, an old, terminally ill woman, who was totally incapable of caring for a child. The emaciated little girl weighed just 22lbs. and was covered from head to foot in scabs and running sores, caused by neglect and filth. Her eyes were completely closed by a skin disease and nobody was sure whether or not she could actually see.

Fanny was brought before magistrates at Dudley charged with ill-treating her child by neglecting it. She tried to argue that her stepmother refused to relinquish the child, calling her sister to corroborate her statement. However, the magistrates did not accept Fanny's explanation and sentenced her to six weeks' imprisonment with hard labour.

14 OCTOBER

1881 Between 13/14 October, the Black Country was particularly badly affected by gales that swept across most of England. At about 10 a.m. on 14 October, a chimney stack blew down in High Street, West Bromwich. The 130ft-high chimney crashed onto the carpenter's and chain workshops below, and Thomas Russell, William Horton and Thomas Atterbury were crushed by the falling masonry. (Another unnamed young man was supposedly buried in the ruins, and later reports of the incident state that four people died.)

At Darlaston, two furnace stacks were blown over, killing thirty-year-old Abraham Wood and seriously injuring two more men. When Wood's body was retrieved, it was reported that nearly every single one of his bones was broken.

15 OCTOBER

1861 Almost immediately after arriving at work at the West Bromwich Foundry, an engineer thought that he felt the earth moving slightly beneath his feet. He immediately suspected that the foundry was about to fall into a disused coal pit and ran for his life. No sooner had he left the engine house than the earth gave way beneath it, swallowing a steam engine and all of the machinery. All that was left of the foundry was the large boiler that was once attached to the engine, which was left teetering on the edge of the abyss.

By a miracle, the engineer was the only man on the premises at the time – had the catastrophe occurred during working hours, loss of life would have been inevitable.

16 OCTOBER

1846 A group of miners broke from their work underground at a pit between Oldbury and West Bromwich to eat their dinner. John Pearson was in charge of the horse that drew the filled skip along an underground railway to the bottom of the shaft. Before eating, he went off to make an adjustment to the rails, leaving the horse with the other miners. Pearson had barely left the group when there was a roof fall, which filled the place where the horse and men had been just seconds earlier, with solid coal. Pearson was so close that part of the coal fell on his leg but he sustained only minor injuries, as did butty Mr Foster, who was approaching the group from the opposite side to give the men some orders.

Hearing the noise, miners flocked to try to rescue the trapped men, and within fifteen minutes Daniel Moss was dug from the rubble, unconscious but still alive. He was taken to his home but died without regaining consciousness. It took almost three hours to dig out John Harvey, Thomas Harpwood and Benjamin Cashmore, all of whom were terribly mutilated and must have died instantly, as did the horse.

The area where the men died was believed to have been one of the safest in the pit and was where the miners chose to sit down and eat their meals. Fortunately, on this occasion, the other miners had not yet arrived, otherwise the death toll would have been considerably higher.

Coroner George Hinchcliffe held three separate inquests, all of which concluded that the pit was carefully worked, with an excellent safety record. The deaths were, therefore, the result of an accident, which human foresight could nether have predicted or prevented.

17 OCTOBER

1932 After the death of his wife, Jeremiah Hanbury of Brierley Hill, began a liaison with Jessie, the wife of his best friend James Charles 'Charlie' Payne. The affair continued for four years until Jessie found a new man and banned Jeremiah from visiting.

He was devastated and asked Charlie why he was no longer welcome at his home. When Charlie replied that it was Jessie's decision, Jeremiah hinted to his friend that she was having an affair, and when Charlie confronted Jessie, she admitted to being unfaithful with Jeremiah but told her husband that it was only once and that she was forced.

During her affair with Jeremiah, Jessie was the subject of police interest regarding an illegal abortion. On 3 October, Jeremiah sought out a police constable in the pub and told him that Jessie had aborted his child, complaining bitterly that she was no longer interested in him now that his money had run out. 'I will find you such a big job one of these days,' Jeremiah told the policeman. That day came on 17 October when, hurt, angry and exhausted through lack of sleep, Jeremiah marched down to Jessie's house, hit her twice over the head with a hammer and cut her throat, before cutting his own.

Covered in blood, he walked home, proudly telling everyone who asked that he had committed murder. After briefly speaking to his niece, he then left home again heading towards the police station but flagged down PC Kirkham, who was at the time cycling as fast as he could to Jessie's house in response to reports from her neighbours that she had been murdered.

After the wound in his throat was stitched, Jeremiah Hanbury recovered sufficiently to stand trial at the Birmingham Assizes on 8 December 1932. He was found guilty and sentenced to death, although he swore that he recalled absolute nothing about the murder.

Law Courts, Birmingham. (Author's collection)

Having failed to convince the jury that Hanbury was insane at the time of the killing, his defence counsel appealed the verdict, but the appeal was unsuccessful and forty-nine-year-old Hanbury was executed at Birmingham Prison on 2 February 1933.

18 OCTOBER

1859 Benjamin and Jane Owen kept The Cottage Spring public house in Wednesbury but the constant presence of alcohol proved too great a temptation for Jane, who became addicted to drink. Her intemperance was worsened by the company of some of her relatives and eventually Benjamin forbade her to see them. However, on returning from his day job as a gas fitter on 18 October, Benjamin discovered that not only was his wife drunk but the prohibited relatives, who Owen referred to as 'those thieves', had spent all day at his house.

Ben told his wife several times to go to bed but she refused. He walked out of the bar to try and calm down but when he returned, Jane was making such a drunken exhibition of herself that he hit her twice. The second blow knocked her down and Benjamin began beating and kicking Jane, who begged for mercy, before running to a neighbour's house to try

and escape her husband's fury. Benjamin followed her, continuing to kick and hit her until she finally died from her injuries.

An inquest into Jane Owen's death returned a verdict of manslaughter against her husband, although magistrates disagreed and ordered him to stand trial at the Staffordshire Assizes for wilful murder. When his trial came to the assizes in December 1859, the Grand Jury returned a bill for murder and it was for this offence that Owen was eventually tried.

Owen's defence counsel maintained that Jane's death was due to apoplexy resulting from excessive drinking and that consequently, her husband should not be facing any charges at all. However, the medical witnesses disagreed and the jury found Owen guilty of manslaughter.

It was the first time that Benjamin Owen had ever hit his wife, who had provoked him intolerably before he finally snapped. Numerous people – including the victim's own mother – gave him such glowing character references that the judge commented that he could hardly bear to sentence such an exemplar. However, the frequency of such ruffianly offences was increasing throughout the country and the judge, therefore, felt duty bound to pass a sentence that might act as a deterrent to others. He sentenced Owen to six years' penal servitude.

19 OCTOBER

1858   As sawyer John Morris walked along the canal towpath at Oldbury, he spotted something strange in the water. He fetched a boathook and guided the object to the bank, where it was found to be a man's body.

The corpse was that of fifty-year-old boatman Charles Thomas, who worked with Thomas Weobley on a boat belonging to a man from Ledbury. The boat was moored nearby but there was no sign of Weobley, whose body was eventually pulled from the canal about 10ft from the spot where Thomas was found.

Both men were drinking at The Cross Guns, Oldbury, on the previous night, leaving at about nine o'clock. The weather was terribly stormy and, at an inquest held by coroner Ralph Docker, it was suggested that the men slipped on the gangplank leading to the boat and fell into the canal. With little more to go on, the inquest jury returned two verdicts of 'found drowned'.

20 OCTOBER

1858   John Powis and John Beddington, of the Wesleyan and General Assurance Society, appeared at Wolverhampton Police Court charged with assaulting Mary Ann Allington on 13 October.

Mrs Allington had been separated from her husband for almost fifteen years when he died in the County Lunatic Asylum. At the time of his death, he had been cohabiting with another young woman and they had several children together, and, according to his will, his mistress inherited his life assurance and property.

When Mr Allington's paramour died, his estranged wife visited Powis at home to demand the proceeds of her husband's life assurance policy. According to Mrs Allington, Powis threw her out of his house and she was then struck by Beddington. Several witnesses were called for the defence, but the Bench decided that Mrs Allington had been assaulted by somebody and fined each of the defendants 1s plus costs.

21 OCTOBER

1893 Nineteen-year-old painter Jesse Burns was fixing guttering on some new buildings in Ryder's Green Road, West Bromwich. Carpenter William Mann wanted to give Burns some instructions about the job and so began to climb the ladder on which Burns was standing. When he reached the tenth rung, the ladder broke and Burns fell, hitting Mann and stunning him before crashing to the ground. Although a doctor was called, by the time he arrived, Burns was dead.

At the inquest on his death, coroner Edwin Hooper told the jury that it was obvious that the ladder broke because it was subjected to undue weight, and that the deceased had lost his life through Mann climbing a ladder meant for the use of one person at a time. He reprimanded Mann for his thoughtless conduct and refused to allow him any expenses for attending the inquest.

22 OCTOBER

1921 A concert was held at the Temperance Hall in Walsall and more than 700 people assembled to watch the show.

At about eight o'clock, singer Arthur Lane was performing when there was an ominous creaking sound and the concert hall ceiling suddenly collapsed. Fortunately, one of the large supporting wooden beams became lodged on the balcony but the audience in the main body of the hall were showered with chunks of plaster and broken timbers. The fall disrupted the electricity supply, leaving the hall in complete darkness.

The mainly female audience were buried under a mass of debris and were forced to crawl around in the dark, groping through clouds of choking dust, to try to find their way out of the hall. More than forty people were injured, seven of those seriously.

Mrs Elizabeth Drew of Walsall suffered a fractured skull and died in hospital at midnight. An inquest into her death concluded on 2 November with a verdict of 'accidental death', after extensive dry rot was discovered in the hall's roof timbers.

23 OCTOBER

1925 Bert Checketts was tried for wilful murder at the Worcester Assizes, where the main dilemma for the jury was deciding if he was sane at the time of the killing.

On 5 July, a man was seen walking round a brickyard in Lye absolutely saturated in blood. 'There's a woman down there who has cut her throat,' he told people, who came to see if he was all right.

A doctor was sent for, but although Dr H.C. Darby arrived quickly, he was too late to save twenty-two-year-old Alice Mary Rowley, who bled to death. Darby was quick to rule out suicide, saying that Alice had met with foul play, and that whoever had cut her throat to the backbone was strong and muscular.

The description fitted the blood-soaked man, Bert Checketts. Although Alice was Bert's stepsister, the two were not blood relatives and Bert was desperately in love with Alice, who spurned his advances. On the day before her death, Bert asked Alice to lend him sixpence, which she said she didn't have. Bert sulked all the next day, before taking a razor to Alice's throat.

Bert's parents had consulted a doctor because of 'certain revolting practices' that he had been engaging in. Various medical witnesses opined that Bert was 'feeble-minded', 'below average intelligence' and suffering from 'a malformation of the mind'. However, at his trial, the consensus of opinion was that Bert was mentally capable of knowing 'the quality and nature of his act', meaning that, in legal terms, he was sane. Found guilty, he was sentenced to death but his sentence was later commuted to detention in a mental hospital at His Majesty's pleasure.

24 OCTOBER

1837 George Hitchinson took his wife Elizabeth to Walsall Market, with the intention of selling her. Elizabeth was led into Walsall by a rope halter around her neck and waist and, within a few minutes, had been sold to Thomas Snape for the sum of *2s 6d.*

Walsall Market, 1961. (Author's collection)

It later emerged that Elizabeth and Snape had already been living together for three years, and that George believed that selling his wife before witnesses in a public market was the equivalent of a divorce and would free him from any liability for her future maintenance and support.

Legally, he was incorrect in his assumptions but, for the time being, all three parties were apparently well satisfied with the transaction.

25 OCTOBER

1864 Matilda Hackett was separated from her husband and lived in Rowley Regis, in a house shared by 'women of loose character'.

When Matilda's baby died, a rumour spread around the area that she had poisoned the infant. The police got to hear of the allegations and, realising that this was actually the fourth of Matilda's children to die in suspicious circumstances, they communicated their concerns to coroner Edwin Hooper, who ordered the exhumation of the baby's body for a post-mortem examination.

At the inquest on 25 October, surgeon Henry Duncalf detailed his findings. According to the doctor, the cause of death was exhaustion through want of food – there were no traces of poison found, but the baby had starved to death. Evidence given by other residents of Matilda's house suggested that the baby was usually filthy and neglected but that it had been eating voraciously until just before its death, when it declined rapidly.

Coroner Mr Hooper told the jury that there was insufficient evidence to commit Matilda for trial and the jury returned a verdict in accordance with the medical evidence, adding that they felt that Matilda was guilty of inhuman and disgraceful conduct. Hooper passed this sentiment on to Matilda, telling her that in future she would be very carefully watched to make sure that no more of her children died in a similar manner.

26 OCTOBER

1861 Coroner Edwin Hooper held an inquest at Tipton into the death of three-year-old James Harris.

James went out to play on 19 October and didn't return home. The area was searched extensively but there was no trace of him until several days later, when his body was found floating in a canal lock, about 100 yards from his home.

Market Place, Great Bridge, Tipton. (Author's collection)

The inquest returned a verdict of 'found drowned', supposing that the little boy had somehow slipped into the water and been unable to extricate himself. James came from a large family and was the third of his parents' children to drown in similar circumstances.

27 OCTOBER

1929 An inquest at West Bromwich returned an open verdict on the death of a man found on the railway line on 22 October.

The body had been identified as that of Oldbury boatman Joseph Chadwick, who had separated from his wife six months earlier. Mrs Chadwick, as well as four of Chadwick's relatives, identified the body and an inquest was arranged for 24 October but Mrs Chadwick began to have doubts. The matter was settled once and for all when Joseph himself turned up, having read about his supposed demise in the newspapers.

On 25 October, a Handsworth woman identified the body as that of her missing husband, Sidney Arthur Smith. Mrs Smith told police that she had received a letter from Sidney a few days earlier, in which he wrote that he was broken-hearted and threatened to commit suicide. However, that very night, police arrested Sidney Smith for drunkenness and causing a disturbance in Birmingham and his wife was taken to Birmingham City Police Court the next morning to confirm his identity yet again.

The true identity of the corpse was never established and his death was recorded as 'Unknown Male'.

28 OCTOBER

1860 George Murray was sitting peacefully by the fire at his Wolverhampton home when his son Thomas burst into the kitchen and told him to 'tumble out of the house'. Thomas then pushed his father violently, knocking him over and breaking his arm.

Mr Murray summoned his son for assault and told magistrates that this was not the first time that Thomas had attacked him but if magistrates could ban the youth from the house that would be punishment enough.

In his defence, Thomas told a completely different story. According to Thomas, his father came home drunk and began to abuse his wife, Thomas's mother. When the youth remonstrated with him, his father threatened the boy with violence and Thomas tried to put him out of the house, breaking his arm in the process.

Thomas's mother corroborated her son's version, telling magistrates that although her husband was the landlord of eighteen tenements, he neglected his family, preferring to spend his money on drink. Mrs Murray begged the magistrates not to ban her son from the house, saying that she needed the 9s a week that he paid as board to keep the rest of her family.

The magistrates chose to believe George Murray. Although they reprimanded him for neglecting his family, they fined Thomas 5s plus costs, and told him that had they not believed that the breaking of the arm was accidental, they would have committed him for trial.

29 OCTOBER

1857 Elizabeth Littlehales of Monmore Green, Wolverhampton, had a violent temper and, after an argument with her husband spilled out onto the street, she threw an iron poker at him. Witnesses were convinced that Elizabeth did not actually intend to hit him, since the poker landed at his feet.

Sadly, two-and-a-half-year-old Sarah Ann McCloud was sitting nearby on a doorstep when the poker rebounded off the road and smacked into her face. It hit her with such force that the sharp end pierced her nostril and went through the roof of her mouth and into her brain. The poker appeared stuck up Sarah's nose and, when well-meaning neighbours pulled it out, blood began to pour from the child's face. She was rushed to South Staffordshire Hospital, where surgeons stitched the wound, but the bleeding continued and Sarah ultimately bled to death.

An inquest held by coroner Mr T.M. Phillips returned a verdict of manslaughter against Elizabeth, who was committed for trial at the Staffordshire Assizes on 10 December. There were several eyewitnesses to the incident but their testimony at the trial differed from that given at the inquest, particularly with regard to the distance that the defendant threw the poker. Nevertheless, the jury needed only a short time to deliberate before finding Elizabeth Littlehales guilty of manslaughter. They did, however, add that they believed that, in one sense, Sarah's death was a tragic accident and, with that in mind, the judge sentenced Elizabeth fairly leniently to two months' imprisonment.

30 OCTOBER

1821 Coroner Henry Smith held an inquest into the death of six miners, killed by a roof fall at the Ebenezer Colliery near West Bromwich. James Nash, Thomas Lawton, John Cotterell, John Butler, John Hicks and Rowland Morris were buried alive by around 30 tons of coal and stone falling from the pit roof. All died instantly, apart from Morris, who was heard to call for help a couple of times before he too died. The men were extricated from beneath the rubble and their bodies taken to their homes to await the attentions of the coroner.

Verdicts of 'accidental death' were recorded on all of the deceased.

31 OCTOBER

1878 Twenty-four-year-old boatman James Musson worked the Stafford and Worcester canal, living as man and wife on his boat with twenty-one-year-old Ann Marie Hillman. The couple had a baby and when they mentioned to a fellow boatman in June 1878 that they were looking for help, he willingly handed over his seven-year-old daughter, to act as a nursemaid, in return for her board, lodging and clothing. Elizabeth Lowke, whose mother was dead, was then a plump, healthy child but, on 31 October 1878, she was found dead on Musson's boat, having apparently been beaten, starved and tortured.

A post-mortem examination disclosed a catalogue of horrific injuries, including two black eyes, along with open cuts and running sores on Elizabeth's shoulder, thighs, ribs, legs, arms, back and even on the soles of her feet. Elizabeth was emaciated and had serious head injuries, which were the main cause of her death, but she also had septic wounds on her back, from which the surgeon drained three-quarters of a pint of blood and pus.

Musson and Hillman explained the wounds by saying that the barge horse had accidentally trodden on Elizabeth. However, witnesses later stated that they had seen the child being beaten with a horse whip or having her head slammed into the cabin door, and that she had also been forced to stand outside naked at night because, according to Miss Hillman, she was 'uncleanly'.

First the coroner and then the magistrates wondered incredulously why nobody had intervened to protect Elizabeth. Her father stated that he had never seen any marks on his daughter except a black eye, which she said happened when she fell over. Everyone swore that Elizabeth had never complained of any ill-treatment.

Musson and Hillman were committed for trial at the Staffordshire Assizes charged with wilful murder. The jury decided that the couple probably hadn't intended to kill Elizabeth, finding them guilty of the lesser offence of manslaughter. The presiding judge seemed surprised at the verdict, commenting that had the jury found the defendants guilty of murder, he would have left them both for execution. As it was, he contented himself with sentencing each of the defendants to twenty years' penal servitude.

Note: There is a tremendous variation in the details, depending on which contemporary newspaper is reporting the case. Musson is also named as Mussom and his forename is given as James, Edward and Frederick. Miss Hillman is named as Hannah Maria, Maria, Annie, and Ann or Anne Marie.

NOVEMBER

West Bromwich, 1934. (Author's collection)

1 NOVEMBER

1869   Those who worked at the process of japanning at Messrs William Evans & Son in Wolverhampton usually cleaned the varnish off their hands with spirits of tar. This was also used as a thinner, hence a big barrel was kept in a basement storeroom.

On 1 November, four or five women and a boy were cleaning their hands when the tap fell out of the barrel. The storeroom was dark and, while the women tried to stem the flow of liquid with their hands, one went in search of a light. Unfortunately, she came back with a piece of lighted paper, which she dropped on the store room floor, causing a fireball. The women's clothes burst into flames and they ran around in a state of panic.

Labourer Edward Craddock had been trying to replace the tap in the barrel. He grabbed Martha Williams in a bear hug and put out the flames consuming her garments – he was later awarded a medal for his bravery. Sarah Harris (14) was also helped by Craddock, who smothered her burning clothes with a tarpaulin, before carrying her to a cab and sending her to hospital, where she later died. Eliza Harrington (17) was completely consumed by fire after tripping over her skirts and falling into the lake of burning spirits on the floor, while Henry Harding (15) took refuge in an adjoining store room but died of suffocation.

Coroner Mr W.H. Phillips opened an inquest into the deaths of Sarah Harris, Elizabeth Harrington and Henry Harding, and adjourned it for three weeks in the hope that some of those in hospital might recover sufficiently to give evidence. By the time the proceedings resumed on 26 November, a fourth victim had died. The inquest jury returned verdicts of 'accidental death' on all of the victims, recommending that more thought and care should be given to the safe storage of inflammable liquids.

Note: It has not proved possible to determine the name of the fourth victim of the fire, although it is believed that there were ultimately five deaths – the three above named and also Maria Farren (18) and Agnes Westwood (33).

2 NOVEMBER

1857   An inquest into the death of a nine-week-old baby concluded at Bilston with a verdict of wilful murder against the baby's mother, Ann Plant.

Ann, of Sedgley, had what was described as 'an improper intimacy' with a married man, which resulted in the birth of baby John. Disowned by her parents, Ann had no home and had to sleep wherever she could find room to lay her head.

On 22 October, she told friends that she was taking John to his father but later returned without the baby. When she was asked where the child was, she spun a tale of meeting a wealthy couple on the road to Wolverhampton, who approached her and said that they had just lost their baby. According to Ann, they asked if she would allow them to adopt John, promising to treat him as their own son, adding that he would never work nor want. The couple took Ann to their new house, which she related 'was carpeted most beautiful'.

Ann's friends didn't believe her and when they continued to question her, she broke down and admitted that she had put John in the canal near Wolverhampton. The police were informed and, when the baby's body was recovered, Ann pleaded, 'I did it from want. I had no home to go to,' and begged to be allowed to jump down a coal pit, saying that this would break her mother's heart.

At the close of the inquest, coroner Mr T.M. Phillips committed her for trial at the next Staffordshire Assizes. She was found guilty, although the jury added a recommendation for mercy in consideration of her distressing circumstances and, although sentenced to death, her sentence was later commuted to one of life imprisonment.

3 NOVEMBER

1924 Coroner Mr J.F. Addison held an inquest at Walsall into the death of James Thomas Marsh. Ten-year-old James tripped and fell in the playground at Croft Street School, banging his head. His teacher washed and cleaned the resultant small graze with iodine and James was able to continue playing, but after returning home that evening, he complained of feeling ill.

His condition worsened rapidly and on 31 October, his worried parents called a doctor. Sadly, by the time the doctor arrived, James was dead from tetanus, arising from the abrasion on his forehead.

At the conclusion of the inquest, Addison mentioned that this was the second fatality from the disease that he had dealt with that month, adding that, in his opinion the soil of Walsall was 'impregnated with the tetanus germ.' He therefore advised people to treat even the most minor injuries with great care.

4 NOVEMBER

1913 Martha Hodgkins shared her home in Wolverhampton with her son, Francis James Hodgkins, nephew Arthur Higgins and a lodger, Josiah Davies. In August 1913, Davies lost his job and was thus without a regular wage.

Davies began taking Martha a cup of tea in bed every morning until Francis asked him to stop, as it was disturbing his mother's rest. However, on 4 November, Francis and Arthur were surprised to find that Davies was up before them and had not only stoked the fire but had also made tea and breakfast.

When Arthur and Francis went to work, Davies and Martha were left alone in the house and, at 7 a.m., a neighbour thought she heard someone shout 'Murder!' Ann Doughty looked out of the window but could see nothing untoward and so went back to bed. Four hours later, she decided to pop next door for a gossip with Martha. Although the doors to the house were open, there was no sign of her until Mrs Doughty went upstairs, where she found her neighbour dead in bed, a silk scarf pulled tight around her neck and half a cup of cold tea under the bed.

The contents of Martha's purse were missing and it seemed obvious that someone had brought her a cup of tea and then strangled her for her money. Josiah Davies was the only person in the habit of taking her tea and, although he had last drawn his unemployment benefit three weeks earlier, he suddenly had the cash to spend in the local pubs.

The evidence against Davies was entirely circumstantial but while in prison awaiting trial for wilful murder, he made a full confession to a warder and the prison surgeon. He was tried at the Staffordshire Assizes in February 1914 and, having been found guilty, was hanged by John Ellis on 10 March.

5 NOVEMBER

1885 Having been separated from her husband for seven years Mary Ann Davies supported herself by working as a cleaner in St Luke's Church School, Wolverhampton. Her alcoholic husband refused to accept that their marriage was over and continued to threaten and harass his wife to try again.

On 5 November, John Davies went to the school where she was working and battered her with a poker. Leaving Mary Ann for dead, he went to the police house at Blakenhall and told PC Milburn, 'I have come to give myself up. I have finished her.'

There was already a warrant out for Davies's arrest for threatening his wife, so Milburn arrested him before going down to the school, where he found Mary Ann lying in a pool of blood. A doctor was on his way, but Mary Ann died from head injuries minutes after his arrival.

John Davies appeared before Mr Justice Wills at the Staffordshire Assizes on 18 February 1886, where he was found guilty of wilful murder and sentenced to death. His sentence was subsequently commuted to one of life imprisonment due to doubts about his sanity at the time of the offence.

6 NOVEMBER

1934 At the Staffordshire Assizes, fifty-seven-year-old Enoch Knowles pleaded guilty to sending obscene and menacing letters to women and was sent to prison for three years.

It emerged that Knowles had been writing poison pen letters for more than twenty-five years, without raising any suspicions. His victims included judges, members of the Royal family and witnesses in criminal trials, and police stated that they had been trying to find out who was behind the letters for years.

Knowles was caught when an eagle-eyed post office sorter spotted a postcard signed 'Enoch and Lizzie' and recognised the handwriting. The police traced Enoch and Lizzie to a council house in Darlaston and matched the handwriting of the anonymous letters to a tenancy agreement.

7 NOVEMBER

1908 Joseph and Charlotte Jones of Wolverhampton had been married for almost twenty years and seemed happy together. However, on 7 November 1908, the couple quarrelled and Joseph hit Charlotte, who immediately packed her bags and went home to her mother. She summoned her husband for assault and on 11 November, magistrates fined him £1.

The next day, Charlotte wanted to collect some things from her marital home so, choosing a time when she thought her husband would be out, she and her mother went to her former house on Merridale Street and Charlotte let herself in through the back door. Minutes later, a shot rang out, after which Joseph appeared at the door, his throat cut.

Charlotte lay dead in a bedroom – Jones was charged with her wilful murder, although he swore that he was innocent, claiming that Charlotte attacked him with a razor then shot herself. At his trial at the Staffordshire

Merridale Road,
Wolverhampton.
(Author's collection)

Assizes in March 1909, the jury found him guilty. Two important factors in reaching their verdict were the testimony of a pawnbroker, who stated that Joseph tried to buy a revolver from his shop on 9 November, and medical evidence that Charlotte's gunshot wound could not possibly have been self-inflicted.

Joseph's defence counsel appealed the verdict, after finding that the man who tried to purchase the revolver was definitely not Joseph Jones but a man named Edward Bailey. Jones had actually owned the gun for years, and the doctor who testified at the trial seemed to know very little about gunshot wounds. The defence produced a firearms expert who believed that the gun could easily have been fired by Charlotte.

The appeal failed, since the Lord Chief Justice saw no reason for Charlotte attempting to kill Joseph and argued that, had she done so, she would most probably have used the gun with which she supposedly committed suicide. Thirty-eight-year-old Joseph Edwin Jones was hanged by Henry Pierrepoint and John Ellis at Stafford Prison on 13 April 1909.

8 NOVEMBER

1890 Wolverhampton locksmith George Henry Smith appeared at the Police Court charged with neglecting his children Annie (11), Hannah (8) and Florrie (9 months). Smith had been married for twelve years and he and his wife had produced nine children, of whom the three girls were the only survivors.

The prosecution was brought by the local branch of the Society for the Prevention of Cruelty to Children and centred round the death of the Smiths' ninth child. Mr C.L. Adams, the Society's Secretary, told the court that he had visited the Smiths' home on Merridale Street on 29 September and found Mrs Smith sitting in a chair next to her dying child. Adams asked her what was being done for the baby and Mrs Smith didn't reply, simply pointing to her husband who had passed out drunk on the floor.

In court, she stated that her husband neglected his work, often not working at all for extended periods and, even when he was working, he refused to give her sufficient money to keep the family, preferring to spend his earnings on drink. When his child was dying, he accused her of a dalliance with a lodger and refused to give her any money at all, so that she was forced to beg what food she could from neighbours.

The magistrates told Smith that his conduct was 'disgraceful in the extreme' and sentenced him to three months' imprisonment with hard labour.

9 NOVEMBER

1929 As bricklayer Frank Hems was motorcycling from Stourport to Kingswinford, he met a cow being driven along the road from market. The headlamp on Frank's motorcycle dazzled the cow, which panicked and rushed blindly towards him, colliding with the motorbike. One of the cow's horns penetrated Frank's chest, severing a main artery and causing his almost instant death. (His pillion passenger escaped unhurt.)

Kingswinford, 1950s. (Author's collection)

The inquest jury returned a verdict of 'accidental death', with a recommendation that cattle on the road should always be led and followed by lights. The coroner promised to convey the recommendation to the authorities.

10 NOVEMBER

1865 An inquest was held by coroner Mr Brooke-Robinson into the death of nineteen-year-old Mary Davis, who was found dead in a stooped position on a dirt bank at High Lane Colliery, Dudley.

On 6 November, Mary went to the pit to collect odd bits of coal and, in bending over to pick it up, she apparently inhaled the noxious gases which sometimes rose from the ground when coal was fired below. Although medical assistance was quickly on hand, Mary was beyond all help and it was assumed that she must have died almost instantly.

11 NOVEMBER

1864 Eighteen-year-old Moses Parker appeared at the Wolverhampton Petty Sessions charged with assaulting fifteen-year-old Hephzibah Foster, who worked in his father's buckle factory in Darlaston. It was alleged that Parker had thrust a red hot spanner up beneath Hephzibah's dress and burned her thigh.

A surgeon told the court that Hephzibah had indeed suffered a burn on the top of her thigh, which was roughly the size of a hen's egg and was fortunately quite superficial. Parker's defence was that she had been standing on some steps close to where he was working and a red hot metal offcut had accidentally flown up her dress and burned her.

Parker produced a witness – a fellow workman – who corroborated his explanation but gave his evidence in such an unbelievable manner that he failed to convince magistrates that he was telling the truth.

Magistrates told Parker that they believed that he had committed a very brutal, very cruel and very indecent assault on Hephzibah and then compounded his offence by persuading someone to commit perjury. They toyed with the idea of forwarding Parker's case for trial at the assizes but decided that since the burn was not too serious, they would deal with it themselves, awarding the most severe punishment permitted. Parker was sentenced to six months' imprisonment with hard labour.

12 NOVEMBER

1831 Eighteen-year-old Jonas Woodall and nineteen-year-old John Poole worked for a chimney sweep and had charge of two younger boys, brothers Benjamin and Joseph Holmes.

On 12 November, the sweeps were asked to clean out a furnace flue at Blower's Green, Dudley. Benjamin was sent into the 2ft-diameter flue but found it unbearably hot and only managed to work for an hour before fainting. When he came round, he found that his brother had been sent up the flue in his place.

Having seen Benjamin faint, Joseph was terrified and repeatedly claimed that he was being burnt to death. Even so, Woodall and Poole insisted that he stayed where he was, swearing at him when he tried to come out and hitting his feet with a shovel to encourage him further up the flue.

When Joseph's sobs finally ceased, Benjamin and Woodall pulled him out barely alive. He survived for only a couple of minutes and a post-mortem examination showed burns on his back, chest and one elbow. The cause of death was suffocation – the inner surface of Joseph's windpipe was completely lined with soot, which had also collected under his tongue.

Woodall and Poole were charged with killing Joseph by compelling him to enter and remain in the flue. They appeared at the Worcestershire Assizes on 6 March 1832, but Mr Justice Littledale ruled that the defendants hadn't intended to kill the boy and, since the medical evidence showed that his death was due to suffocation from inhalation of soot and not from any foulness of the air, he didn't see how manslaughter could apply. The jury found both defendants 'not guilty'.

13 NOVEMBER

1894 On 13 November, twenty-one-month-old Abraham Jones of Willenhall was badly burned when a lamp exploded, dying at Wolverhampton Hospital seventeen days later. When deputy-coroner Mr J.M. Martin opened an inquest, Abraham's mother testified that her husband, who was also named Abraham, had been sitting in a rocking chair in the kitchen. When he stood up, he accidentally bumped the kitchen table, knocking over a lighted petroleum lamp and causing the glass reservoir to explode, showering their son with burning fuel.

However, Daniel Richards and Thomas Huffadine, who went into the house after the explosion, were adamant that Abraham Jones senior was proudly crowing, 'I've done it. I threw the lamp,' and saying he didn't care if they hanged him tomorrow.

Under questioning from the coroner, Mrs Jones admitted that her husband said those words but insisted that he was drunk at the time and didn't know what he was saying. She swore that she and her husband were not quarrelling and was positive that he hadn't thrown the lamp at her.

In the face of such contradictory testimonies, the coroner adjourned the inquest so that further enquiries could be made. When the proceedings reopened on 11 December, the doctors who performed the post-mortem dropped a bombshell. On his death, baby Abraham was suffering from a severe ear infection and the doctors were unable to determine whether it was that or the burns which had killed him.

The inquest jury returned a verdict that Abraham Jones died from disease of the ear accelerated by burns, adding that there was no evidence to show how the burns were occasioned. The obviously dissatisfied coroner had to content himself with heavily reprimanding the little boy's father.

14 NOVEMBER

1872   At about nine o'clock in the morning, desperate cries were heard from a shaft at Pelsall Hall Colliery, near Walsall. A cage was lowered and eleven men were pulled up but when the cage went down again, no more men scrambled on board. The mine had been inundated with a sudden influx of water, which rushed through the workings, sweeping all before it. Pumping began immediately to try and reduce the level of the water but it was six days before the first body was recovered, that of eighteen-year-old Thomas Starkey, who became jammed in the pump.

The final death toll stood at twenty-two: Charles Astbury (28), Frank Dilkes (27), Thomas Orcutt (30), George Baugh (39), John Heyward (38), John Quarter (45), Charles Capewell (89), Joseph Hollis (27), Tom Richards (30), Charles Cash (21), Thomas Hollis (28), John Roberts (14), Michael Cash (48), John Hubbard (17), John Starkey (26), George Cassel (28), Richard Hyde (28), Thomas Starkey (18), Thomas Coleman (14), Stephen Lawton (13), Thomas Starkey (70) and Edward Williams (48). Those miners who didn't drown were killed by chokedamp gas and their corpses were laid out in a room at the back of The Station Inn. (One body, believed to be that of Stephen Lawton, was never recovered.)

The dead were commemorated by a granite memorial in Pelsall churchyard. It was fortuitous that, when the disaster occurred, twenty men had just come to the surface for breakfast, otherwise the number of fatalities would have undoubtedly been higher.

15 NOVEMBER

1923   Thirty-three-year-old gardener John Samuel Totby appeared at the Staffordshire Assizes charged with demanding money with menaces at Walsall.

The court was told that Totby wrote to a relieving officer demanding £200 and threatening 'you and yours will die' unless the money was forthcoming, claiming to have formed a Klu Klux Klan gang to carry out the murders.

After a prison doctor testified that Totby suffered from delusions and had written threatening letters to numerous recipients, including the Home Secretary, the jury found him guilty but insane. The judge ordered him to be detained at the King's pleasure and, as he left the dock, Totby threatened him, 'I'll have you shot.'

16 NOVEMBER

1886 Abraham Earp appeared at the Police Court in Wednesbury charged with being drunk in charge of a tramcar.

Magistrates heard that on 13 November, Earp was returning his tramcar to the South Staffordshire and Birmingham District Tramways depot at Darlaston, when he drove it 'with great force' down a slope and collided with a car attached to another engine, doing £69 worth of damage. The consequences might have been fatal had the conductor been standing on the platform at the time.

Earp was found to be intoxicated and was handed over to the police, although he was allowed bail. He explained his drunkenness by saying that he had accidentally missed his tea break and, being thirsty, purchased half a pint of ale. Not being in the habit of drinking, the alcohol affected him badly.

Earp pleaded with the Bench for leniency, promising never to drink again. In view of his previous good character and the fact that he had been dismissed from his job, a fine of 20s plus costs was agreed, or one month's imprisonment with hard labour in default.

17 NOVEMBER

1927 The coroner for West Bromwich was scathing in his condemnation of the A4123 – the new arterial road between Birmingham and Wolverhampton – as 'a death trap.'

The twelve mile stretch of road was one of the first ever to be constructed specifically for the use of motor traffic and, after three years of construction work, was opened on 2 November 1927 by the then Prince of Wales, later King Edward VIII.

Two weeks later, there had already been a number of fatal accidents, two of which were on the Oldbury section. According to the coroner, the road encouraged fast driving but the planners had made no provision for pedestrians and, in combination with speeding drivers, this was causing carnage.

Despite multiple improvements over the years, the road remains an accident black spot.

HRH the Prince of Wales. (Author's collection)

18 NOVEMBER

1887   Coroner Mr E. Percy Jobson held an inquest at Guest Hospital, Dudley, into the death of sixteen-year-old Rose Smith.

Rose was a domestic servant who worked for Mr and Mrs George F. Thompson of London Fields, Dudley. As Rose and another servant were dusting a bedroom, Rose spotted a large cobweb over the mantelpiece, near a wall-mounted bracket.

Guest Hospital,
Dudley, 1905.
(Author's collection)

She pointed the cobweb out to the other maid, who, without looking, told her to 'knock it off'. Rose took a swipe at the cobweb with the hand brush she was holding and knocked down an ornament, behind which was propped a revolver.

As the revolver hit the floor there was a loud bang and Rose fell, mortally wounded. A post-mortem examination found that she had been shot once in the abdomen, the bullet travelling to her spine before moving through her body in a downwards direction.

The inquest jury returned a verdict of 'death from misadventure'.

19 NOVEMBER

1892   Fifteen-year-old Richard Jukes was employed to assist Mr D. Howard to construct a gasholder at the West Bromwich Corporation Gasworks.

It was Richard's job to heat the rivets and carry them to Howard. In order to do so, he had to walk along a plank and step across a small gap onto some brickwork. Witnesses would later say that the plank was quite steady and that Richard was not being hurried but that, as he took the step, he somehow fell though the 18-inch gap between plank and bricks, plummeting 31ft to the ground.

He was rushed to the West Bromwich District Hospital but died on the way there from a fractured skull. The inquest jury returned a verdict of 'accidental death'.

20 NOVEMBER

1857   At Messrs Motteram and Deeley in Tipton, a large cylindrical boiler – weighing between eight and 9 tons – needed to be moved. In order to do this, chains were wrapped around the boiler and horses attached to the chains to pull it to its final location.

After the boiler had travelled about 150 yards it had to be turned. A number of workmen put their backs against the boiler to lift it so that a prop could be put underneath. Somehow, George Lester had managed to get a little further beneath the boiler than his companions and, when it was lowered, it fell onto the lower half of his body, crushing him from the waist downwards.

Although medical assistance was quickly sought, Lester's condition was hopeless. Even so, he lingered for three days before dying, and was conscious and lucid almost throughout.

From Lester's statements, as well as the testimony of eyewitnesses, the coroner deduced that nobody was to blame for the tragedy other than Lester himself, who had no business venturing as far under the boiler as he did. The inquest jury returned a verdict of 'accidental death'.

21 NOVEMBER

1860 As thirty-year-old Elizabeth Lewis was scrubbing a floor in the house in Wallbrook which she shared with her husband, the couple's lodger crept into the room and propositioned her. When Elizabeth rejected his improper advances, John Stephenson began to slash at her with a cut-throat razor, severely lacerating her hands, the back of her neck and her throat, before cutting his own throat.

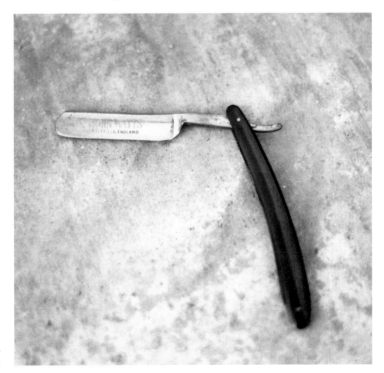

A cut-throat razor.
(© R. Sly)

Elizabeth Lewis had a severed windpipe and was not expected to survive. Nevertheless, under the skilful care of surgeon Mr Smith, she slowly recovered. By the New Year, she could talk and eat solid food again and was amusing herself by sewing. However, she grew bored with being confined to her bed and on 6 January 1861, against Mr Smith's orders, she persuaded her husband to take her downstairs for a little while.

Sadly, she caught a cold and within two days bronchitis set in and she died on 23 January. Mr Smith conducted a post-mortem examination and was of the opinion that the primary cause of death was the wound in her throat, inflicted by Stephenson. At an inquest held by deputy coroner Mr W.H. Phillips, the jury returned a verdict of wilful murder against Stephenson, almost two months after one of suicide was returned in respect of his own demise.

22 NOVEMBER

1874 Wolverhampton grocer William Nendick died in hospital, six days after being attacked in his home by two men. Shortly before his death, the borough magistrate was summoned to take his deposition but failed because Nendick refused to acknowledge that he was dying. Instead, he implored the policeman standing guard by his bed to hunt 'every court and alley' to find his attackers.

An inquest concluded on 8 December with a verdict of 'wilful murder by person or persons unknown'. At that time, the police already had two men in custody for Nendick's murder, Richard Hickson and Edward Carter.

It was said that Hickson had been overcome by guilt and had confessed to somebody in the pub on 24 November. When arrested, Hickson initially said, 'I hope the Lord will have mercy on my soul.' However, when he was formally charged with Nendick's murder, Hickson insisted that the police had made a mistake and that he knew nothing about it. The second person in custody was Edward Carter, who lodged with Hickson. Carter had fashioned the murder weapon by sharpening an old file into a dagger, although he swore he had never used it.

When the two men were brought before magistrates, more than one witness thought that they had seen Hickson and Carter close to Nendick's premises, shortly after the grocer was attacked. One witness, Cornelius Gorton, actually heard Nendick shouting 'Murder!' and saw a man climbing out through the grocer's window. Gorton gave chase and would have caught the man had he not become tangled in wire netting – he identified Hickson to the police by his 'shambling gait'.

However, magistrates found insufficient evidence against either Hickson or Carter to send them for trial and both were released. Nendick's murder has remained unsolved, in spite of a £100 reward offered for the detection of his killer(s).

23 NOVEMBER

1866 Coroner Edwin Hooper held an inquest at Wednesbury into the death of five-year-old Samuel Kendrick Cattell.

Samuel drowned after falling into an unfenced stream, which ran through land belonging to a Mr Elwell. Mr Hooper clearly recalled holding an inquest in 1865 on another child who drowned in the same stream, at which the jury recommended that a fence should be put along the side of the stream facing some houses. Hooper communicated the jury's recommendations in a letter to Elwell and, having not received a reply, assumed that his suggestions had been acted on. Now, he was surprised and grieved to find that they had not, stating that had they been, a child's life would have been spared.

The inquest jury returned an open verdict, asking Hooper to write to Elwell again. Hooper agreed to do so, adding that if his recommendations were not followed this time he would take stronger steps.

The child who drowned in 1865 was Samuel's sister, Eliza Ann Cattell, who died aged two years and nine months.

24 NOVEMBER

1920 As PCs Taylor and Lewis patrolled their beat in Walsall they heard a man and woman quarrelling above a shop in Lower Bridge Street. A couple of hours later, the policemen were in the area again and heard a crash followed by a heavy thud coming from the rear of the building. When they checked, they found Sidney William Derry lying semi-conscious in the yard, having jumped from an attic window and bounced off a shed roof. He had a deep cut on his throat.

The constables sent for a doctor, who dispatched Derry to Walsall General Hospital. Strangely, nobody in the living quarters above Sidney's barbers and tobacconist's shop had stirred during the commotion and, unable to rouse Derry's wife, the policemen forced an entry.

They were immediately struck by a strong smell of gas permeating the property and, when they reached the bedrooms, were horrified to find Derry's wife and two daughters with gunshot wounds and their throats cut. Thirty-one-year-old Emma and three-year-old Gwendoline Annie were dead but six-year-old Irene Clara was still alive, although she died on 6 December. Meanwhile, her father clung to life and was able to attend the adjourned inquest on 3 January 1921, where he sat staring blankly ahead as the horrific details of the deaths of his wife and daughters were discussed.

The inquest reached three verdicts of wilful murder against Derry and he was discharged from hospital to Winson Green Prison in Birmingham. On 12 February, he appeared at the Staffordshire Assizes charged with three counts of murder and one of attempted suicide, but as he stood in dock, it was obvious that his mental state had deteriorated. He was found guilty but insane and ordered to be confined as a criminal lunatic until His Majesty's pleasure be known. He is believed to have died in 1949.

25 NOVEMBER

1864 At the colliery owned by Messrs Yardley and Roberts at Darlaston, the clerk of the works happened to walk past the engine house and realised that the steam engine wasn't running. He went to see why and found twenty-seven-year-old engineer William Bate trapped in the workings of the engine.

It was quickly thrown into reverse but when Bate was extricated from the machinery his heart had been completely torn out of his body by the crank.

An inquest later recorded that Bate suffered an accidental death by coming into contact with the crank of a steam engine. He left a wife and two young children.

26 NOVEMBER

1900 In West Bromwich, Rebecca Coleyshaw was late returning home, so her mother sent her younger sister Matilda to look for her. However, when Rebecca arrived back, she was alone and told her mother that she had not seen Matilda. The next person to see the nine-year-old was a farm bailiff, who found her body in a field the next day.

A post-mortem examination concluded that Matilda died from suffocation, having been violently raped. During house-to-house enquiries, police were informed that twenty-eight-year-old Joseph Lowe was out late on the night of her disappearance, returning home from the pub wet and muddy. His mother-in-law saw him trying to clean his trousers and became suspicious. She surreptitiously examined his wet jacket, finding spots of blood on the sleeves, and when she challenged Joseph, he told her that he had slaughtered a duck a few days earlier. Lowe's mother-in-law revealed her suspicions to the police, who found more blood on his shirt and a bloody handkerchief in a jacket pocket. Lowe was arrested and charged with Matilda's murder, although he denied even having seen her.

Mr Justice Phillimore. (Author's collection)

When Lowe appeared before Mr Justice Phillimore at the Stafford Assizes in March 1901, the evidence against him was circumstantial. Three people had seen Matilda with a man, and others had seen Lowe in the area at around the same time – nobody could place them together. A physical examination after Lowe's arrest showed no signs that he had recently engaged in violent intercourse with a child and after analysis, Dr Alfred Bostock Hill, the Professor of Chemistry and Toxicology at Queen's College, Birmingham, was unable to identify the stains on the handkerchief and Lowe's waistcoat, although the small spots on his shirt and jacket sleeves tested positive as blood.

The crux of the prosecution's case was that it took Lowe three-quarters of an hour to walk the short distance home from the pub. Lowe's defence team insisted that he had passed much of that time talking to friends, but they believed that they parted from Lowe at 11.15 p.m. and he didn't arrive arrived home until 11.58 p.m.

The jury found Lowe guilty and Mr Justice Phillimore passed the mandatory death sentence, advising Lowe to hold out no hope for a reprieve. However, on 2 April, it was announced that Lowe's death sentence had been commuted to one of life imprisonment.

27 NOVEMBER

1894   Fifty-eight-year-old Samuel Cooper was working in a clay pit in Dudley. As he swung his pick, the head became embedded in the sides of the pit and refused to budge.

Cooper tugged at his pick, which suddenly freed itself, sending him tumbling backwards. He fell 7ft and sustained a broken rib and two slight scalp wounds. None of the injuries should have proved fatal, but it hurt Cooper so much to breathe that he developed bronchitis, to which he succumbed on 10 December.

At an inquest held by coroner Mr Jobson, Dr Griffiths, who had treated Cooper since the day of his accident, stated that the cause of death was bronchitis but that the bronchitis was a direct consequence of his fall. The jury returned a verdict of 'accidental death'.

28 NOVEMBER

1860   At Bull Pleck Coal Pit near Wolverhampton, engineer Joseph Newill went down the shaft to attach a new bucket on a pump. To save time, he wrapped a chain around his waist and secured the ends to the draw chain, by which material was lowered and raised to and from the workings.

Newill had barely begun his descent into the pit when the two chains parted company. About halfway down the shaft, Enoch Mason was working on scaffolding and Newill hit the scaffold boards so hard that the platform on which Mason was standing disintegrated. Both men crashed to the bottom of the pit, narrowly missing miner William Francis, who had heard something falling and stepped back out of the way. Both Newill and Mason were terribly mutilated and died before medical help could be summoned.

29 NOVEMBER

1861   Twenty-year-old boatman William Edwards appeared before magistrates at Wolverhampton charged with an aggravated indecent assault on a respectable young woman named Elizabeth Hodnett.

The assault occurred when Edwards was leading a horse along the canal towpath and was witnessed by David Hordern, who was aboard the boat that the horse was pulling. Although Hordern didn't leave the boat, he watched the assault and shouted encouragement and instructions to Edwards throughout. Magistrates therefore determined that he was an accomplice.

Found guilty, Edwards was fined £10 plus costs or three months' imprisonment, while Hordern was fined £3 plus costs or six weeks' imprisonment.

30 NOVEMBER

1893   At Messrs James Wright & Co. Bottle Works at Brierley Hill, one of the furnaces used to heat the glass developed a slight leak. Normally, water was sprayed on leaks until the molten glass solidified and sealed them, but as labourers played a hose on this one, a firebrick slab in the furnace fell out, releasing 30 tons of molten glass.

Charles Pearson escaped with his life, although he was severely burned. Brothers Elijah and Sylvanus Grainger were also burned, as was a man named Thompson. However, Albert Ryder (or Rider) and Enoch Oliver died instantly and their charred remains – recovered several hours later – were barely recognisable as having once been human.

Deputy-coroner Mr A.B. Smith held an inquest where it was determined that the firebrick slipping out was a complete accident, which couldn't possibly have been foreseen or prevented. Thus, verdicts of 'accidental death' were recorded on both Ryder and Oliver. Ryder's brother, William, was working alongside him until seconds before the accident, when he stepped out for some fresh air. He heard a thunderous noise and turned to see the firebrick falling and the resulting flood of molten glass. William managed to outrun the lava-like flow, although he suffered burns and scalds and was choked by the sulphurous fumes.

Note: Some contemporary accounts state that the men were entombed in molten metal rather than glass.

DECEMBER

Wolverhampton from the West Park, 1910. (Author's collection)

1 DECEMBER

1906 Ethel Clarke went shopping, leaving her husband Edmund dozing at their home in Quarry Bank. When she returned, she was unable to open her front door until her father, who lived with the couple, opened it from the inside. Edmund was still stretched out on the sofa, but now his head was bleeding.

Mr Justice Walton. (Author's collection)

'Father, what have you done?' Ethel asked.

'He started on me,' Joseph Jones replied, before leaving the house in search of a policeman and, on finding one, demanding to be arrested for 'knocking Edmund's head in with a poker.'

Edmund had been hit on the head several times and his throat cut with a razor and, when he died, his father-in-law was charged with wilful murder. According to his daughter, Jones was addicted to drink. The house that the Clarkes shared with Jones used to be his but, having got into money difficulties, he signed it over to his son-in-law in 1905.

Sixty-year-old Joseph was tried at the Staffordshire Assizes before Mr Justice Walton. The victim was portrayed as a happily married family man, a Sunday school teacher and someone of high moral character but according to Jones he was a bully, who was not above using his fists on his wife and father-in-law. Although Jones swore that he was acting in self-defence, the house showed no signs of a struggle, and the prosecution contended that Jones had simply hit Edmund as he lay snoozing on the sofa.

The jury found Jones guilty and although they tempered their verdict with a recommendation of mercy, he was hanged by Henry Pierrepoint and William Willis at Stafford Gaol on 26 March 1907.

2 DECEMBER

1858 When Eliza Slater broke off her long-term relationship with Elijah Knowles, he visited her at the nail-making shop where she worked and asked if she 'was in the same temper she always was'. When Eliza confirmed that her feelings towards him hadn't changed, Knowles threatened, 'If you won't have me, I'll make you so as no-one else shall.'

On 2 December, Eliza spotted Knowles outside the nail shop with something that looked like a gun in his hand. The door was pushed ajar and she saw a sudden flash and heard a bang. Eliza fainted from terror and, although physically unhurt, she remained almost senseless for three days.

Knowles appeared before magistrates at the Court House in Wordsley with a man named Enoch Partridge, who was suspected of being involved in the shooting. Although Partridge was discharged due to lack of evidence, two people apart from Eliza swore that they saw Knowles firing the gun round the workshop door and, when arrested, his boots were a perfect match to footprints found nearby. Hence he was committed for trial at Staffordshire Assizes charged with maliciously shooting, with intent to kill and murder.

His trial took place on 10 March 1859 and produced a shock result. After several witnesses had provided Knowles with an alibi by swearing that he was at home on the day in question, Enoch Partridge suddenly stood up in court and confessed that it was he who fired the gun. The jury had no choice other than to discharge Knowles and there is nothing to suggest that Partridge was ever tried for the shooting.

3 DECEMBER

1863 A ferocious gale was blowing in the Lower Gornal area when, at around midday, two ten-year-old girls walked along the canal close to Foster's Works. Suddenly, the wind blew one of them into the canal.

Sarah Fellows screamed desperately for help as she watched her friend, Honor Bennett, struggling in the water but her cries were lost to the howling of the wind. By the time someone heard Sarah shouting, Honor had sunk beneath the surface of the water and drowned. An inquest later held by coroner Mr T.M. Phillips returned a verdict of 'accidental death'.

4 DECEMBER

1895 Coroner Mr E. Thorneycroft held an inquest at Springfield, Wolverhampton, on the death of four-year-old Thomas Henry Roberts.

On 1 December, Mrs Roberts left Thomas and his younger brother locked in the house together while she popped out for a few groceries.

Within minutes, neighbours heard terrible screaming and, on breaking down the door, found Thomas with his clothes on fire. The flames were extinguished and Thomas was taken to hospital, where he died later that day. On the journey to hospital, the little boy kept repeating, 'Sammy done it,' and when the parents questioned two-and-a-half-year-old Samuel, he cheerfully admitted to deliberately setting his brother on fire. The inquest jury returned a verdict of 'accidental death'.

5 DECEMBER

1860 Seventeen-year-old William Startin appeared at the Staffordshire Assizes charged with manslaughter.

Startin worked for a Darlaston carpetbag manufacturer, whose workshop was laid out over two storeys, with a ladder leading to a trapdoor connecting the two floors. A 40lb block of iron was used in the manufacturing process and Startin had taken it to the upper storey. Wanting to get it back downstairs, he pushed it through the trapdoor without first checking that it was clear below. Sadly, thirteen-year-old Stephen Thomas was walking up the ladder at the time and the weight fractured his skull.

The judge pointed out to the jury that, if Startin caused the boy's death as a consequence of negligence, he was guilty of manslaughter and therefore the jury must decide whether he had thrown the iron downstairs in such a manner as to endanger life and limb. The jury found him not guilty.

6 DECEMBER

1857 Schoolmaster Mr Horton appeared at Wolverhampton Police Court charged with cruelly beating a four-year-old boy.

The child's father stated that his son attended St Peter's Infants' School, Wolverhampton, and on one day the previous week, returned home very late for his lunch.

When the boy got home he was hoarse with crying. He had a black eye, a bruise on the top of his head and cuts behind one ear and on his right cheek, as well as cane marks across his shoulders.

A school class. (Author's collection)

Magistrates heard from two assistant teachers, who related that the boy was 'obstinate', refusing to answer a simple sum or write on his slate. The assistants and Horton all argued that the boy deserved his punishment, adding that the only reason for the marks on his face was that he wouldn't stand still while he was being caned, leading to his face being accidentally hit.

The magistrates recognised the need to maintain discipline but agreed that in this case, more severity than necessary had been used. They told Horton that using a birch rod rather than a cane might have been more justifiable, and imposed a token fine of 1s plus costs to show their disapproval.

7 DECEMBER

1863   Carter John Howells appeared at Willenhall Police Court charged with violently assaulting three-year-old William Morris Chester.

Howells was employed by James Brevitt, who kept a number of carts parked on the public highway near his premises at Portobello. The carts proved a magnet for local children, and both Brevitt and Howells frequently had to shoo them away.

On 29 November, Howells confronted some children playing on the carts and threatened to cut off all of their heads. He then lashed out wildly with his heavy driving whip, twice hitting William in the face.

Surgeon Mr Pitt sent a medical certificate to the Court, stating that William had sustained an injury to his cheek and was likely to be permanently blind in one eye.

Howells did not appear in court but magistrates described his behaviour as 'scandalous' and fined him £2 in his absence, of which 35s went to pay for William's medical treatment.

8 DECEMBER

1865   In the early hours of the morning, a group of Irish people caused a disturbance at an inn at Willenhall. PC William Butler heard the ruckus and went to see if he could assist and, although the boisterous drinkers left the pub, once they got outside the policeman was savagely attacked. Butler had a firm grasp of one man's collar and was defending himself with his free hand when PC Enoch Augustus Hooper came to his aid. However, Hooper had barely entered the fray when Butler saw him fall.

With the help of a member of the public, Butler got the man he was holding to the police station, where he was identified as John McCue. Meanwhile, Hooper bled to death from a stab wound in his chest.

The identities of most of the combatants were known to the police, who quickly arrested Patrick and Mary Kane, their son, James (or John), John Leonard (or Lennon), and James Brown. John Brown, Patrick Kelly, Patsy Rowan, Edward (aka Owen) O'Donnell and John Kelly were also implicated, but absconded before the police could arrest them.

Magistrates determined that Patrick and Mary Kane should be tried for wilful murder. However, when they appeared at the Staffordshire Assizes in March 1865, it was impossible to prove the case against them and they were acquitted. The descriptions of the missing men were circulated in the *Police Gazette* and in February 1866 Patrick and John Kelly and John

Brown were arrested in Blackburn. However, as with the Kanes, there was little hope of securing a conviction.

Patsy Rowan and Edward O'Donnell were never traced, thus the only person who paid any legal penalty for the incident was John McCue, who was fined £10 for assaulting PC Butler and sent to prison for two months.

9 DECEMBER

1856 At the Wednesbury Petty Sessions, seventeen-year-old George Paddock was charged with cruelty to a dog.

Superintendent Wemyss of the Royal Society for the Prevention of Cruelty to Animals stated that Paddock was a former employee of the South Staffordshire Railway Company. On 27 November, a Skye terrier dog happened to wander into the goods shed at Great Bridge Station and together with a colleague, James Kenyon, Paddock immersed the dog in turpentine, surrounded it with straw and set fire to it, burning the poor animal alive.

Both men were dismissed from their jobs and immediately absconded. Paddock was the first to be caught and although he maintained that he had only intended to scorch the dog, the magistrates gave him the harshest penalty within their power, sentencing him to three months' imprisonment with hard labour.

There was a warrant out for Kenyon's arrest but it wasn't until March 1857 that he was apprehended and appeared at the Wednesbury Petty Sessions, charged with having been an accomplice to Paddock in roasting a dog alive. Kenyon pleaded guilty and was treated relatively leniently by the magistrates who, after giving him a severe reprimand, fined him £2 plus costs.

10 DECEMBER

1888 Thirty-four-year-old Joseph Taylor of Coseley left home at four o'clock in the afternoon to go to work. Normally, Taylor would have returned from the Eagle Ironworks at four o'clock the next morning but this time he didn't come home.

Joseph's wife, Alice, contacted the Ironworks and found that her husband had left at half-past ten the previous night, in the company of his friend and colleague James Baker. There was a dense fog at the time and Baker told Alice that, as the two men walked home, he accidentally fell into the canal.

Taylor was quick to rescue him and escorted him home safely, even though Baker's house was out of his way. In view of the terrible weather, Taylor was asked to stay the night at Baker's house, but he was afraid that his wife would be worried and was determined to go home. Baker provided him with a lamp and a candle and watched his friend disappear into the thick fog. It was the last time that he was seen alive.

The police made exhaustive enquiries, the canals were dragged several times and disused pit shafts were searched but no trace of Taylor was found until his bloated and decomposed body surfaced in the canal near Tipton Green at the beginning of January 1889. An inquest held by coroner Edwin Hooper heard that Taylor was somewhat shortsighted and it was assumed that he had accidentally wandered into the canal and drowned, less than two hours after saving his friend from a similar fate.

11 DECEMBER   **1900**   Baby Minnie Violet Degville, of Walsall, was suddenly taken ill for no apparent reason. On 14 December, somebody noticed that she had a tiny scratch on her chin, which looked as though it might have been made by a pin. The scratch grew more and more inflamed and only two days later gangrene had set in and the seven-month-old baby was dead.

On 17 December, the inquest jury heard medical evidence that the cause of death was syncope resulting from a pin scratch. They returned a verdict of 'accidental death'.

12 DECEMBER   **1890**   Coroner Edwin Hooper held an inquest at Tipton on the deaths of six children, who drowned after falling through ice.

John William White (7), Joseph Moreton (7), Samuel Webb (8), William Beddoe (8), Thomas Henry Arch (6) and Thomas Henry Tabberner (6) were all pupils of the Bloomfield Infants' Board School and had been cautioned numerous times by their parents and teachers about the dangers of 'Shenton's Pool', an old colliery pool close to the school.

On 9 December, it was very foggy and the children were let out of school a little earlier than normal. In spite of all the warnings they had been given, knowing that the pond was frozen over, the six boys went straight there. Twelve-year-old William Moseley saw them sliding and running across the ice and, when it broke beneath them, he ran straight off to find a grown-up.

Labourer Thomas Law pulled four of the boys from the water, which was approximately 4ft deep. They were passed to the bank, where surgeons worked on trying to revive them but without success. All six boys were pronounced dead at the scene.

Although satisfied that the deaths were accidental, the coroner said that he believed it his duty to write to the owners of the pool suggesting that it should be securely fenced off. The boys were buried in one grave at the Toll End Cemetery in Tipton.

A Victorian winter funeral. (Author's collection)

13 DECEMBER   **1859** Eleven-month-old Edward Davis of Wolverhampton always slept with his mother and father but at 2 a.m., Mrs Davis woke and found that the baby was no longer in the bed. She woke her husband, who struck a light and found his son dead and cold. It appeared that Edward's legs and body had slipped under the bed head, but the gap was too small for his head to pass through, leaving him hanging by the neck on the bedstead, dangling between the wall and the bed.

Edward's parents were known to treat their son well and, since there were no other marks of violence on the baby's body, an inquest later recorded a verdict of 'accidental death'.

14 DECEMBER   **1855** Butty collier David Millard sent nine-year-old Thomas Lear back to his house to fetch some gunpowder from the cellar. Thomas was given the gunpowder by David's wife, Jane, and set off to return to the mine. On his way back, he met Millard's son, Samuel, who had also been sent on an errand, to fetch some corn for the horses.

Samuel had to wait for the corn and decided to go home to warm himself for a few minutes. He had barely arrived home when there was an explosion, which razed the Millard family's cottage and the two adjoining dwellings to the ground. Jane Millard died in the explosion, as did nine-year-old Samuel and two of his siblings – Hannah, aged seven and Absalom, aged eleven months. Three-year-old David's head and legs were injured, while the children's nursemaid, ten-year-old Fanny Allen, was so badly hurt that she was not expected to survive.

Eliza Jackson, who lived next door, sustained serious injuries to both legs, while the other next-door neighbour, Hannah Stevens, suffered severe head injuries.

When the bodies were examined, Samuel Millard was found to have gunpowder in his pockets. It was surmised that he was jealous of the fact that Thomas Lear was entrusted with the gunpowder and had been determined to get some of his own, taking a candle into the cellar to find it and causing an explosion.

15 DECEMBER   **1889** Simon Parker lived at Greet's Green, West Bromwich, close to a marlhole worked by his father.

On 15 December, Parker had arranged to help his father with some blasting and was sent to fetch some gunpowder. Having collected about 3lbs of powder in a can, Parker went home for breakfast, placing the can on the table while he ate.

Minutes later, the house was shaken by a huge explosion, the force of which was so great that a horse in a nearby stable was blown right over, and Parker's wife ran out screaming hysterically that everyone had been killed.

When people could get into the house they found twenty-seven-year-old Parker in the kitchen, with a compound fracture of his right leg. (It was later necessary to amputate the limb.) His six-year-old son, Simon, was badly burned and died later that day in hospital, while four-year-old Thomas lay dead and terribly mutilated at the foot of the stairs.

Mrs Parker was taken to hospital for treatment. Only days earlier, her father and brother had been involved in an explosion at Sandwell Park Colliery and although both were recovering, Mrs Parker now had to face the consequences of another explosion. For some time, nobody broke the news of Thomas's death to her and she was under the impression that he had gone to his grandmother's house.

Coroner Mr F.W. Topham opened an inquest into the deaths of the two little boys at the West Bromwich District Hospital on 17 December. The jury were able to speak to Simon Parker senior, who explained that he was sitting close to the fire while eating his breakfast, with the can of gunpowder on the table. Although the lid was on the tin, Parker stated that he was not aware that the powder might explode when it became hot.

The inquest jury returned verdicts that the deceased died from the effects of injuries received by the explosion of gunpowder, although there was insufficient evidence as to how the explosion occurred.

16 DECEMBER

1849 As she did every Sunday evening, sixteen-year-old Elizabeth Cockin left her uncle's house at Rowley Regis to walk to the Independent Chapel at Halesowen. It was very foggy and Elizabeth's path from the house to the public road led over a dam, across a large fish pond.

Unfortunately, she wandered off the path in the fog and fell into the pond, her desperate screams alerting the occupants of a nearby house to her plight. They rushed to her aid but the fog was so thick that they could barely see their hands in front of their faces and the lighted candles they carried were instantly extinguished by the mist.

By the time they reached her, Elizabeth had sunk in more than 10ft of water and, although the pond was dragged, it took more than an hour for her body to be recovered. The jury at the subsequent inquest on her death returned a verdict of 'accidentally drowned'.

17 DECEMBER

1852 Samuel Thompson heard a strange noise at the Bromford Iron Works, West Bromwich and felt a few small particles of grit falling onto him. He stepped out of the way and almost immediately the wall near which he had been standing collapsed.

Abraham Barton and William Williams were buried beneath the rubble and when they were dug out, Barton was dead and Williams was barely alive, dying in hospital two hours later.

An inquest heard that the wall which had collapsed was about 7ft high and built inside an arch. Two weeks earlier, it was decided to demolish the wall but, as a temporary measure, some bricks were removed to make a way through it. The work was done by a bricklayer, who said at the inquest that he was completely satisfied that the upper portion of the wall within the arch had sufficient support. However, new machinery at work within the mill may have caused more than normal vibration, shaking the wall and causing it to fall.

The inquest jury returned two verdicts of 'accidental death' but commented that the wall should have been completely removed, or that there should have been additional support to the brickwork over the new doorway.

18 DECEMBER

1892 Twenty-seven-year-old Charlotte Bates left her husband, William, numerous times because of his drunkenness and violence, yet somehow William always managed to persuade her to come back. In November 1892, he beat her so badly that she finally decided to leave him for good. With the couple's two children, Charlotte moved in with her parents in Whitehall, Walsall, and took out a summons, charging William with assault.

On 18 December, William appeared unexpectedly at the home of his parents-in-law. Charlotte was out, so William sat down and suggested that Mr and Mrs Busst sent out for beer while they waited for her to return. Mrs Busst refused but instead made a pot of tea and the three sat talking almost companionably. Suspicious of William's motives, Mrs Busst stepped outside and waited for Charlotte, begging her not to go into the house but Charlotte said, 'I may as well face him as not,' and went indoors.

William seemed intent on persuading Charlotte to live with him again. Three times he asked her to kiss him and three times she refused, moving away from her husband until he finally sat down on the couch and lit his pipe. 'Isn't she a pretty girl?' he asked his father-in-law, before suddenly rushing across the room and seizing his wife's hands, raising her arms above her head as if to kiss her. Instead, he drew a razor from his pocket and swept it across Charlotte's throat. She gave a loud, gurgling scream as the blood gushed down the front of her dress, and while everyone rushed to her assistance, William calmly drew the razor across his own throat and sat down on the couch waiting to die.

Wanting to get her daughter to hospital, Charlotte's mother began to walk her up the street but after a few yards, she collapsed and died. As Charlotte's body was carried back to her home, two policemen took William off to hospital but he died before arriving.

An inquest into the two deaths heard that William had apparently planned to kill his wife and to commit suicide and had told his colleagues and father-in-law that he intended to 'do for' his wife. Sadly, nobody took him seriously. The inquest returned verdicts of 'wilful murder' against William Bates in respect of the death of his wife and 'suicide' in respect of his own death, adding that there was nothing to indicate the state of his mind at the time.

19 DECEMBER

1871 An inquest concluded at Bilston, on the deaths of three children from the same family. Eliza Griffiths had given birth to twelve children, three of whom died in 1871 – eight-month-old Thomas on 16 September, thirteen-year-old Mary Jane on 28 September and six-year-old William on 10 October. By December 1871, she had just one surviving child.

Infant mortality was high at the time and little attention was paid to the first of the three recent deaths, which was said to have been from 'consumption of the bowels'. When Mary Jane fell ill shortly afterwards, a surgeon was called but the medicine he prescribed had little effect on the girl's symptoms, and the doctor suspected that her mother hadn't given her the treatment. The cause of Mary Jane's death was given as cholera but the coroner halted the girl's funeral so that a post-mortem examination could be carried out. This was done on 1 October and revealed certain inconsistencies.

When surgeon Henry William Larkin performed the post-mortem, he was made aware of another sick child in the house. Larkin treated William, initially for sickness and diarrhoea then for general fever. By the time William died on 10 October, analysis of Mary Jane's remains by Dr Alfred Bostock Hill revealed the presence of antimony. The poison was also found in William's organs and, when baby Thomas was exhumed, he too had antimony in his system.

Antimony could have been medicinally administered, most commonly as tartar emetic, although nobody could recall it having been bought or prescribed for the Griffiths children. Since neither Eliza or her husband William could explain how antimony came to be ingested by their children and, having learned that all three children were insured for a cash sum payable on death, the coroner's jury found three verdicts of 'wilful murder' against Eliza Griffiths.

By the time the case came before magistrates, various articles from the children's home had been analysed, including their medicine bottles. Not the slightest trace of antimony was found and the magistrates declined to forward the case for trial. However, Eliza Griffiths had already been committed for trial on the coroner's warrant and appeared at the Staffordshire Assizes on 11 March. The prosecution offered no evidence against her and she was acquitted and discharged.

20 DECEMBER

1864 Coroner Mr A.A. Fletcher held an inquest at Walsall into the death of labourer Thomas Law.

On 10 December, Law was holding a pig while butcher Mr T.L. George slaughtered it. The animal reflexively kicked out as it died and caught George's hand, causing him to accidentally stab the inside of Law's right arm. The knife severed Law's brachial artery, and no less than four surgeons were consulted about the advisability of amputating the limb.

The doctors finally decided that it was too dangerous to attempt to amputate Law's arm but by that time, his wound had turned gangrenous and he died on 18 December. The jury found that the injury had been accidental and that it had ultimately caused Law's death, although his demise was accelerated by the effects of heart disease.

21 DECEMBER

1858 At the Wednesbury Petty Sessions, railway signalman John Riley was charged with obstructing two other signalmen, Webb and Vines, in the execution of their duty.

The magistrates heard that Riley arrived at Dudley Port to begin his shift at six o'clock on the evening of 10 December, but the stationmaster quickly realised that he was drunk and ordered him to go home, asking Webb and Vines to stay on and man the signals.

Riley became very angry and refused to leave the station. In spite of being physically removed from the signal box several times, for the next four hours he repeatedly harassed Webb and Vines, during which time thirteen trains passed along the line. The London and North West Railway

Company were so concerned about the possible consequences of Riley's behaviour that they dismissed him immediately and asked magistrates to inflict the most severe penalty that the law allowed.

In his defence, Riley argued that, in seven years' service, this was the first time that he had ever been drunk on duty, adding that he had been forced to drink by Webb and Vines. The magistrates were less than sympathetic, fining Riley £5 and costs or three months' imprisonment in default. They added that it showed a considerable 'want of energy' on the part of the stationmaster in not locking Riley up and in taking four hours to have him removed from the premises.

22 DECEMBER

1894 Brothers William and Job Caddick worked in a cycle factory in Wolverhampton and, on 21 December, William had occasion to complain to his younger brother about the quality of his work. Job resented his brother's criticism and, later in the day, he refused to work late to complete a foreign order. When Job arrived for work the next morning, William wanted to know why he had left early and Job told him that he was tired. The two brothers argued and William eventually told Job to leave for the day, paying him his week's wages before he left.

Both brothers spent much of the afternoon drinking before meeting at their brother-in-law Jesse Sayers's house later that evening. They began quarrelling and Job called his brother a monkey and hit him. In order to avoid further trouble, Jesse put Job outside in the yard to calm down but as soon as Jesse turned his back, Job hopped over a wall, walked round the house and went back in through the front door.

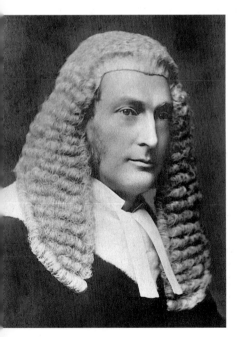

There were several people in the house at the time and each later gave a different version of events. All agreed that Job rushed at William and there was a massive fight, ultimately involving other people, who tried to separate the brothers. When they were finally pulled apart, Job had a stab wound in the side of his neck and another in his abdomen and bled to death within minutes.

Twenty-six-year-old William appeared at the Staffordshire Assizes on 9 March 1895 charged with wilful murder. Nearly all of the witnesses had been drinking heavily but all agreed that Job had been the aggressor, even his wife. There was argument about when the knife was drawn and whether it was actually in William's hand when his brother rushed him. William himself stated that Job was brandishing a knife and that he had drawn his only in self-defence.

Mr Justice Grantham summed up the contradictory evidence with a diatribe against drink, but suggested that the jury gave William the benefit of any doubt they might have. The eventual verdict was guilty of 'manslaughter under provocation' but, in sentencing William to five years' penal servitude, Grantham pointed out that he could have defended himself with his fists rather than a knife or alternatively he could have just walked away from his brother's violence.

Mr Justice Grantham, 1905. (Author's collection)

23 DECEMBER   **1854**   As Elizabeth Gamion stood on the platform at the Swan Village Station the express train from Birmingham approached, travelling at about forty miles an hour. Suddenly, one of the metal tyres flew off a wheel and hit the platform, breaking off a huge chunk of wood, which hit Elizabeth on the head. Bleeding heavily, she was carried to a waiting room, where, in spite of medical attention, she died within half an hour.

An inquest was opened into her death by coroner George Hinchcliffe, who adjourned the proceedings to allow an engineer to examine the tyre. When the inquest resumed on 1 January 1855, civil engineer Thomas Tertius Chellingworth of Birmingham stated that he had examined the tyre, which came from a 6ft driving wheel and was 2½ inches thick and 5½ inches wide.

The tire had fractured but not at the weld, where it should have been at its weakest. Closer examination showed that there was a defect in the iron, which could not possibly have been detected either by the manufacturer, the fitter who placed the tyre on the wheel or the train driver. The inquest jury therefore ruled that Elizabeth's death was accidental. A second person was knocked unconscious by the piece of wood that killed her but made a full recovery.

24 DECEMBER   **1894**   Seventeen-year-old domestic servant Hannah Mason from Wednesbury was a sturdy girl with a fresh, ruddy complexion. However, in 1894, sturdy, fresh and ruddy weren't fashionable and every girl aspired to being pale and thin.

Somebody told Hannah that in order to look good she should drink vinegar and eat starch, raw oatmeal and uncooked rice. Hannah embraced the diet whole heartedly and it soon had the desired effect – she became pale and thin but, not surprisingly, she also became unhealthy and suffered from a constant pain in her side.

When she died on Christmas Eve, the cause of death was given as a perforation of the stomach resulting from an abscess. The inquest jury returned a verdict of 'accidental death' and the coroner strongly condemned the foolhardiness of young girls in pursuit of beauty.

25 DECEMBER   **1914**   A man walking along the canal near Windmill End Railway Station at Dudley spotted a woman's hat floating on the water. Since three young people from Netherton were known to be missing, the canal was dragged and three bodies were recovered.

Samuel Crew (21) was courting Phyllis Chandler (19), who worked at a pen factory in Birmingham. On Christmas Eve, Samuel travelled to Birmingham to meet Phyllis and they came home by train, accompanied by her friend and colleague Mary Ann Wells (17).

The area was shrouded in heavy fog and it was assumed that the three had lost their bearings while walking home from the station, accidentally falling into the canal. When their bodies were found, Samuel and Phyllis were tightly locked in each other's arms.

26 DECEMBER   **1852**   An inquest was held at The Swan Inn, Wolverhampton, into the death of forty-six-year-old Daniel Onions. On Christmas Eve, Onions was working as a furnace man at Blackwell's Works in Wolverhampton. The furnaces were equipped with tuyers and when some water accidentally got into one, the furnace exploded, sending a shower of molten metal over Onions, who was dreadfully burned and subsequently died from his injuries.

The inquest returned a verdict of 'accidental death', although the dead man's workmates preferred to view it as Divine retribution for an act of gross barbarity. Some weeks before his death, Onions was seen to throw the foal of an ass into the furnace, where it was roasted alive.

27 DECEMBER

1862 Isaac Thompson of Sedgley, Staffordshire, thrust a sharp-pointed poker into the head of his eight-year-old daughter, causing a fatal wound. What made Thompson's actions more deplorable was that, at the time, he was awaiting trial for roasting another of his children alive and, only fourteen months earlier, was charged with unlawfully wounding a third child.

Thompson first appeared before magistrates in August 1862, after he smacked his thirteen-year-old daughter Rachel in the mouth and threw a metal spike at her, which penetrated one inch into her back. Thompson excused his actions by claiming that his wife was a drunkard, who neglected the family, and that he was angry at his daughter for leaving her siblings crying when she was supposed to be caring for them. Magistrates sympathised with Thompson for having 'a thorough bad wife' and fined him just 5s plus costs.

Two months later, Thompson took seventeen-month-old Martha downstairs to feed her. The next morning, he asked Rachel where the baby was, having forgotten where he had put her. Martha was eventually found lying dead and badly burned on the floor near the fire. Her father made a statement, relating that his 'thorough bad wife' was out drinking and had neglected to feed the children. He got Martha up and shared his food with her then, suddenly needing to use the lavatory, laid her down on the rug. When he returned, he sat down and before he knew it, he was asleep.

The inquest jury returned a verdict of manslaughter against Thompson, who was allowed bail until his trial at the Staffordshire Assizes. It was while on bail that he 'accidentally' threw the poker at eight-year-old Hannah, having come home from the pub and found his 'thorough bad wife' not at home.

Thompson was tried in March 1863 for having feloniously killed and slayed Hannah, which was, of course, a terrible accident 'of a most lamentable kind' that was all the fault of his 'thorough bad wife'. Thompson himself 'had been kindly and indulgent to his children and had tried so far as he could to supply the mother's place and it was not to be supposed that he could ever have contemplated injuring his child'.

The jury found Thompson guilty but recommended mercy on account of his 'thorough bad wife'. The prosecution then informed the jury that there was another indictment against Thompson for having killed Martha in October 1862, adding that they did not propose to offer any evidence against him on that charge.

Accordingly, the judge ordered the jury to find Thompson 'not guilty' of the manslaughter of his daughter Martha. For taking Hannah's life Thompson was sentenced to two weeks' imprisonment with hard labour, the sentence to be backdated one week.

28 DECEMBER

1845 Twenty-six-month-old Joseph Revell Pitt of Bilston climbed onto a chair while playing. The chair overbalanced and fell onto Joseph but his mother could find no injury apart from a small bruise on Joseph's lower lip and upper gum. The boy certainly wasn't in any pain and was soon playing again.

While feeding Joseph that evening, Mrs Pitt noticed that his gum had bled a little. She took the boy to surgeon Mr T.W. Dickenson, who dressed the gum and stopped the bleeding, although it began bleeding afresh about an hour afterwards and continued to ooze a little blood all night.

The following morning, Mrs Pitt went back to Dickenson, who applied something to Joseph's gum and bound it with tape. She went back again the next day, when the gum was still bleeding, and then went to another surgeon, who suggested that she rinsed her son's mouth with alum water three times a day. She continued to do this until 2 January, when Joseph died.

Coroner Mr T.M. Phillips held an inquest at The White Lion, Bilston on 3 January 1846. The inquest was told that no less than sixteen people in the same family had bled to death from minor injuries. Although medical evidence nowadays would suggest that Joseph was a haemophiliac, in 1846 Dickenson attributed his death to watery blood and a relaxation of the system, and the inquest jury returned a verdict in accordance with the medical evidence.

29 DECEMBER

1933 Stanley Eric Hobday was hanged at Winson Green Prison, Birmingham, having been found guilty at the Staffordshire Assizes of the murder of Charles William Fox on 27 August.

Fox disturbed Hobday while he was in the process of burgling the house that Fox shared with his wife at West Bromwich. Mrs Fox heard someone cry out, after which her husband staggered upstairs, a bowie knife embedded to the hilt in his back. Hobday broke into another house in the area that night, where he calmly used the householder's razor to shave and darned his jacket, before making off with money and silver. He then broke into a garage and stole a car.

The police had a good description of Hobday and, for the first time ever on 28 August, they broadcast an appeal on the BBC for a man 'aged 21, height 5ft 5in., brown eyes, very dark brown hair, sallow complexion, slim build. Hair brushed back with oil. He speaks very quietly and has a reserved disposition. Last seen dressed in a blue serge jacket and trousers and no waistcoat, soft collar and tie and a striped shirt. He may be wearing a brown trilby hat with fawn band, turned down in front.'

The stolen car was involved in an accident and abandoned in Cheshire, and, a few days later, Hobday was recognised in Cumberland and arrested. When charged with murdering Fox he responded, 'Murder? I have not done any murder.'

The evidence against him convinced the jury at his three-day trial otherwise, and Hobday was found guilty and sentenced to death. After an appeal to the Court of Criminal Appeal failed, the Home Secretary announced that he saw no reason to interfere with the course of justice.

30 DECEMBER

1879 Coroner Mr R.J. Watts re-opened an inquest at the Guest Hospital, Dudley, into the death of six-year-old Hannah Williams.

Hannah was given some peanuts by her stepfather but accidentally ate a shell, which lodged in her throat. The little girl retched and coughed all night but was unable to dislodge the blockage, so, the following morning, her stepfather took her to hospital. Hannah's throat was operated on but the surgeon was unable to find the obstruction.

When the child weakened and died, the coroner adjourned the inquest for a post-mortem examination, which revealed the nutshell about an inch from the surgeon's incision. Surgeons Mr Walford and Mr Messiter explained that Hannah was suffocating from the effects of the nutshell when she arrived at the hospital. The surgery involved placing a silver tube in her throat to enable her to take a full breath and hopefully cough up the obstruction. The surgery itself was dangerous and left the child weak and, according to the surgeons, the only reason she had not been able to dislodge the nutshell after surgery was because it was pointed.

The inquest jury returned a verdict of 'death from exhaustion consequent upon swallowing a nutshell'.

31 DECEMBER

1933 Martha Tonks, George Pritchard and Gertrude Robinson attended a New Years' Party and were walking home when Pritchard offered to show the girls a short cut along the canal banks at Wednesfield.

It was a very foggy night and the three linked arms, with George in the middle and Martha nearest the water. As they neared the lock, Martha gave a sudden squeal and disappeared.

Without hesitation, George stripped off his overcoat and jumped into the water after her. Gertrude stood on the bank screaming for help and eventually a man came to her aid. However, by that time, George and Martha had sunk beneath the surface. The police were informed and began dragging the canal immediately, although George and Martha's bodies were not recovered until the early hours of 1 January.

An inquest suggested that Martha had either slipped on the icy brickwork around the lock or had simply wandered off the towpath in the fog. The coroner commended George Pritchard for his courage in trying to rescue her without thought for his own safety.

BIBLIOGRAPHY

Berrow's Worcester Journal
Birmingham Daily Post
Black Country Bugle
Daily Mail
Daily News
Dudley Herald
Guardian / Manchester Guardian
Illustrated Police News
Lloyd's Weekly Newspaper
Midland Chronicle
Morning Chronicle
Morning Post
Reynolds's Newspaper
Staffordshire Sentinel
The Times
Ten Towns' Messenger
Wolverhampton Chronicle
Wolverhampton Express & Star
Worcester News & Times
Worcestershire County Express.

INDEX

Because they are mentioned so frequently throughout the text, Bilston, Birmingham, Dudley, Stafford, Walsall, Wednesbury, West Bromwich and Wolverhampton have been omitted from the index.

Phillips, Mr W.H. 18, 67, 76, 83, 130, 143, 149, 170, 180
Phillips, Richard 26
Phipson, John 101–2
Pierrepoint, Henry 173
Pierrepoint, Thomas 58, 134
Piggott, Mr Baron 113
Piper, Walter, 67–8
Pitcock, Frederick 99
Pitt, Joseph Revell 199
Plant, Ann and John 170
Plant, Joseph 98
Plimmer, Ernest Harry 64
Poole, John 175
Portman, Samuel 62
Pountney, Elijah & Alice Gertrude 42–3
Powell, Enoch 146
Powell, George 70–1
Powell, Maria 18
Power, John 141
Powick Asylum 26–7
Powis, John 163
Prendergast, Tom 110
Price, David 30
Price, Enoch 112
Price, Thomas 97
Pritchard, George 201
Pritchard, Thomas 28
Probert, Robert 130
Pugh, Mr & Mrs 30
Pumphrey, Mary Ann 125–6
Purnell, Mr 77–8

Quarlter, Thomas 97
Quarry Bank 114, 134, 186
Quarter, John 176

Ramsell, Silvanus 75–6
Reed, John 142–3
Reynolds, John 157–8
Reynolds, Louis 64
Richards, Daniel 176
Richards, Edith 44
Richards, Tom 176
Ridley, Mr Justice 111
Riddle, Henry 21
Riley, John 195–6
Riley, PC 83
Roberts, Henry 102
Roberts, John 176
Roberts, Joseph 68
Roberts, Thomas Henry & Samuel 187–8
Roberts, William 148
Robins, Benjamin 50
Robins, Mary Ann & Lucy 91
Robinson, Charles Christopher 133
Robinson, Gertrude 201
Robinson, John 155
Robinson, Maria 75
Robinson, Muriel 130–1
Robinson, Noah & William 86
Robinson, PC 86
Robinson, Mr W. 98
Robinson, William 51–2
Rogers, Henry & Sarah Jane 102–3, 105
Rotchell, Caroline 107

Round, Job 15
Rowan, Patsy 189
Rowden, Jane 97
Rowley, Alice Mary 164–5
Rowley, James 16
Rowley Regis 22, 30, 45–6, 47, 59, 62, 75, 107, 138, 157, 165, 193
Russell, Joseph, Ellen & Eliza 38–9
Russell, Thomas 160
Russell, William, Ann & Joseph 154
Ryder, Albert & William 184

Sankey, Sarah 90
Sayers, Jesse 197
Sayers, Joseph & Eliza 32
Scott, Mr J.W. 100
Seagar, Harriet 133
Sedgley 135–6, 157, 170, 198
Shakespeare family 96
Shearman, Mr Justice 43
Shee, Mr Justice 76
Sheen, John Thomas 110
Sheldon, John 29
Sheldon, Thomas 122
Shelley, Joseph 149
Shoot, Lily Mary 123
Silletto, Eliza 122
Simmonds, John 66–7
Simpson, Mark 37
Siviter, Joyce 62
Skidmore, Jane 83
Skidmore, Mr A.C. 21
Slater, Eliza 186–7
Slater, Joseph 107
Slater, Julia 23
Slaughter, Harry 91–2
Smart, Minnie 13
Smethwick 7, 41, 54, 138
Smith, Eliza & father 17
Smith, Esther & Samuel 34
Smith, George 150
Smith, George Henry 173–4
Smith, Henry 23, 140, 146, 168
Smith, Joseph 127
Smith, Joseph, Abraham & Samuel 96
Smith, Josiah 156
Smith, Mary 47–8
Smith, Mr 179–80
Smith, Mr A.B. 84, 105, 184
Smith, Mrs 23
Smith, Rosannah 56
Smith, Rose 178
Smith, Sidney Arthur 166
Smith, William John 129
Snape, Thomas 165
Sones, James 93
Southall, Joseph 99
Southwell, John 28
Sowden, Daniel 22
Spence, Dr J.B. 116
Spencer, Robert 118
Stackhouse, Florence 87
Stanley, Joshua 76
Stanley, Mr T.H. 18, 87
Starkey, Thomas 176